BROOKLANDS
BOOKS

Austin-Healey
SPRITE
1958-1971

Compiled by
R.M. Clarke

D1592651

ISBN 0 907073 409

Distributed by
Brooklands Book Distribution Ltd.
'Holmerise', Seven Hills Road,
Cobham, Surrey, England

Printed in Hong Kong

BROOKLANDS BOOKS

BROOKLANDS BOOKS SERIES

AC Ace & Aceca 1953-1983
AC Cobra 1962-1969
Alfa Romeo Giulia Berlinas 1962-1976
Alfa Romeo Giulia Coupés 1963-1976
Alfa Romeo Spider 1966-1987
Aston Martin Gold Portfolio 1972-1985
Austin Seven 1922-1982
Austin A30 & A35 1951-1962
Austin Healey 100 1952-1959
Austin Healey 3000 1959-1967
Austin Healey 100 & 3000 Collection No. 1
Austin Healey 'Frogeye' Sprite Collection No. 1
Austin Healey Sprite 1958-1971
Avanti 1962-1983
BMW Six Cylinder Coupés 1969-1975
BMW 1600 Collection No. 1
BMW 2002 1968-1976
Bristol Cars Gold Portfolio 1946-1985
Buick Riviera 1963-1978
Cadillac Automobiles 1949-1959
Cadillac Automobiles 1960-1969
Cadillac Eldorado 1967-1978
Cadillac in the Sixties No. 1
Camaro 1966-1970
Chevrolet 1955-1957
Chevrolet Camaro Collection No. 1
Chevelle & SS 1964-1972
Chevy II Nova & SS 1962-1973
Chrysler 300 1955-1970
Citroen Traction Avant 1934-1957
Citroen 2CV 1949-1982
Cobras & Replicas 1962-1983
Cortina 1600E & GT 1967-1970
Corvair 1959-1968
Daimler Dart & V-8 250 1959-1969
Datsun 240z 1970-1973
De Tomaso Collection No. 1
Dodge Charger 1966-1974
Excalibur Collection No. 1
Ferrari Cars 1946-1956
Ferrari Cars 1962-1966
Ferrari Cars 1969-1973
Ferrari Dino 1965-1974
Ferrari Dino 308 1974-1979
Ferrari 308 & Mondial 1980-1984
Ferrari Collection No. 1
Fiat X1/9 1972-1980
Ford Falcon 1960-1970
Ford Mustang 1964-1967
Ford Mustang 1967-1973
Ford RS Escort 1968-1980
High Performance Escorts MkI 1968-1974
High Performance Escorts MkII 1975-1980
Hudson & Railton Cars 1936-1940
Jaguar Cars 1957-1961
Jaguar Cars 1961-1964
Jaguar Cars 1964-1968
Jaguar MK2 1959-1969
Jaguar E-Type 1961-1966
Jaguar E-Type 1966-1971
Jaguar E-Type V12 1971-1975
Jaguar MK2 1959-1969
Jaguar XKE Collection No. 1
Jaguar XJ6 1968-1972
Jaguar XJ6 Series II 1973-1979
Jaguar XJ6 & XJ12 Series III 1979-1985
Jaguar XJ12 1972-1980
Jaguar XJS 1975-1980
Jensen Cars 1946-1967
Jensen Cars 1967-1979
Jensen Interceptor Gold Portfolio 1966-1986
Lamborghini Cars 1964-1970
Lamborghini Cars 1970-1975
Lamborghini Countach Collection No. 1
Lamborghini Countach & Urraco 1974-1980
Lamborghini Countach & Jalpa 1980-1985
Lancia Stratos 1972-1985
Land Rover 1948-1973
Land Rover Series II & IIa 1958-1971
Land Rover Series III 1971-1985
Lotus Cortina 1963-1970
Lotus Elan 1962-1973
Lotus Elan Collection No. 1
Lotus Elan Collection No. 2
Lotus Elite 1957-1964
Lotus Elite & Eclat 1974-1981
Lotus Turbo Esprit 1980-1986
Lotus Europa 1966-1975
Lotus Europa Collection No. 1
Lotus Seven 1957-1980
Lotus Seven Collection No. 1
Maserati 1965-1970
Maserati 1970-1975
Mazda RX-7 Collection No. 1
Mercedes 230/250/280SL 1963-1971
Mercedes 350/450SL & SLC 1971-1980
Mercedes Benz Cars 1949-1954
Mercedes Benz Cars 1954-1957
Mercedes Benz Cars 1957-1961
Mercedes Benz Competition Cars 1950-1957
Metropolitan 1954-1962
MG Cars 1929-1934
MG TC 1945-1949
MG TD 1949-1953
MG TF 1953-1955

MG Cars 1957-1959
MG Cars 1959-1962
MG Midget 1961-1980
MG MGA 1955-1962
MGA Collection No. 1
MGB Roadsters 1962-1980
MGB GT 1965-1980
Mini Cooper 1961-1971
Morgan Cars 1960-1970
Morgan Cars 1969-1979
Morris Minor Collection No. 1
Old's Cutlass & 4-4-2 1964-1972
Oldsmobile Toronado 1966-1978
Opel GT 1968-1973
Pantera 1970-1973
Pantera & Mangusta 1969-1974
Plymouth Barracuda 1964-1974
Pontiac GTO 1964-1970
Pontiac Firebird 1967-1973
Pontiac Tempest & GTO 1961-1965
Porsche Cars 1960-1964
Porsche Cars 1964-1968
Porsche Cars 1968-1972
Porsche Cars in the Sixties
Porsche Cars 1972-1975
Porsche 356 1952-1965
Porsche 911 Collection No. 1
Porsche 911 Collection No. 2
Porsche 911 1965-1969
Porsche 911 1970-1972
Porsche 911 1973-1977
Porsche 911 Carrera 1973-1977
Porsche 911 SC 1978-1983
Porsche 911 Turbo 1975-1984
Porsche 914 1969-1975
Porsche 914 Collection No. 1
Porsche 924 1975-1981
Porsche 928 Collection No. 1
Porsche 944 1981-1985
Porsche Turbo Collection No. 1
Reliant Scimitar 1964-1986
Rolls Royce Silver Cloud 1955-1965
Rolls Royce Silver Shadow 1965-1980
Range Rover 1970-1981
Rover 3 & 3.5 Litre 1958-1973
Rover P4 1949-1959
Rover P4 1955-1964
Rover 2000 + 2200 1963-1977
Rover 3500 1968-1977
Rover 3500 & Vitesse 1976-1986
Saab Sonett Collection No. 1
Saab Turbo 1976-1983
Singer Sports Cars 1933-1934
Studebaker Hawks & Larks 1956-1963
Sunbeam Alpine & Tiger 1959-1967
Thunderbird 1955-1957
Thunderbird 1958-1963
Triumph 2000-2.5-2500 1963-1977
Triumph Spitfire 1962-1980
Triumph Spitfire Collection No. 1
Triumph Stag 1970-1980
Triumph Stag Collection No. 1
Triumph TR2 & TR3 1952-1960
Triumph TR4.TR5.TR250 1961-1968
Triumph TR6 1969-1976
Triumph TR6 Collection No. 1
Triumph TR7 & TR8 1975-1982
Triumph GT6 1966-1974
Triumph Vitesse & Herald 1959-1971
TVR 1960-1980
Volkswagen Cars 1936-1956
VW Beetle 1956-1977
VW Beetle Collection No. 1
VW Golf GTi 1976-1986
VW Karmann Ghia 1955-1982
VW Scirocco 1974-1981
Volvo 1800 1960-1973
Volvo 120 Series 1956-1970

BROOKLANDS MUSCLE CARS SERIES

American Motors Muscle Cars 1966-1970
Buick Muscle Cars 1965-1970
Camaro Muscle Cars 1966-1972
Capri Muscle Cars 1969-1983
Chevrolet Muscle Cars 1966-1972
Dodge Muscle Cars 1967-1970
Mercury Muscle Cars 1966-1971
Mini Muscle Cars 1961-1979
Mopar Muscle Cars 1964-1967
Mopar Muscle Cars 1968-1971
Mustang Muscle Cars 1967-1971
Shelby Mustang Muscle Cars 1965-1970
Oldsmobile Muscle Cars 1964-1970
Plymouth Muscle Cars 1966-1971
Pontiac Muscle Cars 1966-1972
Muscle Cars Compared 1966-1971
Muscle Cars Compared Book 2 1965-1971

BROOKLANDS ROAD & TRACK SERIES

Road & Track on Alfa Romeo 1949-1963
Road & Track on Alfa Romeo 1964-1970
Road & Track on Alfa Romeo 1971-1976
Road & Track on Alfa Romeo 1977-1984
Road & Track on Aston Martin 1962-1984
Road & Track on Auburn Cord & Duesenberg 1952-1984
Road & Track on Audi 1952-1980
Road & Track on Audi 1980-1986
Road & Track on Austin Healey 1953-1970

Road & Track on BMW Cars 1966-1974
Road & Track on BMW Cars 1975-1978
Road & Track on BMW Cars 1979-1983
Road & Track on Cobra, Shelby & Ford GT40 1962-1983
Road & Track on Corvette 1953-1967
Road & Track on Corvette 1968-1982
Road & Track on Corvette 1982-1986
Road & Track on Datsun Z 1970-1983
Road & Track on Ferrari 1950-1968
Road & Track on Ferrari 1968-1974
Road & Track on Ferrari 1975-1981
Road & Track on Ferrari 1981-1984
Road & Track on Fiat Sports Cars 1968-1987
Road & Track on Jaguar 1950-1960
Road & Track on Jaguar 1961-1968
Road & Track on Jaguar 1968-1974
Road & Track on Jaguar 1974-1982
Road & Track on Lamborghini 1964-1985
Road & Track on Lotus 1972-1981
Road & Track on Maserati 1952-1974
Road & Track on Maserati 1975-1983
Road & Track on Mazda RX7 1978-1986
Road & Track on Mercedes 1952-1962
Road & Track on Mercedes 1963-1970
Road & Track on Mercedes 1971-1979
Road & Track on Mercedes 1980-1987
Road & Track on MG Sports Cars 1949-1961
Road & Track on MG Sports Cars 1962-1980
Road & Track on Mustang 1964-1977
Road & Track on Peugeot 1955-1986
Road & Track on Pontiac 1960-1983
Road & Track on Porsche 1951-1967
Road & Track on Porsche 1968-1971
Road & Track on Porsche 1972-1975
Road & Track on Porsche 1975-1978
Road & Track on Porsche 1979-1982
Road & Track on Porsche 1982-1985
Road & Track on Rolls Royce & Bentley 1950-1965
Road & Track on Rolls Royce & Bentley 1966-1984
Road & Track on Saab 1955-1985
Road & Track on Toyota Sports & G T Cars 1966-1986
Road & Track on Triumph Sports Cars 1953-1967
Road & Track on Triumph Sports Cars 1967-1974
Road & Track on Triumph Sports Cars 1974-1982
Road & Track on Volkswagen 1951-1968
Road & Track on Volkswagen 1968-1978
Road & Track on Volkswagen 1978-1985
Road & Track on Volvo 1957-1974
Road & Track on Volvo 1975-1985

BROOKLANDS CAR AND DRIVER SERIES

Car and Driver on BMW 1955-1977
Car and Driver on BMW 1977-1985
Car and Driver on Cobra, Shelby & Ford GT40 1963-1984
Car and Driver on Datsun Z 1600 & 2000 1966-1984
Car and Driver on Corvette 1956-1967
Car and Driver on Corvette 1968-1977
Car and Driver on Corvette 1978-1982
Car and Driver on Ferrari 1955-1962
Car and Driver on Ferrari 1963-1975
Car and Driver on Ferrari 1976-1983
Car and Driver on Mopar 1956-1967
Car and Driver on Mopar 1968-1975
Car and Driver on Pontiac 1961-1975
Car and Driver on Porsche 1955-1962
Car and Driver on Porsche 1963-1970
Car and Driver on Porsche 1970-1976
Car and Driver on Porsche 1977-1981
Car and Driver on Porsche 1982-1986
Car and Driver on Saab 1956-1985
Car and Driver on Volvo 1955-1986

BROOKLANDS MOTOR & THOROUGHBRED & CLASSIC CAR SERIES

Motor & T & CC on Ferrari 1966-1976
Motor & T & CC on Ferrari 1976-1984
Motor & T & CC on Lotus 1979-1983
Motor & T & CC on Morris Minor 1948-1983

BROOKLANDS PRACTICAL CLASSICS SERIES

Practical Classics on Austin A40 Restoration
Practical Classics on Land Rover Restoration
Practical Classics on Metalworking in Restoration
Practical Classics on Midget/Sprite Restoration
Practical Classics on Mini Cooper Restoration
Practical Classics on MGB Restoration
Practical Classics on Morris Minor Restoration
Practical Classics on Triumph Herald/Vitesse
Practical Classics on Triumph Spitfire Restoration
Practical Classics on VW Beetle Restoration
Practical Classics on 1930S Car Restoration

BROOKLANDS MILITARY VEHICLES SERIES

Allied Military Vehicles Collection No. 1
Allied Military Vehicles Collection No. 2
Dodge Military Vehicles Collection No. 1
Military Jeeps 1941-1945
Off Road Jeeps 1944-1971
V W Kubelwagen 1940-1975

CONTENTS

ACKNOWLEDGEMENTS

Austin-Healey followed in the steps of MG, Morgan and Austin itself by introducing in 1958, a small, light, practical and economical sports car. It was based mainly on components used in the A35 and Morris Minor of the period and was powered by the BMC four cylinder 948cc unit. Although fitted with twin SU carburettors it produced only some 42.5 bhp.

The Mark II appeared in May 1961 with a less distinctive body shape and a modified engine. The compression was raised to 9.1 and the unit now produced some 46.5 bhp. The Sprite still needed more power and this was forthcoming in October 1962 when the capacity was increased to 1,098cc and power boosted to 55 bhp. This gave the car a respectable 0—50 time of a 11 sec with a fuel consumption of over 30 mpg.

The power output was upped again in March 1965 to 59 bhp when the Mk III was unveiled which came equipped with a curved windscreen, lockable doors and hinged quarter-lights.

There were major changes to the Sprite in October 1966 when a version of the 1275cc Cooper engine was incorporated in the Mk IV. This gave a useful increase in bhp bringing it up to 65 at 6000 rpm.

In late 1968 the final drive was raised from 4.22 to 3.9:1 and subsequently the 30-50 mph time was reduced to a sporty 9.6 seconds. Only minor changes in appearance were made to the model for 1970 and the most notable improvement for 1971 was the introduction of reclining seats.

Shortly after this Donald Healeys contract with BLMC came to an end and the marque passed into motoring history.

The Motor staff fairly summed up the Sprite in their final road test in 1970 by saying ". . . a splendid little sports car . . . fun to drive . . . practical".

Further information on this model can be gleaned from a companion book MG Midget 1961-1979 which deals with the Sprite's twin.

The copyright articles contained in this book are reprinted with the permission of the original publishers. Austin-Healey enthusiasts will I am sure wish to join with me in thanking the management of Autocar, Autosport, Car & Driver, Modern Motor, Motor, Motor Racing, Motor Sport, Motoring Life, Road & Track, Sports Cars Illustrated, Track & Traffic and Wheels, for their generosity in allowing these articles to be reproduced in this form.

R.M. Clarke

AUSTIN-HEALEY

One-litre Sports Car with Integral Structure and Quarter-elliptic Rear Springs

FOR some months past, persistent rumours of a new small sports car under development by B.M.C. have circulated amongst those with trade and sporting interests in such a vehicle. Most of these legends suggested a new M.G.; in fact, the mystery car now described is designated an Austin-Healey, for the good reason that it owes its conception to the Healey design office in Warwick.

From this stage Longbridge took over, and the new Healey was "productionized"—that is, its constituents and layout were adapted where necessary to simplify their production and assembly in very large numbers. Two prototype cars were next made by Austins, who did the initial type-testing; then the whole project was handed to the M.G. team at Abingdon, to develop further, and ultimately to assemble.

Announcement of this new car—the Sprite—was delayed until the production line at Abingdon (where its larger stablemate, the Austin-Healey 100-Six, is made also) was flowing freely; during the past several weeks, large numbers of these little sports cars have been completed and despatched to distributors in this country and overseas.

Essential factors in a project of this nature are, of course, interrelated weight and price. Excess weight of material increases cost and decreases road performance, and to ensure that the Sprite should be competitive with its rivals in these respects, a light integral structure of body and chassis has been adopted.

This description requires qualification, in that very few of the outer body panels are stressed. For instance, the bonnet, front mudguards, lamps and radiator cowl are combined in a single unit, hinged on the scuttle in front of the windscreen to give unimpeded access to the power unit, steering and suspension components. Indeed, two experienced fitters can complete an engine change in about 20 minutes. Incidentally, these body and chassis units are made by Pressed Steel at Swindon, then rust-inhibited and painted at the Morris works near Oxford before they arrive at Abingdon.

At the front of the chassis is a very substantial boxed structure, including a wide cross-member outrigged to carry the front suspension and steering mechanisms, and to provide a firm lock-mounting for the rather heavy bonnet. A secondary cross-member bridging this main member braces the upper

spring pads of the front suspension. Two boxed longerons, parallel with the chassis centre-line, connect the forward cross-member with a second one approximately in line with the forward door hinges. Behind this the long body sills 'and the propeller shaft tunnel unite with the floor to support a raised, transverse structure carrying the rear suspension spring and torque link mountings, and the Armstrong lever-type dampers. Two L-shaped members of top-hat section run beneath the front seats from the central cross-member to this rear structure, to help support the weight of the luggage boot, spare wheel and fuel tank.

A full-width scuttle superstructure integrates with the forward ends of the body sills to add frame stiffness, and is arranged to absorb some front suspension loads by the provision of a bracing strut at each side, connecting with the front cross-member.

There is no exterior boot lid because the panel is stressed, and its contents must be reached from behind the seats—a manœuvre rendered difficult because the floor of the boot is swept up locally to clear the axle casing. Stiffening plates welded into each rear-wheel arch give added support to the overhung tail.

The scuttle is formed in the shape of separate boxes around each occupant's legs at either side of the engine compartment, which extends slightly into the cockpit. This structure is extended upwards to carry the bonnet hinges, windscreen frame and facia.

For the front suspension, standard Austin A.35 coil spring and wishbone components are used, in conjunction with lever-type Armstrong hydraulic dampers. Only the lower arm of each suspension assembly is, in fact, a wishbone, the single upper arm being also the lever of the damper, the body of

Prominent head lamps and a simple radiator grille give the new Austin-Healey Sprite an almost animate expression. The bonnet and front wing assembly is hinged just forward of the windscreen. The doors are opened by interior handles

AUSTIN-HEALEY
Sprite

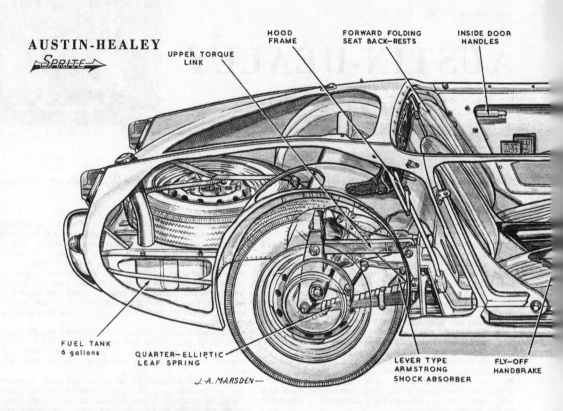

HOOD FRAME

FORWARD FOLDING SEAT BACK-RESTS

INSIDE DOOR HANDLES

UPPER TORQUE LINK

FUEL TANK 6 gallons

QUARTER-ELLIPTIC LEAF SPRING

J. A. MARSDEN —

LEVER TYPE ARMSTRONG SHOCK ABSORBER

FLY-OFF HANDBRAKE

which is bolted to an upward extension of the front cross-member. Morris Minor type rack-and-pinion steering is fitted of which the rack forms the centre of a three-piece track-rod. Although the ratio gives 2½ turns of the steering wheel from lock to lock, this is much higher than would appear at first sight, the short wheelbase (6ft 8in) giving the car a very compact turning circle.

Rear suspension details are of particular interest, in view of the reversion to quarter-elliptic leaf springs—a feature of the famous Austin 7 which was in production for most of the years between the wars. This system, with its spring anchorages well ahead of the rigid axle, concentrates suspension stresses within a very short frame. Incidentally, the new Healey might well be considered a successor to those small sporting versions of the Austin 7, the Speedy and Nippy, which were produced up to 1937.

Each spring has 15 leaves, and its "free" length—between its mounting bracket and attachment to the axle—is 16in. It is located by four studs and one dowel; the front two are fitted studs and pass through holes in the spring leaves, while the rear two straddle the spring; the dowel is placed at the approximate centre of the four studs and also passes through all the spring leaves. Each pair of studs is threaded into a bridge stepped to fit over the upper spring leaf, and a pressed steel

Above: There are individual bucket-type front seats, and elbow room is generous. The facia is trimmed in plastic material and the instrument layout is simple and neat. Below: A three-piece Vibak panel gives excellent rearward vision and admits plenty of light to the interior. A section of each sidescreen folds upwards for reaching the door handle. Access to luggage and the spare wheel is from behind the folding seat squabs

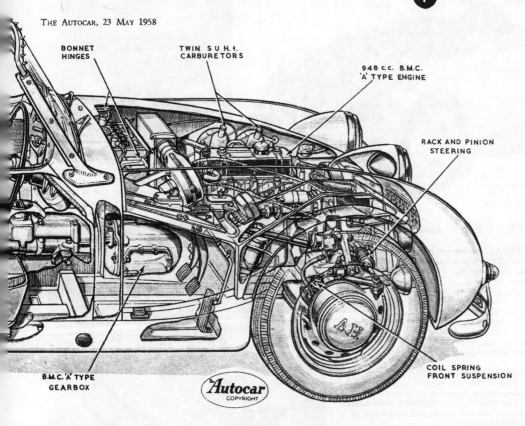

BONNET HINGES

TWIN S U H.1. CARBURETORS

948 c.c. B.M.C. 'A' TYPE ENGINE

RACK AND PINION STEERING

COIL SPRING FRONT SUSPENSION

B.M.C. 'A' TYPE GEARBOX

Autocar COPYRIGHT

plate of ⅛in thickness spreads the load by sandwiching the car frame between the base of the spring and the clamping nuts.

Each spring eye is formed from the two main leaves and carried below the axle centre line in a bracket welded to the axle casing, this bracket also extending above the axle tube to locate the rearmost eye of the upper torque link. These links

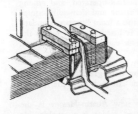

The rear axle is located by its quarter-elliptic springs and torque links; rubber blocks and flexible straps limit its vertical travel. Inset is the right spring fixture, with two fitted bolts passing through it, two straddling it, and a central dowel

Front end details (right) include rack-and-pinion steering, coil spring and wishbone suspension and Armstrong lever - type dampers

are fabricated from channel steel pressings welded to form a box-section. They are mounted at each end on rubber bushes, so that lateral location of the axle is governed entirely by the springs. A rubber bump stop is attached to the top of this axle bracket by split-pins passing through it, and rubberized canvas straps limit rebound movement.

Braking is by a conventional Lockheed hydraulic system having two-leading shoes in the front drums, leading-and-trailing in the rear; a cable and rod hand-brake linkage, with its compensating gear, is anchored to the axle casing and operates in the wheel cylinders by the cam action of pivot levers. Although the brake shoes are only 1⅜in wide, the drum faces are much wider than this, perhaps to allow braking effort to be stepped up when the car is tuned above standard performance.

Under the bonnet is that admirable and exceptionally tough B.M.C. A-type four-cylinder engine of 948 c.c. capacity, with pushrod-operated o.h.v. and heart-shaped combustion chambers. For the Sprite it is fed by two S.U. 1⅛in carburettors set at a slight angle to the horizontal, and protected by individual

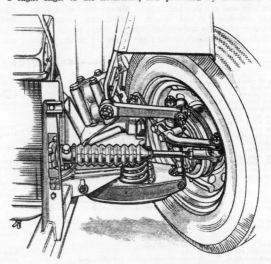

This exhibition "chassis" shows how the main structure is self-supporting without the outer body panels. Heating and ventilation equipment is optional

Vestigial front mudguards are revealed with the bonnet opened. It is locked shut by horizontal sliding bolts and a T-handle

AUSTIN-HEALEY SPRITE

Cooper air filters. The A.C. mechanical fuel pump, incidentally, is new to Abingdon. The exhaust valves have Stellited seats and the valve springs are special, but the compression of 8.3 to 1 is identical with those for the Austin A.35 and Morris Minor.

In this form the unit develops 43 b.h.p. (nett) at 5,000 r.p.m., and the makers claim a top speed in the early eighties, a 0-60 m.p.h. figure of about 22sec, and fuel consumption between 30 and 45 m.p.g., depending on driving methods. The gear box is as fitted to the Minor and A.35, with the remote-control lever sprouting from the transmission tunnel. Hydraulic operation and extra-strong release springs characterize the Borg and Beck clutch.

Final drive ratio of the conventional hypoid rear axle is 4.2 to 1, and the rear track of 3ft 8¾in accords with that of the A.35—the casings being similar except in the arrangements for spring mountings. The exhaust pipe, suspended from rubber-in-shear brackets, passes under the axle and terminates in a Burgess straight-through silencer.

Turning now to body details, one is struck immediately by the width of the cockpit, which is, in fact, more spacious than that of the M.G. A. Comfortable bucket seats give good lateral support, and are trimmed in P.V.C.-coated material over foam rubber on the cushions, rubberized horsehair on the backrests. The latter fold forward to give access to the spare wheel and luggage.

The hood, in P.V.C.-coated fabric, it attached to the upper screen rail and to the tail panel by fasteners of three different types. When not required, it folds neatly out of sight behind the seats, and is secured by straps beneath the lip of the luggage boot —one section of the hood frame being first dismantled, folded and stowed in special sockets. The sidescreens are attached to the doors by screws with knurled heads. Interior door handles only are fitted, which entails placing a hand through a flap in the sidescreen to open the door from outside. Since the hood can be unfastened easily from outside, the car cannot be locked.

A wide beading of polished aluminium puts a neat finishing touch to the boot's leading edge and the door tops, but the facia and its surround are sheathed in matt plastic material to avoid creating reflections in the screen. Instruments comprise a speedometer (with trip and total mileage recorders), petrol gauge, and combined water thermometer and oil pressure gauges. There

As specially developed for the Sprite, the 948 c.c. B.M.C. engine has two S.U. carburettors and develops 43 b.h.p. (nett) at 5,000 r.p.m.

are small lamps to indicate dynamo discharge, head lamp main beams and signal flashers, the latter operated by a switch which is not self-cancelling.

The head lamp dipping switch is foot-operated, and among the listed extras are a tachometer, heating and demisting equipment, screen washer, tonneau cover and a front bumper (standard on export cars). When the heater is fitted, it feeds air to the occupants' legs through trap doors in each side of the central engine and transmission housing.

There is a choice of five bright colours for the Sprite—cherry red, white, blue, primrose and dark green, and a variety of contrasting trims to go with them. In each case, the hood is available only in black.

At £678 17s including tax, this new Austin-Healey is the cheapest four-cylinder sports car listed, which is a considerable achievement in view of its mechanical merit and standards of both finish and equipment. It is many years since the name of Austin was associated with a small sports car of this nature, and there is certainly a large market awaiting it.

SPECIFICATION

ENGINE

No. of cylinders ...	4 in line
Bore and stroke ...	62.9 x 76.2mm (2.48 x 3.0in)
Displacement ...	948 c.c. (57.87 cu in)
Valve position ...	o.h.v., pushrods
Compression ratio ...	8.3 to 1
Max. b.h.p. (gross) ...	48 at 5,000 r.p.m.
Max. b.h.p. (nett) ...	43 at 5,000 r.p.m.
Max b.m.e.p. (nett)	136 lb sq in at 3,300 r.p.m.
Max. torque (nett) ...	52 lb ft at 3,300 r.p.m.
Carburettor	2 S.U. H.1
Fuel pump	A.C. mechanical
Tank capacity ...	6 Imp. gal (27.3 litres)
Sump capacity ...	6⅞ pints (3.34 litres)
Oil filter	Tecalemit or Purolator (renewable element)
Cooling system ...	Pump, fan and thermostat
Battery	12 volt 43 amp hr

TRANSMISSION

Clutch	B. and B. 6¼in dia (hydraulic operation)
Gear box	Four speeds, synchromesh on 2nd, 3rd and top, central lever
Overall gear ratios ...	Top, 4.22; 3rd, 5.96; 2nd, 10.02; 1st, 15.31
Final drive	4.22 to 1

CHASSIS

Brakes	Lockheed hydraulic
Drum dia., shoe width	7in; 1¼in
Suspension: front ...	Independent coil springs and wishbones
rear ...	Quarter-elliptic springs and trailing links
Dampers	Armstrong lever-type hydraulic
Wheels	Pressed steel
Tyre size	5.20—13
Steering	Rack and pinion
Steering wheel ...	16in
Turns, lock to lock ...	2⅓

DIMENSIONS

Wheelbase	6ft 8in (203 cm)
Track: front	3ft 9¾in (116 cm)
rear	3ft 8¾in (114 cm)
Overall length ...	11ft 0⅝in without front bumper (337 cm) 11ft 5¼in with front bumper (349 cm)
Overall width ...	4ft 5in (135 cm)
Overall height ...	4ft 1¾in (126 cm) 3ft 8⅛in (112 cm), hood down
Ground clearance ...	5in at exhaust pipe (13 cm)
Turning circle: right...	31ft 2½in (9.5 m)
left	32ft 1½in (9.8 m)
Kerb weight	1,328 lb (602 kg)

PERFORMANCE DATA

Top gear m.p.h. per 1,000 r.p.m. ...	15.4
Torque lb ft per cu in engine capacity ...	.89
Brakes surface area swept by linings ...	110 sq in

PRICES

Basic ... £455; Purchase tax ... £223 17s; Total ... £678 17s

Extras: Heater-demister, £20 16s 3d. Radio, £25. Front bumper, £6. Tonneau cover, £6. Tachometer, £4 10s.

Hail to thee, blithe Sprite

New Austin Healey venture in a classic tradition

Since the end of the war, motoring editors' desks have been piled high with letters asking manufacturers to investigate the possibility of making a genuine touring car which could be sold at the price of a small saloon. These letters showed that the market was certainly there. And now comes the new Austin Healey Sprite, a car which is just the answer to the demands of the touring car enthusiast. The new Sprite is a very pretty little car, with a lot of clever ideas under its sleek body. Unitary construction is used, resulting in a great saving of weight and an overall smoothness of line to bring joy to the eyes of a connoisseur. And it's as practical as it is pretty. The whole bonnet and wings assembly of the Sprite lifts up to give quick accessibility to the engine and front suspension. This should make home maintenance

delightfully easy. There's fresh thought, too, in the rear suspension. Trailing links are used for improved road-holding and to reduce unsprung weight. The Sprite engine is the brilliant BMC 'A' series 948 cc. engine. Twin S.U. carburettors lift its maximum output to 43 BHP at 5,200 rpm—making this great little engine an ideal power unit.

Not the least of the many delightful features of this car is the price. At £668 17s. tax paid, it is the most astounding value offered to the enthusiast today. For the Sprite is everything a touring car ought to be and yet costs no more than a small saloon.

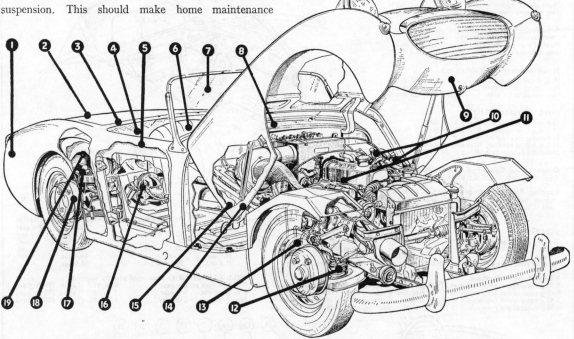

HERE IT IS—POINT BY POINT

1 BODY, of unitary construction to give tremendous strength without unnecessary weight, is roto-dipped against corrosion. Low total weight (approximately 11.9 cwts.) gives brilliant performance.

2 LARGE LUGGAGE COMPARTMENT is accessible from inside car.

3 PVC HOOD is easily and quickly assembled. Stows completely out of sight behind seats.

4 INDIVIDUAL BUCKET SEATS. Driver's seat adjustable. Foam rubber seating upholstered in toughest Vynide.

5 TRIM includes map pockets in doors.

6 STEERING is by rack and pinion, 2¼ turns from lock to lock. New two-spoke steering wheel.

7 WINDSCREEN is curved, toughened glass. Twin windscreen wipers standard.

8 INSTRUMENTS include oil pressure and petrol gauges, thermometer, ignition warning, headlamp main beam, direction indicator lights. Rev. counter is an optional extra.

9 EASY ACCESS FRONT. Cowl, bonnet and front wing assembly hinge as one

unit for complete access to engine and front suspension.

10 TWIN S.U. CARBURETTORS are fitted for maximum power output.

11 ENGINE is the latest development of the BMC 'A' Series 948cc. engine which holds several world records. Compression ratio 8.3 :1.

12 INDEPENDENT FRONT SUSPENSION with coil springs and hydraulic shock absorbers.

13 WHEELS are fully ventilated for maximum brake cooling. Tubeless tyres.

14 GEARBOX has four forward speeds. Ratios—first 3.628, second 2.374, third 1.412. Short, remote control gear lever ensures quickest possible gear changes.

15 HANDBRAKE is centrally mounted for quick access.

16 HYPOID REAR AXLE. Ratio is 4.22 :1.

17 REAR SUSPENSION is by quarter elliptic springs with trailing links. Independently mounted hydraulic shock absorbers are fitted.

18 BRAKES are Lockheed hydraulic with 2 leading shoes on front wheels. Total brake area is 67.2 square inches for safe stopping at all speeds.

19 FUEL TANK holds approximately 6 gallons (27 litres).

The **Motor** Road Test No. 15/58

Make: Austin-Healey   **Type:** Sprite

Makers: Austin Motor Co. Ltd., Longbridge, Birmingham.

Test Data

World copyright reserved ; no unauthorized reproduction in whole or in part.

CONDITIONS: Weather : Warm and dry with moderate breeze. (Temperature 70°—74°F., Barometer: 30.2–30.4 in Hg.). Surface: Dry tarred macadam. Fuel: Premium-grade pump petrol (Approx. 95 Research Method Octane Rating).

INSTRUMENTS

Speedometer at 30 m.p.h.	3% fast
Speedometer at 60 m.p.h.	5% fast
Speedometer at 80 m.p.h.	8% fast
Distance recorder	2% fast

WEIGHT

Kerb weight (unladen, but with oil, coolant and fuel for approx. 50 miles) .. 12¾ cwt.
Front/rear distribution of kerb weight .. 55/45
Weight laden as tested .. .. 16 cwt.

MAXIMUM SPEEDS

Flying Quarter Mile
Mean of four opposite runs .. .. 82.9 m.p.h.
Best one-way time equals .. .. 86.5 m.p.h.

"Maximile" Speed (Timed quarter mile after one mile accelerating from rest).
Mean of four opposite runs .. .. 81.1 m.p.h.
Best one-way time equals .. .. 83.3 m.p.h.

Speed in Gears (at 6,000 r.p.m.).
Max. speed in 3rd gear .. .. 65 m.p.h.
Max. speed in 2nd gear .. .. 39 m.p.h.
Max. speed in 1st gear .. .. 25 m.p.h.

FUEL CONSUMPTION

52.5 m.p.g. at constant 30 m.p.h. on level.
54.5 m.p.g. at constant 40 m.p.h. on level.
53.5 m.p.g. at constant 50 m.p.h. on level.
38.0 m.p.g. at constant 60 m.p.h. on level.
36.0 m.p.g. at constant 70 m.p.h. on level.

Overall Fuel Consumption for 1,696 miles, 50.5 gallons, equals 33.6 m.p.g. (8.4 litres/100 km.)

Touring Fuel Consumption (m.p.g. at steady speed midway between 30 m.p.h. and maximum, less 5% allowance for acceleration) 43.0 m.p.g.
Fuel tank capacity (maker's figure) .. 6 gallons

STEERING

Turning circle between kerbs :
   Left .. .. 28½ feet
   Right .. .. .. 29⅓ feet
Turns of steering wheel from lock to lock 2⅓

BRAKES from 30 m.p.h.

0.97 g retardation (equivalent to 31 ft stopping distance) with 90 lb. pedal pressure.
0.75 g retardation (equivalent to 40 ft stopping distance) with 75 lb. pedal pressure.
0.49 g retardation (equivalent to 61½ ft stopping distance) with 50 lb. pedal pressure.
0.22 g retardation (equivalent to 137 ft stopping distance) with 25 lb. pedal pressure.

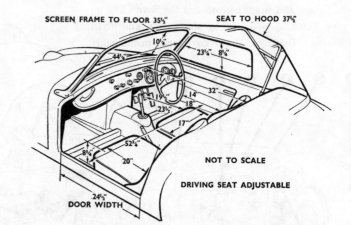

TRACK:— FRONT 3'-0" REAR 3'-8¾"
OVERALL WIDTH 4'-5¼"
3'-11¼"
16'-7"
GROUND CLEARANCE 4⅜"
21½"
11½"
6'-8"
11'-4¼"
AUSTIN-HEALEY SPRITE

SCREEN FRAME TO FLOOR 35½"
SEAT TO HOOD 37½"
10¼"
44¼"
23¼" 8½"
11½"
14" 32"
18"
23½"
17"
52¼"
8¼"
20"
24½"
DOOR WIDTH
NOT TO SCALE
DRIVING SEAT ADJUSTABLE

ACCELERATION TIMES from standstill

0-30 m.p.h.	5.1 sec.
0-40 m.p.h.	8.5 sec.
0-50 m.p.h.	13.7 sec.
0-60 m.p.h.	20.5 sec.
0-70 m.p.h.	31.1 sec.
Standing quarter mile	21.8 sec.

ACCELERATION TIMES on Upper Ratios

	Top gear	3rd gear
10-30 m.p.h.	13.7 sec.	8.6 sec.
20-40 m.p.h.	12.6 sec.	7.7 sec.
30-50 m.p.h.	12.6 sec.	8.6 sec.
40-60 m.p.h.	14.4 sec.	11.4 sec.
50-70 m.p.h.	18.5 sec.	—

HILL CLIMBING at sustained steady speeds.

Max. gradient on top gear .. 1 in 11.7 (Tapley 190 lb./ton)
Max. gradient on 3rd gear .. 1 in 7.5 (Tapley 295 lb./ton)
Max. gradient on 2nd gear .. 1 in 4.5 (Tapley 485 lb./ton)

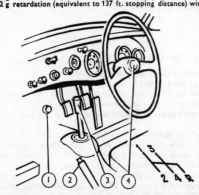

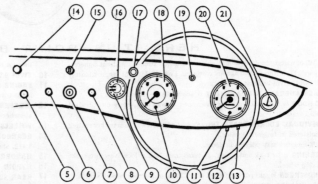

1, Headlamp dip switch. 2, Handbrake. 3, Gear lever. 4, Horn button. 5, Windscreen washers button. 6, Windscreen wipers control. 7, Ignition and lights switch. 8, Heater control. 9, Water thermometer. 10, Headlamp high-beam indicator lamp. 11, Dynamo charge warning lamp. 12, Panel light switch. 13, Trip resetting knob. 14, Choke control. 15, Direction indicator switch. 16, Oil pressure gauge. 17, Starter switch. 18, Tachometer. 19, Direction indicator warning lamp. 20, Speedometer and distance recorder. 21, Fuel contents gauge.

The AUSTIN-HEALEY Sprite

LOW built to corner with minimum roll, the Sprite combines protection for the driver with good all-round vision.

Motoring That is Fun at Very Modest Cost

WERE it possible to define quantitatively a pleasure-to-price ratio for cars, the new Austin-Healey Sprite would undoubtedly register an amazingly high figure for this desirable virtue. Costing about as much to buy as do many popular saloons of similar 1-litre engine size, and perhaps even cheaper than such saloons to run, this open two-seater offers much better acceleration up to a top speed which is higher by some 10 m.p.h., but responsiveness to the slightest touch on the controls is what really makes it such a joy to drive.

Small in size, the Sprite is certainly not a "miniature" car nor should it be regarded as merely a fragile toy. Modern full-width styling of the low-drag body enables it to provide generous room for two big men on excellent seats and there is substantial (if awkwardly arranged) accommodation for luggage also. Almost entirely in evenings and at week-ends,

and unable to attend motor races or other public functions in a still-secret car, members of our staff nevertheless ran the Sprite some 2,000 miles in a period of 20 days, at the end of which period a car which came to us with just over 2,000 miles on its speedometer merely seemed rather better for this extra running-in mileage.

Weighing 2-3-cwt. less than the saloons which use a basically similar power unit, and with wind resistance minimized by a 10-15-inch saving in overall height, the Sprite has required only mild engine tuning to gain performance fully comparable with lively modern saloons of double its size. There are two carburetters, and some valuable mechanical refinements inside the engine to ensure its stamina, but it retains a compression ratio which is moderate enough to tolerate the use of intermediate-grade fuels, a cast iron exhaust manifold with central hot-spot, and a camshaft giving touring valve timing. It is a docile engine, starting easily and quite happy to pull down to 15 m.p.h. in top gear if the car must be lent to some driver of non-sporting tastes. But it is an engine which only begins to sound alive in top gear at more than 30 m.p.h. and thereafter remains smooth and hard-working until the rev. counter needle reaches the far end of the scale, use of 5,000 r.p.m. in the gears when accelerating seeming entirely natural, and cautionary markings on the rev. counter dial between 5,500 and 6,000 r.p.m. being quickly reached. The exhaust note is sharp at wide throttle openings and high r.p.m., but with reasonably restrained handling the Sprite runs through towns without much noise.

Oil consumption during our test was only about 1 pint per 1,000 miles, but in exceptionally warm spring weather the coolant temperature rose sharply enough in London traffic or around Devon trials hills to suggest the desirability of some air outlet louvres on top of the bonnet.

Contributing much to the merit of this car is a four-speed synchromesh gearbox, third gear being useful up to an over-60 m.p.h. speed which is in sensible relation to an over-80 m.p.h. maximum in top gear. The gap between 3rd and 2nd ratios is too wide to please really hard drivers, the useful limit of speed in 2nd gear being less than 40 m.p.h., but this ratio will, if required, start the car from rest and carries it up almost any hill which is used by normal traffic. Located with its knob rather high up and close to the facia, the remote-control gear lever is positive in action, but became stiff to use when the car was really well warmed up.

Rack and pinion steering is geared at only 2¼ turns from extremity to extremity of a steering lock which lets the car swing round between low kerbs a mere 30 feet apart. With no evident lost motion whatever, seemingly negligible friction, and quite light self-centring effect, this steering lets the car be guided by use of fingers and wrists rather than by arm movements —the near-vertical two-spoke wheel is set too close to the seat to permit the straight-arm driving position which is fashionable with racing drivers of cars with lower-geared steering. Naturally enough, this is a car which corners fast with little or no roll, squealing its tyres only under very severe provocation, and in a corner it shows a modest degree of

In Brief

Price £455 plus purchase tax £223 17s. 0d.
    equals £678 17s. 0d.

Capacity	948 c.c.
Unladen kerb weight ..	12¾ cwt.
Acceleration :	
20-40 m.p.h. in top gear	12.6 sec.
0-50 m.p.h. through gears	13.7 sec.
Maximum direct top gear gradient	
	1 in 11.7
Maximum speed ..	82.9 m.p.h.
"Maximile" speed ..	81.1 m.p.h.
Touring fuel consumption	43 m.p.g.

Gearing : 15.4 m.p.h. in top gear at 1,000 r.p.m. 30.8 m.p.h. at 1,000 ft./min. piston speed.

The AUSTIN-

COCKPIT of this simple sports car shows the central gear lever and handbrake, individual bucket seats, two-spoke steering wheel, optional rev. counter and neatly fitted rubber floor covering.

pressures. Ordinary buyers of this car should never have any worry with brake fade, but the harder treatment imposed by competitions might disclose that whilst a single stop from 80 m.p.h. merely produces a warm smell, three or four stops from 60 m.p.h. in rapid succession cause a considerable temporary loss of front brake effectiveness. Set close against the passenger seat, the pull-up handbrake (of touring rather than fly-off pattern) works excellently. Low build and proximity of the radiator air intake to the ground limit this car's ability to negotiate fords or flood-water, but ground clearance beneath the chassis proves to be rather more adequate than it appears, as the underside of the body is a smooth metal surface almost devoid of vulnerable projections.

Habitability

In respect of touring car amenities a sensible compromise seems to have been struck, the Sprite having most of the essentials included in its moderate price but being very evidently capable of improvement by the subsequent addition of extra equipment. Two front-hinged doors (with interior handles only) give acceptable ease of entry to the low body, and capacious pockets in the lower halves of unlined doors leave generous elbow width available above them. Two sidescreens have simple and secure fixings, and the fully detachable hood has a three-piece rear window of wrap-around proportions. Two wiper blades operate on a curved glass windscreen of large area, which gives good protection although inducing appreciable back-draught in the cockpit. Flashing turn indicators do not cancel themselves but their control is conveniently placed at the centre of the facia panel. An excellent driving light is given by the headlamps, though in misty weather the fact that their mountings are almost in the driver's short-range sight line over the low bonnet might prove a handicap. Unluckily, the pattern of air flow around the body at speeds above 60 m.p.h. tends to flutter the hood, and blows rainwater or insects into the body through gaps which open up between an easy-to-erect hood and the top of the windscreen, and between the windscreen and sidescreens. An optional extra, the fresh-air heater with air valve and booster fan controlled from the facia panel worked well on our test car, and by turning off the under-bonnet water tap it could be used to blow cool air into the cockpit.

Accommodation for a considerable volume of luggage is available behind the seats, in a long and reasonably wide compartment of moderate height, but this space can be reached only from the front

stable "understeer" until the limit of tyre adhesion is transgressed. Perhaps because the natural sensitivity of the steering is magnified by flexible rubber bushes in some of the front and rear suspension pivots, the car needs a decidedly delicate touch on the controls to put it into a corner fast and accurately on a chosen line without initial "oversteering" by the driver, and too heavy a hand on the controls will accentuate a slight tendency to weave on the straight at maximum speeds. Once a sensitive driver has the feel of this car however, he can revel in hustling it along winding roads, totally forgetting a tendency for the car to pull slightly to the right during acceleration or left on the over-run which

at first acquaintance was fairly evident. Wet and slippery roads do nothing to diminish the pleasure of driving this light and outstandingly responsive car, and rough roads do not jolt it unduly despite the suspension being much firmer than on most modern touring cars.

Toe and Heel

Three pedals which are spaced to accommodate reasonably wide shoes are set conveniently level with one another, and the headlamp dipper acts as a rest for the left foot beside the clutch pedal. It is possible to "blip" the accelerator for a downward gearchange whilst braking, and the brakes give instant and powerful response to modest pedal

BENEATH the lift-up body nose is this 948 c.c. engine, with twin carburetters and modified internally to withstand sustained operation at high r.p.m.

HEALEY Sprite

past tilted-forward seat backrests, and small items can become lost in its depths. The hood fabric and sidescreens must be stowed in the luggage space when they are not in use, the folded hood frame fitting neatly into sockets where it encircles the mouth of the luggage compartment, but contributing to the variety of minor rattles evident around

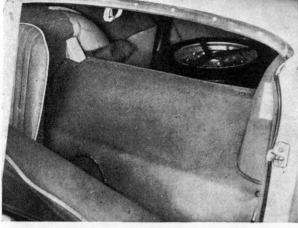

TAILPIECE of the small Austin-Healey is a luggage locker accessible only from inside the body. Weather protection includes a quickly erected hood with wrap-around rear window.

what is in essentials a sturdily rigid body. Simple in its mechanical design, and using a large proportion of well-tried components this should not be in any way a difficult car to maintain. Proper

provision is made, for example, for access to the gearbox dipstick, a secure cover being disclosed when the moulded rubber floor covering is rolled back. Concealed hinges do not allow the awkwardly heavy

lift-up nose of the steel body to rise as far as is desirable for comfortable access to the engine, but two self-locking struts can be supplemented by a third prop to ensure the safety of anyone working on the mechanism. Even when driven quite hard this car gives over 30 m.p.g. fuel economy, and gentler treatment readily produces well over 40 m.p.g. on long runs when the petrol tank capacity of 6 gallons begins to seem less meagre.

It is safe to predict that this inexpensive new Austin-Healey will have a very wide appeal, both in Britain and in many other parts of the world. Good performance which asks to be used to the full, controls of a responsiveness which many touring car owners have never even imagined possible, and a complete lack of temperament will make it a desirable and possible purchase both as an " only " car and also as " second car " in households already using a four-seat saloon.

Specification

Engine:

Cylinders	4
Bore	62.9 mm.
Stroke	76.2 mm.
Cubic capacity	948 c.c.
Piston area	19.29 sq. in.
Valves	Pushrod o.h.v.
Compression ratio	8.3/1
Carburetter	2 inclined S.U. type H1
Fuel pump	AC mechanical
Ignition timing control	Centrifugal and vacuum
Oil filter	Tecalemit or Purolator, full-flow
Max. power (net) 43 b.h.p. (gross, 50 b.h.p.) at	5,200 r.p.m.
Piston speed at max. b.h.p.	2,600 ft./min.

Transmission

Clutch	Borg and Beck 6¼-in. s.d.p.
Top gear (s/m)	4.22
3rd gear (s/m)	5.96
2nd gear (s/m)	10.02
1st gear	15.31
Reverse	19.69
Propeller shaft	Hardy Spicer open
Final drive	Hypoid bevel
Top gear m.p.h. at 1,000 r.p.m.	15.4
Top gear m.p.h. at 1,000 ft./min. piston speed	30.8

Chassis

Brakes	Lockheed hydraulic (2 l.s. front)
Brake drum internal diameter	7 in.
Friction lining area	67.5 sq. in.
Suspension:	
Front	Independent by coil springs and wishbones
Rear	Quarter elliptic springs and rigid axle
Shock absorbers	Armstrong hydraulic, lever-arm type
Steering gear	Rack and pinion
Tyres	5.20-13 tubeless

Coachwork and Equipment

Starting handle	Yes
Battery mounting	Behind engine on scuttle
Jack	Bipod screw type with ratchet handle
Jacking points	External sockets on body sides
Standard tool kit: Jack and ratchet handle, tyre pump, grease gun, wheel nut spanner, ignition screwdriver/feeler, tyre valve key, sparking plug spanner, plug and tappet feeler gauge, screwdriver, toolbag.	
Exterior lights : 2 headlamps, 2 sidelamps/flashers, 2 stop/tail lamps, number plate lamp.	
Number of electrical fuses :	2
Direction indicators : Flashers (white front, amber rear), non self-cancelling.	
Windscreen wipers : 2-blade electrical, self-parking.	
Windscreen washers :	Optional extra.
Sun vizors :	None
Instruments : Speedometer with decimal trip distance recorder, oil pressure gauge, cool-	

ant thermometer, fuel contents gauge (tachometer optional extra).

Warning lights : Headlamp main beam, direction indicators, dynamo charge.	
Locks : With ignition key : Ignition switch.	
With other keys :	None
Glove lockers :	None
Map pockets :	Two in doors
Parcel shelves :	None
Ashtrays :	None
Cigar lighters :	None
Interior lights :	Instrument lighting only
Interior heater : Optional extra, fresh-air type with screen de-misters.	
Car radio :	Optional extra
Extras available : Rev. Counter, Heater, Radio, Screen washers, laminated glass screen, front bumper, tonneau cover, locking petrol cap.	
Upholstery material :	Leathercloth
Floor covering :	Moulded rubber mats
Exterior colours standardized.	Five
Alternative body styles :	None

Maintenance

Sump 6 pints, plus ⅞ pint in filter, S.A.E. 30 (below freezing, S.A.E. 20W)	
Gearbox	2½ pints, S.A.E. 30
Rear axle 1¾ pints, S.A.E. 90 hypoid gear oil	
Steering gear lubricant	S.A.E. 90 hypoid gear oil
Cooling system capacity	5¾ pints (2 drain taps)
Chassis lubrication : By oil gun every 1,000 miles to 10 points	
Ignition timing	5° before t.d.c. static
Contact breaker-gap	0.014–0.016 in.
Sparking plug type	Champion N5 (14 mm. long reach)
Sparking plug gap	0.025 in.

Valve timing Inlet opens 5° before t.d.c. and closes 45° after b.d.c.: Exhaust opens 40° before b.d.c. and closes 10° after t.d.c.	
Tappet clearances (Hot) Inlet and exhaust	0.012 in.
Front wheel toe-in	0 – 1/8 in.
Camber angle	1°
Castor angle	3°
Steering swivel pin inclination	6½°
Tyre pressures :	
Front	18 lb.
Rear	20 lb.
Brake fluid	Lockheed
Battery type and capacity : 12 volt, 43 amp. hr. Lucas B.T.W.7A.	

CAR CHARM!

The Editor drops the clutch on the Speedwell Sprite which he found to be a most potent little machine with no vices, and surprising tractability. Sidescreens and windscreen permit high speeds with no need for hat. Slight bulge on nearside of bonnet is the only distinguishing feature from standard Sprite

A WEEKEND WITH THE AUSTIN-HEALEY SPRITE   *by CHARLES MEISL*

IF I had an 18-year-old son (and the money) I would certainly not hesitate in giving him a Sprite.

Even on briefest acquaintance the car impresses with its "built-in" safety. I refer particularly to road-holding which is outstanding in such a small and mass-produced car.

Neutral steering is prevalent with perhaps the slightest bias towards oversteer, and any over-enthusiastic cornering is checked with a flick of the wrist. We purposely induced four-wheel "driftlets" during the prevailing damp weather and the Sprite behaved like a full-grown racing machine, being controllable to an inch. Poor roads set up a slight fore and aft pitch, especially at slowish speeds, this also produces sundry rattles and squeaks. Some of the rattles on the test car were traced to the choke and throttle cables drumming against the bonnet, and in fairness it must be said that the test car had had a tough life! The squeak seemed to come either from one of the rubber bushes of the rear torque arms or perhaps from excessive dryness of one of the rear quarter elliptic springs.

The brakes are adequate without being outstanding, repeated applications from the higher speed ranges produced slightly uneven pulling, but this might be curable by fitting harder linings. The rev-counter (optional fitting) indicated 4,500 r.p.m. at 70 m.p.h. on the speedometer, and this is an agreeable cruising speed.

The well-proven and willing A35 engine of 948 c.c. revs very freely up to 6,000 without stress or vibratory periods and the hydraulically operated clutch is certainly man enough for its job—it took performance and repeated acceleration testing in its stride. The A35 gearbox ratios are very suitable for the Sprite, but when the box is really used hard, bottom and second become progressively more difficult to engage. I disliked the length of the gear lever. It is too easy to bark one's knuckles (I did, twice) on the lower edge of the facia in bottom and third gear positions.

The small overall size of the Sprite and the more than adequate leg-room even for six-footers enables one to drive the car well and quickly right from the start and visibility is excellent, even with the hood up and side screens in place.

Some might prefer a slightly lower-geared steering, especially if they are not too experienced.

Appearance is really quite good, the sticking-up head-lamps together with the radiator grille giving the little car a cheerful "smiling" countenance. The height of the headlamps is necessitated by American lighting regulations.

Trim is reasonable within the price structure of the car, the seats earning high marks for the way they hold driver and passenger during rapid cornering—they also support the back of the thighs well, a boon for long-distance driving. There are large pockets in the doors but no cubby on the facia.

The interior bent tin door handles are placed so that an energetic manoeuvre brings them into violent and painful

Large enough for even six-footers the roomy cockpit has two bucket seats which effectively hold the driver and passenger when cornering rapidly. The short gear lever is well positioned but it is possible for the hand to touch the facia in 1st and 3rd gears

contact with the driver's elbow, they are unworthy of such a delightful little car.

The hood with its removable tubular hood-sticks is cleverly engineered and easily erected. Even at high speeds it does not flap unduly and is quite rainproof. The optional heater and windscreen washer do their job very well.

The whole of the bonnet is hinged from the scuttle and can be secured with a strut that is safe. Accessibility to the engine and front suspension is good, although when closed the bonnet tends to flutter up and down a little at speed. Stronger hinges might obviate this trouble. Improvement of the bonnet lock would also be desirable; again it is likely to trap unwary fingers and knuckles. The horn sounds like a hysterical canary.

In warm weather the engine starts without the choke even after 12 hours' inactivity and soon settles to even running.

The Sprite has undeniable charm, it is fun to drive, eminently safe and B.M.C. together with Donald Healey have jointly produced a real money spinner.

Performance Figures

0–30 m.p.h.	.. ..	6.2 sec.
0–50 ,,	.. ..	15.3 ,,
0–60 ,,	.. ..	25.0 ,,
30–50 ,,	.. ..	9.4 ,,
50–70 ,,	.. ..	15.0 ,,
Maximum speed	..	81.4 m.p.h. ★

BRIEF ENCOUNTER
THE EDITOR SAMPLES THE "SPEEDWELL SPRITE"

WITH memories of the highly enjoyable time I had with the "Speedwell A35" last month still fresh in my mind I was delighted to be invited by Speedwell director John Sprinzel to try the modified Austin-Healey Sprite which his company ultimately intends to market in the same manner as their current A35 saloon.

When I collected the car from Speedwell's new premises at 763 Finchley Road, London, N.W.1, it was looking very travel-stained, but it turned out to be anything but weary. Completely standard-looking, except for a slight bonnet bulge to accommodate the raised carburetters, it was appropriately finished in Speedwell Blue.

As if to warn me of its potentialities, Development Engineer George Hulbert informed that the speedometer had cried "enough", but that the rev-counter was functioning well and performance figures would be easy enough to obtain.

One's first reaction is that here is a tiny 1-litre, mass-produced sports car that goes and handles as well as many 1½-litre "thoroughbred" cars of not so many years ago. I can remember spending much money and midnight oil on the modification of a sports car of very high repute, within the last 10 years, and it did go awfully well, but I'm sure the Speedwell Sprite would run rings round it—and the *conducteur* wouldn't be tired out!

After collecting a friend who insisted on accompanying me, and who claimed that he was the best stop-watch driver in Bucks, we set off to collect some acceleration times, etc. It must be pointed out in fairness to the car (but not to my friend) that he weighs very nearly as much as I do, and that is *circa* 15 stone. Please make the necessary mental adjustments.

Engine modifications to the Speedwell Sprite have not unnaturally been based on and developed from their well-known converted A35 and Morris Minor units. S.U. carburetters of 1⅛ in. diameter are fitted as standard on the production Sprite, but Speedwell replace these with 1¼-in. instruments, and like their A35 saloons, the cylinder head has reshaped combustion chambers, flowed ports, and stronger valve springs. The standard camshaft is retained but the valves are reground with a different under-head radius. Compression ratio is raised from 8.3 to 8.7 : 1 which results in a claimed power output of more than 50 b.h.p. Great attention to the lining-up of manifolding and ports, and the standard coil and distributor is used in conjunction with a 6.5 deg. advance. These engine modifications designated Stage I can be carried out to existing standard Sprites at a cost of £65, plus £7 10s. fitting charge.

It is certainly "some mill" as the Americans would have it. Even with 29 stones aboard the car. 0 to 30 m.p.h. took 4.5 sec.; 0–40 m.p.h., 7.8 sec.; 0–50 m.p.h., 12.4 sec.; 0–60 m.p.h., 20 sec.; 0–70 m.p.h., 28 sec., and 0–80 m.p.h., 38 sec. The way the rev-counter swung round to 5,000 in

Speedwell Sprite has larger, 1¼ in. S.U. carburetters and stronger valve springs. The carburetters are high-mounted on the long Speedwell light-alloy induction pipes. Rocker cover is dull-plated, and power-output in Stage I form is claimed to be more than 50 b.h.p. but a more powerful Stage 2 version as fitted for the Apline Rally, is on the way

the gears was most impressive, the little engine bellowing away but retaining remarkable smoothness throughout the whole of the test.

There was no time to seek an airfield where maximum speeds could be tried in comparative comfort, so we set out to get as near maximum as we could without frightening ourselves too much. After several runs up and down a well-surfaced highway near Beaconsfield we managed 88 m.p.h. with the hood down, and although there was undoubtedly a bit left, the accident was getting awfully close, so *we* shut off.

Maximum speeds in the gears were 25–40–65, and the gear change was delightful in the B.M.C. manner.

The Speedwell anti-roll bar made the Sprite a very manageable car, although I think it would be a better car for the "ordinary" motorist (and at the price a lot of "ordinary" motorists are going to buy this car) if the steering were a little less high geared. It is necessary to hold the wheel very lightly indeed, and roundabouts are "wished" round rather than steered.

I was sorry to return the Sprite so soon, but I look forward to trying it in its latest Alpine Trial form with 60 b.h.p. engine, special camshaft—the lot! Even this is not the end of the Speedwell plan for the Sprite. They are developing a new "front bonnet", probably of fibre-glass, and a hard-top for the car, besides considering the marketing of wire wheels for the model.—D.A.
★

SPORTS CARS ILLUSTRATED

WITH THE INTRODUCTION of their latest product, BMC has changed the spelling of the word "fun." It's now a six letter word: Sprite. This newest concept from the fertile minds of Donald Healey and son Geoff even *looks* happy.

On first look you feel as if you would like to pat it on the head — if it had one to pat. Virtually everyone who has driven it has much the same reactions. First the feeling described above, then a sort of "cute car but will it go?" feeling. One block of driving and nobody cares *how* fast it is. The pure enjoyment of handling this willing little box is such that true performance doesn't matter very much — you're having too much of a ball to dither about trifles. It pounces around in traffic like a playful kitten, goes when it's told and stops when bidden. Its steering is the sort of thing automobile writers dream about and seldom experience, even on pure-bred racing machinery. Light withal, it gives a definite feeling of utter reliability, and only three days after the A-H Sprite was introduced, a car appeared in Class H Production at Put-In Bay, Ohio.

Sprites are ideal first sports cars for either the beginner in The True Motoring whose tastes formerly leaned toward the titanic, or the novice to sports racing who wants to feel his way around the race course. Its 948 cc displacement places it well up in the 750 cc to one liter class; and more important, though it's not a true race car, most of the others in its class are even less so.

We must admit we felt far from cocky as we gunned our Sprite from the pit area at Lime Rock onto the course for its performance testing, easing it into the slot between a Mercedes 190 SL and a very hot Alfa Veloce. Under no condition could we compare it with the latter, but all things considered, we were able to at least play a bit with the 190 in the turns.

Pulling through the hairpin, through the esses and into the serpentine we were aware of the lightness and quickness of the steering. At low speed the Sprite has the feel that the tail might hop out, but somewhere between 50 and 60 mph the feel turns to one of dead neutrality. At no time is there a feel of plowing, if the machine is handled correctly. The tail *is* reluctant to flick out, and the best technique is to punch the brake as the wheel is cut into the turn. This throws the rear wheels into a slip attitude which, if moderate, can be held at high speed (for the Sprite) if the driver adheres to his "line" smoothly. If he tries for too much drift, he will just slow down, as it is impossible to sustain big slip angles on turns. The engine just isn't strong enough. (Incidentally, this is also true of most "road" cars). Despite this, the Sprite is extremely easy to take around the course, and properly handled can make its presence known to bigger cars on the tighter turns.

The powerplant is the sturdy BMC A-type engine equipped with dual S.U.'s and heavier valve springs. Output is 48 horses at 5000 and 52 lb/ft of twist at 3300 rpm. The torque comes in at the mid point of the rev range (600-6000), and coupled with the 3.63 first gear and 2.37 second cog, the Sprite jumps off briskly until it is popped into 3rd. In 1.41 torque multiplication niche the acceleration curve starts to flatten, reaching what seems the almost horizontal at about 4500 ticks on the tach. The engine pulls the last 1500 to indicated 60 mph much more slowly, requiring approximately the last half of the standing quarter for the last 1500 revs in third. Going into 4th at 60, acceleration is steady if not flashing. Since 4000 revs is 60 mph in top, the Sprite is capable of 90 mph indicated without over-revving, and there is every indication that over a prolonged stretch of still-air, level-ground road (all right, maybe assisted by a down grade or two) the Sprite will reach its red line in fourth. We were somewhat reluctant to try, because the day's testing at Lime Rock, with every staff member driving BMC's new baby, the car had run the equivalent of ten 10-lap races without inspection. An insurance policy will do just so much for courage and morale!

One interesting feature is the rear suspension. The expected live rear axle is suspended by a pair of quarter elliptic leaf springs, similar to those used on the 3.4 Jaguar. The axle is located by a pair of sturdy radius brackets that run parallel to the wheel-base line, and is equipped with a strap that over a spring busting bump will transfer some of the impact overload on the shocks to the base of the spine. Shocks on both ends, incidentally, are non-tubular and smack very strongly of our own GM practice in the 40's. They are probably oversize, for they do a really good job. Despite the short wheel base the Sprite rides extremely well over choppy roads, and aside from a tendency to scrape.

AUSTIN-HEALEY
Sprite

Cavernous trunk is accessible when twin bucket seats are tilted forward, accomodates a lot of luggage plus spare wheel.

Hood, fenders are unit, hinge from cowl to expose inner fenders that protect pepped-up BMC A-type engine.

Spacious cockpit is leather covered and full instrumented. Shift lever is long, probably be shortened by do-it-yourself.

the license plate on either end (shades of the 100-6!), handles the dipsy doodles very well.

Front end is conventional A-35 *ifs* with the single shock arm incorporated into the suspension as an upper arm. Coil springs are based on the bottom A-frame, and Morris Minor rack and pinion steering linkage is fully shielded by rubber covers.

In appearance, the Sprite is basically Healey, seasoned strongly with M.G.A. (and according to a few Porsche-pushing critics, Crosley Hotshot, too). But it does have a personality all its own. Aside from those silly headlights that should be faired into somewhere, the front is Ferrari in concept, with the slightly protruding-from-the-recessed snout very much like the front of the 250 TR. From the side, we admit the Porsche pushers had us very much on the defensive; however, from the rear the little one at speed could very well be mistaken for an Ace or a Siata, depending on what one expected to see.

Twin bucket seats face a leather-covered fully-instrumented panel. The small instruments are identical to those in the 100-6; however, the speedo and the tach are indigenous to the new breed. The former group functions perfectly, but both the speedo and the tach have a tendency to be very vague. For example, when accelerating the tach needle seems to stick at the 5000 rev mark, suddenly taking a dive into and over the shaded area; one expects loud noises until he realizes that these two dials are of the "about" variety. The tach is an optional extra that costs $17.50.

For a small car, the luggage area is deceivingly spacious. Prior to testing the Sprite, the writer thoroughly accustomed himself to the habits of the 100-6 by weekending at the Bridgehampton Road Races. All luggage was crammed into one fibreglass suitcase of proportions that the trunk capacity successfully defied. Since this particular 100-6 had an "occasional" seat, the

case was just plain ungainly. The suitcase was truly *tolerated.*

In the Sprite, there is no trunk lid. Cavernous trunk is accessible through a comparatively small opening which is exposed by tilting both seats forward. The suitcase under discussion, plus others, fit with no difficulty. But our prayers protecting us against flats were answered, as it is necessary to crawl into the cramped rearward recesses to remove the spare. After the first such mishap, BMC would have no trouble marketing, as an optional extra, a trained monkey to load and unload the spare and the tools.

But one feature that will sell a lot of Sprites is its complete happiness in close traffic. Under these conditions, like its big brother, the water temperature creeps to 190° plus on a hot day, but the cockpit stays cool. The hydraulically actuated clutch is easy to engage without a lot of slippage and the engine picks up the load at low revs. It is possible to run in top

Live rear axle is suspended from quarter elliptic leaf springs, is located by radius bracket. Hole is for brakes.

Front ifs bases coil on bottom A-frame, single arm from chassis-mounted shock acts as top member. Steering is Morris.

Very distinctive rear styling. We had looks from people on the road who wondered what kind of car we were in.

the *Sprite*

A real sweetheart on the turns. It's easy to get the tail out, and if you don't demand big slip angles, you can keep it there.

AUSTIN-HEALEY SPRITE

PERFORMANCE

TOP SPEED:
Estimated .... 80-85 mph

ACCELERATION:

From zero to	seconds
30 mph	6.0
40 mph	10.5
50 mph	15.9
60 mph	25.2
Standing ¼ mile	22.8
Speed at end of quarter	58 mph

SPEED RANGES IN GEARS: (1000-5200 rpm)

I	0-21 mph
II	7-34
III	11-55
IV	15-top

SPEEDOMETER CORRECTION:

Indicated	Timed
30	29
40	39
50	49
60	58

FUEL CONSUMPTION:
26 mpg

SPECIFICATIONS

POWER UNIT:
BMC A Series .... Water-cooled in-line four
Valve Operation .... pushrod ohv, in-line
Bore & Stroke .... 2.47 x 3.00 in (62.9 x 76.2 mm)
Stroke/Bore Ratio 1.21/1
Displacement .... 57.8 cu in (948 cc)
Compression Ratio 8.3/1
Carburetion by .... Two S.U. H-1 semi-down-draft
Max. Power .... 48 bhp @ 5000 rpm
Max. Torque .... 52 lbs-ft @ 3300 rpm

DRIVE TRAIN:
Transmission ratios
I 3.63
II 2.37
III 1.41
IV 1.00
Final drive ratio .. 4.22
Axle torque taken by radius arms

CHASSIS:
Frame .... Pressed steel monocoque body-frame
Wheelbase .... 78 in
Tread, front and rear ..... 45¾, 44¾ in
Front Suspension .... Coil springs and wishbones
Rear Suspension .... Rigid rear axle, quarter-elliptic Springs and radius arms
Shock absorbers .... Lever action hydraulic
Steering type .... Rack and pinion
Steering wheel turns L to L .. 2⅓
Turning diam., curb to curb .. 32 ft
Brakes .... Lockheed 2LS front, 1LS rear
Brake lining area .... 67.5 sq in
Tire size .... 5.20 x 13

GENERAL:
Length .... 137 in
Width .... 53 in
Height, top up and down ... 44, 50 in
Weight, as tested .... 1740 lbs
Weight distribution,
F/R as tested 49/51
Fuel Capacity .... 7.2 U. S. Gallons

RATING FACTORS:
Specific Power Output ..... 0.83 bhp/cu in
Power to Weight Ratio ..... 36.3 lbs/hp
Piston speed @ 60 mph ..... 1935 ft/min
Braking Area .... 78 sq in/ton
Speed @ 1000 rpm in top gear .. 15.5 mph

Price at East Coast POE $1795
U. S. Importer: Hambro Automotive Corp.
27 West 57th St.
New York 19, N. Y.

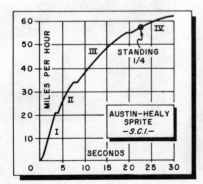

Only three days after introduction, a Sprite raced at Put-In-Bay.

gear at speeds between 15 and 20 mph and accelerate smoothly to top. The shifting lever is beautifully placed, but is long enough to smash knuckles attached to energetic arms into dash panel simultaneously with third gear. It's not difficult to envision this lever shortened, a la MGA, when the gear box becomes more tractable through break in.

The top is a lot easier to erect than that of the 100-6. Instead of the myriad of snaps at the rear, two slide fasteners (MGA) engage the bottom half and the front drops into place. The bow is still mounted and pivoted down. The windshield is removable, and one staff member noticed immediately the availability of screws to peg on racing shields. The side curtain brackets slide easily into non-removable locking screws, but they are not of the best possible design. More attention was given to cost and useability than styling and convenience. It is necessary to reach inside through the curtain to open the doors. There is no glove box, but there is a spacious pocket in each door.

BMC has introduced a new concept of Sports Car for Americans. The Sprite is not a "big" car, like the 100-6; nor is it a "pocket-size" car. It's fully useable for two people, spacious, comfortable (heater is available) and extremely roadable. The price, at $1795 P.O.E., N. Y., will go a long way toward sugar coating any short comings in styling or otherwise. In our opinion, it's an awful lot of car for the money; and BMC will sell a lot of Sprites. All you have to do is try one and you're sold.

Though not exactly designed for the 1-mile straight at Put-In-Bay, is was well up in class and very much a race car.

Reader's Report

Austin-Healey Sprite

I HAVE just come in from driving my five-seater family saloon. I nearly turned it over, ambling down to the post office and back. The trouble was I was travelling at Sprite "ambling" speed.

This is the first lounge-suit sports car I have owned and driving it from Abingdon with a bare mile showing on the mileage recorder as I turned out of the MG works, I began to make comparisons with my previous cars. Away from the gates we accelerated. H'mm! Not as good as a Cooper 100 JAP. Then into a few bends. Not, I'm afraid, the hard taut feel of the Lotus. The brakes were, however, as good as any I have used. Arriving home, having been merely running-in at two and a half thousand revs. and, at the same time, unfairly comparing the machine with out and out racng machinery, I was not wildly impressed. Now three and a half weeks and two race meetings later, there is a different story to tell, and the car which I though of as just another touring car has proved me wrong to the extent of a "first" in the Leinster Trophy Race and very nearly leaving me upside down in another make of car through driving it as though it were a Sprite.

Four days after collecting from Abingdon the car was on its way up to Liverpool to be shipped over to Kirkistown. At incredibly short notice we now had fitted a Sprinzel head and carbs., Mintex M20 brake linings, balanced wheels (with tubes, thank you very much, for a sports car on tubeless tyres seems an incredible thing for anyone to produce, to my way of thinking), and a rev-counter from Smith's to cope with the Speedwell conversion, which sends the revs. straight off the standard instrument. There were roughly 900 miles on the clock, by way of running in! We are going to have a rush to make the boat, so despite the maker's recommendation not to use full power until 2,000 miles were completed, the foot went down (after all, we were racing the car next day) and although at this stage not impressed with the performance myself, I did not notice that every other car on the A5 was going backwards for some reason.

Then it began raining, and remarkably, the water stayed outside, no gushes through the floor or drips down the back. Here, indeed, was something quite new to me in sports car behaviour. If it rains now I go out on purpose and drive through all the puddles I can find just to get my money's worth. But reverting to the run to Liverpool, the most incredible feature of the car was now revealed. The cornering in the wet is, without question, the best I have ever experienced. I tried consistently to slide the car for the rest of the journey but, without doing something completely insane, found it to be quite impossible to do so. Greasy, smooth, bumpy, whatever the surface. it made no difference, and bends were taken at speeds which would have thrown any previous car I have driven off the road. This combined with the wide rev-range is the car's simply outstanding feature and before the Dunboyne race one driver was actually praying for rain, which, unhappily for the organisers and other competitors, came down heavily. At least two competitors in racing cars spun whilst keeping company with the Sprite in bends, and avoiding them as they gyrated was made simple by the road-holding of the car. The rev. range was also useful in passing more powerful cars, which was done as follows: wait a fair way behind until a third-gear bend, enter bends faster than car in front (simple in the Sprite), and get alongside coming out of the bend, then hold onto the revs. until he changes gear and one can slip ahead in the inevitable pause in his acceleration and then change down at leisure. This technique took the Sprite past cars of double the capacity, which were supposed to catch and pass it.

The racing over, the car was driven three up, full of luggage (it is a two seater officially), down to Killarney and then through the Gap of Dunloe. I'd like to have tried that, three up, in the Lotus! No snags. No trouble. The car is not, as I by this time realised, a sports racer in the traditional sense, but a sports car which can be raced. It is a sports car to be used for enjoyment and remarkably good value.
Radlett, Herts.

J. Anstice-Brown.

AUTOSPORT, OCTOBER 3, 1958

DONALD HEALEY with the Sprite, designed to meet the need for a low-priced sports car with a small-capacity engine.

sible with all-metal shells. The dream of an ultra-light sporting two-seater with a high power-weight ratio could have been realized, but production costs would have far exceeded the price bracket for which "the Tiddler" was intended.

The well-tried Austin A35 engine was a "natural" for the power plant. Fitted with twin-carburetters and modified porting, it was good for 42.5 b.h.p., which Healey and his technicians calculated would produce a maximum speed of around 80 m.p.h., and give all-day cruising at 70 m.p.h. It was also decided to retain the four-speed B.M.C. gearbox.

● SPOTLIGHT ON—

The Austin-Healey Sprite

Yet Another Spectacular Success for the Warwick-Longbridge Enterprise—80 m.p.h. from 1000 c.c. Sports Car of Infinite Charm

ONE of the best pieces of business that Sir Leonard Lord has ever done for Austins and B.M.C. was to take over the manufacturing rights of the Healey "Hundred", after its sensational début at the 1954 Earls Court Motor Show. As the Austin-Healey 100, the car made a considerable impact on the export market, particularly in the U.S.A. The car was, of course, powered by the four-cylinder Austin A90 engine, modified for a higher performance in a sporting chassis. Then followed the 100-Six, utilizing the well-proved Austin "105" power-unit, which has made an even more universal appeal than the original "four".

However, B.M.C. were interested in a new small sports car; the M.G. had grown up to such an extent that it could hardly be said to cater for the type of market that was satisfied in the 1930s by Austin Seven, M.G. Midget, Singer Nine, Triumph Super Seven and other small, high-performance machines. Donald Healey applied his mind to this

particular problem, and for some time it was no real secret that the works at the Cape, Warwick, were experimenting with a little machine affectionately known as "the Tiddler". There were, of course, the usual wild rumours: "it was a 2-o.h.c. . . . it had all-independent suspension . . . it was a flat-four . . . it had a space frame . . . and so on". In point of fact, Donald's intention was to make his new creation as simple as possible, and to utilize existing B.M.C. components to keep production costs down to the minimum.

There was no use in tooling for a machine with all-independent suspension when no other B.M.C. product was available. With the U.S.A. in mind, steel was adopted for the body shell; aluminium is definitely not popular with American service stations and repairers, as few concerns are equipped to do light-alloy welding. Again, "fibreglass" was not considered to have reached the point where such units could be turned out in thousands, with the workmanship pos-

When the car was originally submitted to Sir Leonard, it had retractable head-lamps. However, legal requirements made these impracticable, and despite the loss of aesthetic appeal, the somewhat "sexy" shrouded lamps were adopted. Whatever one may think of their appearance, there is one thing certain—they are just about the most efficient road lamps ever fitted to a small-capacity production car.

I first tried the "Sprite", as it was named, last May during the period of the Monaco G.P. In the mountains around the Principality, it showed itself to be a really first-rate little machine. It possessed excellent acceleration, a sound gearbox, powerful brakes and the feeling that it could be caned unmercifully for ever. There was, at first, a suggestion of oversteer which was most disconcerting, but attention to tyre pressures completely cured that. Also, although the hood was fairly easy to erect, and fitted snugly, the car could hardly be said to be completely weather-

WEATHERPROOFING (above) has been carefully studied: the rear window gives excellent visibility. LIDLESS boot (right) is surprisingly roomy.

proof or draught-proof. However, this was a very early car, more or less a pre-production vehicle; eventual production cars have far more efficient all-weather equipment.

Later, in the Austin-Healey showrooms in South Audley Street, London, Mort Morris-Goodall let me examine a machine from which the bodywork had been removed. Without question, the Sprite is a finely engineered job in every way. The entire structure looks, and is rigid; obviously it will not batter itself to pieces on Belgian pavé, or on those dreadful tracks which pass as roads, off the state highways of the New World. Subsequently the design was thoroughly proved when a team of Sprites came successfully through the 1958 "Coupe des Alpes", completely dominating the small-capacity classes.

You see, Don Healey is a competitions driver of immense experience. New-comers to the sport of motoring may not be aware of the fact that Healey won the Monte Carlo Rally outright in a 4½-litre Invicta, and was outstandingly successful as a works driver for the old Triumph concern. Whilst agreeing that very lightweight cars are essential for modern sports car racing, Donald's vast experience convinced him that longevity was far more important than weight-pairing, and thus the Sprite is by no means an ultra-light vehicle; kerb weight is precisely 12¼ cwt. However, progress has enabled Austins to produce a car of under 1,000 c.c., with the almost comparable performance of the 1½-litre H.R.G. of a decade ago—a notable achievement whichever way one looks at it.

The Sprite has, of course, no chassis frame proper, being designed as a body-cum-chassis structure; surely an innovation in quantity produced light open cars! The use of quarter-elliptic springs at the rear is unconventional, but I will say that there is a complete absence of axle-tramp, a failing of several small-

capacity British machines with semi-elliptics. Taking it by and large, the suspension is in direct contrast to the sports cars of the pre-war era, providing an extremely soft ride, and remarkably good road-holding. Actually the independent front suspension is the simplest possible form of wishbone and helical spring assembly. A triangulated steel pressing forms the bottom wishbone, on which the spring is located, contained by the front sub-frame. A lever-type damper forms the top link. Steering is by rack-and-pinion, and is notable for its lightness. It is this light feeling, combined with fairly high gearing, which tends to make one believe that the car has built-in oversteer; this is far from the case, and within a few miles the feeling disappears, to be replaced by one of supreme confidence in the little car's fast cornering abilities. In point of fact, after experiences over a considerable mileage, the characteristic seems to be on the side of a slight understeer.

The gearbox is delightfully quick, but I do wish that closer ratios could have been incorporated, particularly between 2nd and 3rd. The high-revving properties of the engine emphasize this gap, especially when changing up on a slope. Third itself is an admirable ratio, giving about 65 m.p.h., but second, even at 6,000 r.p.m., is under 40 m.p.h. Consequently there is a considerable speed drop after changing, and one also has to guard against over-revving when making a quick down-change. During acceleration tests, the best results were obtained by limiting second gear r.p.m. to 5,000, and pulling the lever through as smartly as possible even although there was a tendency to beat the synchromesh, which I must admit seems to be more sluggish in operation than on many other modern cars. Treating the box as a "crash-type", and adopting double-declutching methods, would appear to be the most satisfactory method of ensuring fairly quick and positive changes. In any case this is a *must*

for bottom gear, which, like all B.M.C. productions, has no synchromesh.

On the car tested a rev-counter was fitted, but there was no red marking to denote r.p.m. limits; however, there was a shaded sector between 5,500 and 6,000 r.p.m., so presumably the makers feel that the very willing power-unit should not be pushed too long in the higher ranges. The Series A engine is virtually standard, with the exception of twin H.1 semi-downdraught SU carburetters, and a special exhaust system; the latter produces quite a pleasant note, without being in the least offensive.

Naturally, at its low price the Sprite is by no means luxurious. Nevertheless equipment and general trim are excellent. The facia panel is finished in P.V.C.-coated fabric, and the adoption of a two-spoked steering wheel provides good visibility for the various instruments. The bucket seats are very comfortable indeed, obviously having been designed by someone who goes in for a fair amount of long-distance motoring. The doors have generous recesses, but no outside handles. A grab-handle is provided on the facia panel for the passenger.

Luggage accommodation is quite remarkable for such a small car, although it has to be reached from behind the seats. Presumably the part played by the bodywork in ensuring rigidity has dictated the absence of a locker-lid.

COMPETITIONS: Already the Sprite has done well in motoring sport, such as in the recent Liverpool Jeans Cup Rally, and (right) in the very arduous "Alpine", in which the little cars carried off the class award—a fine performance on their first appearance in a Continental event.

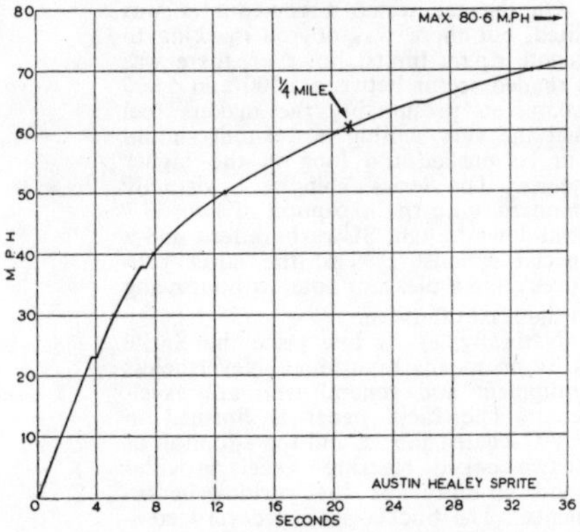

Acceleration Graph

Specification and Performance Data

Car Tested: Austin-Healey Sprite. Price £668 17*s*. including P.T. Extras: r.p.m. counter, heating and demisting units, tonneau cover, windscreen washers, laminated glass screen, radio, plated front bumper.

Engine: Four cylinders, 62.9 mm. x 76.2 mm. (948 c.c.). Pushrod-operated overhead valves; 8.3 to 1 compression ratio; 42.5 b.h.p. at 5,000 r.p.m. Twin SU carburetters; Lucas coil ignition; A.C. mechanical fuel pump.

Transmission: Borg and Beck 6¼ ins. single-plate dry clutch. Four-speed B.M.C. gearbox with short central lever on top of box. Ratios: 15.31, 10.02, 5.96 and 4.22 to 1. Reverse: 19.68 to 1. Hardy-Spicer open propeller shaft; hypoid-bevel rear axle.

Chassis: Integral steel construction. Independent front suspension by helical springs and wishbones. Rack-and-pinion steering. Quarter-elliptic rear springs with radius arms; hydraulic lever-type dampers. Lockheed hydraulic brakes (2LS at front) in 7 ins. x 1¼ ins. drums; 13 ins. x 3½ ins. pressed steel wheels (four-nut fixing), with 5.20 x 13 four-ply tubeless tyres.

Equipment: 12-volt lighting and starting (38 amp./hr. battery). Speedometer with trip-recorder, combined water temperature and oil pressure gauges, petrol gauge, headlamp beam, dynamo and flasher warning lights.

Dimensions: Wheelbase, 6 ft. 8 ins. Track (front), 3 ft. 0 in.; (rear) 3 ft. 8¼ ins. Overall length, 11 ft. 4½ ins.; width, 4 ft. 5¼ ins.; height (hood erect), 3 ft. 11¼ ins. Turning circle, 32 ft. Ground clearance, 5 ins. Weight (as tested), 12¾ cwt.

Performance: Maximum speed, 80.6 m.p.h. Speeds in gears: third, 65 m.p.h.; second, 38 m.p.h.; first, 23 m.p.h. Standing quarter-mile, 21.2 secs. Acceleration: 0-30 m.p.h. 5.2 secs.; 0-40 m.p.h. 7.8 secs.; 0-50 m.p.h. 12.8 secs.; 0-60 m.p.h. 20.3 secs.; 0-70 m.p.h. 33.5 secs.

Fuel Consumption: (Driven hard) 32 m.p.g.; at 50-60 m.p.h. (cruising), 44 m.p.g.

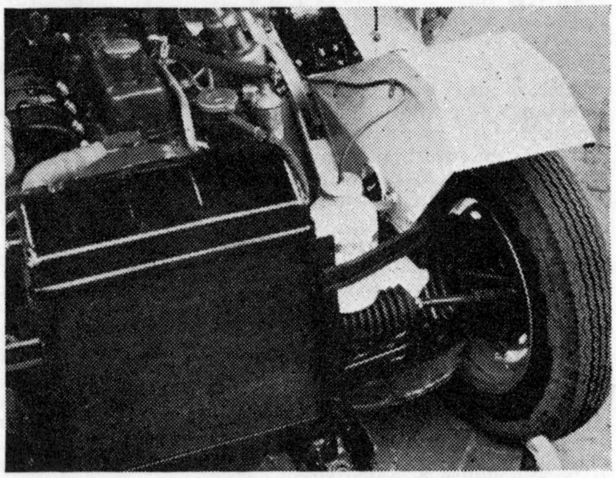

★

Front suspension and anti-splash guard details on the Sprite. When the bonnet section is lifted, accessibility of the engine and components is extremely good.

★

However, as one well-known driver pointed out, "It's always something less to rattle!"

The ratchet-type handbrake is inclined to be awkward to use, being placed between the seats where it gets mixed up with the passenger. I would have much preferred to see a "fly-off" type used, in keeping with the car's sporting character. Whilst on the critical side, I feel that something should be done about making the bonnet-section lighter to operate. It requires a more than considerable amount of effort to lift it, and one has to guard against losing one's hands when it is being lowered, as it certainly comes down with an almighty thump.

Accessibility of engine and components is first-class, making servicing no problem at all. When a heater unit is installed, a large intake tube is located on the off-side of the power-unit. The car itself is easy to keep clean: the only plated parts on the car tested were bumpers and over-riders, front grille, lamp rims, wiper blades and wheel hub-covers.

Normally speaking, speed is expensive in terms of fuel consumption, but I found that no matter how hard the car was driven, it never used petrol at the rate of less than 32 m.p.g. It could, however, with advantage have a slightly larger fuel tank to give it a longer cruising range, the existing unit holding about six Imperial gallons.

The brakes are extremely good, and during the time the car was in my hands displayed not the slightest tendency to "fade", grab, pull or do anything other than stop the car surely and progressively. The engine starts first time from cold, but was inclined to stall in traffic: adjustment of the slow-running stops to give 550-600 r.p.m. tick-over completely cured this. Oil consumption was precisely nil.

Whilst I was using the Sprite, I became firmly attached to it, and fervently hope that the makers keep it at under 1,000 c.c. Already some people are talking in terms of a 1½-litre power-unit, but I am convinced that an increase in capacity would completely spoil the part it is playing in bringing sporting motoring within the pockets of thousands of people who are perfectly satisfied with its performance. Naturally competitions-minded people will hot-up their Sprites, and in fact equipment for increasing performance is already on the market. However, the basic fact remains that in production form the conception is just right, and every credit is due to the manufacturers for instigating what will undoubtedly prove to be a new era in the popularity of small-capacity, open car motoring.

Gregor Grant.

★

Unusual today is the use of quarter-elliptic springs for the rear suspension.

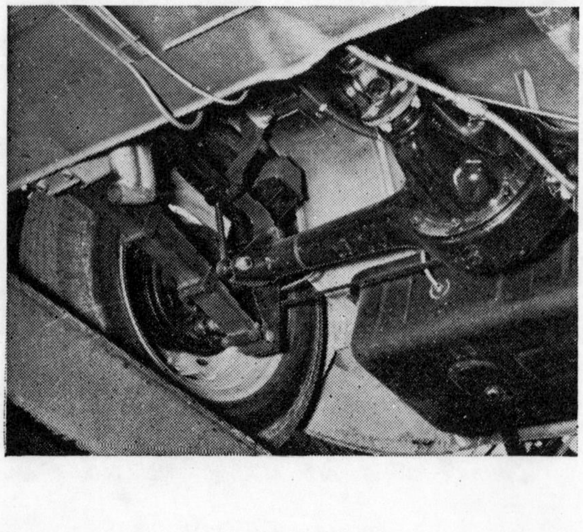

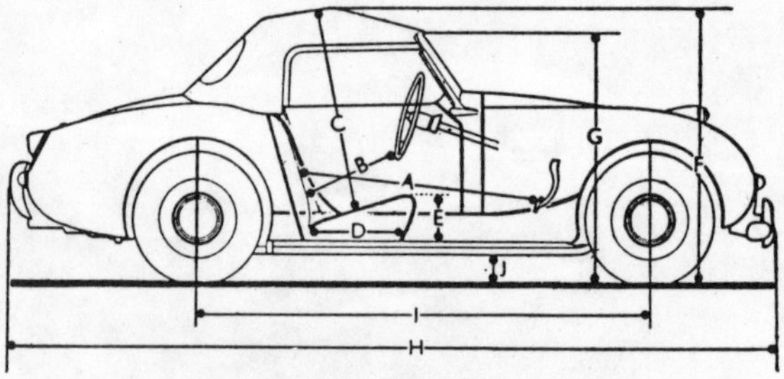

SPRITE DIMENSIONS

- **A** *Squab to accelerator pedal, 3 ft. 7¼ ins.*
- **B** *Squab to steering wheel, 1 ft. 5 ins.*
- **C** *Height to top of hood frame from seat, 2 ft. 10½ ins.*
- **D** *Depth of seat cushion, 1 ft. 7 ins.*
- **E** *Height of seat cushion, 7¾ ins.*
- **F** *Overall height, 4 ft. 1¼ ins.*
- **G** *Height from ground to top of screen, 3 ft. 8⅛ ins.*
- **H** *Overall length, 11 ft. 5¼ ins.*
- **I** *Wheelbase, 6 ft. 8 ins.*
- **J** *Ground clearance, 5 ins.*

The Motor

April 22, 1959

90-PLUS SPRITE

A Warwick-tuned Austin-Healey

Hardtop, disc brakes, wire wheels and dual exhaust system make the car about half a hundredweight heavier, even though the front bumper is removed.

ROADWORTHINESS, an engine which is already lively and has proved its ability to withstand the stress of developing much more power, even the name Austin-Healey Sprite itself, have been an open invitation from the start to specialist tuners of production cars. From the Healey works in Warwick there came into our hands recently a Sprite which has "got about as far as they can go," possessing not only a considerably modified engine but altered transmission ratios and several changes in the chassis specification, of which the most notable are centre-lock wire wheels and disc front brakes.

The result is a machine lifted out of the amusing runabout class into the ranks of serious sports cars, breaking from modern tradition in providing high performance with a fair amount of noise and fuss (but complete reliability) from a very small engine.

It is unfortunate that an aggressive and tiring bark from the exhaust, resonating at between about 2,300 r.p.m. and 3,000 r.p.m., is the most immediately noticeable characteristic of the car, the more so as the noisy speeds are not those corresponding with the greatest increase in performance. The biggest gains are to be found, as might be expected, at the upper end of the scale, where better breathing of the engine is exploited to achieve a mean maximum speed of 91.6 m.p.h., equal to just under 6,500 r.p.m.

A table on this page shows the cost of the several items and operations applied to the test car. So far as the engine is concerned they mainly represent "Tuning Condition 4" in the Sprite Tuning Booklet, a condition which apart from the afore-mentioned exhaust note leaves the engine flexible, easy to start from hot or cold and perfectly docile, although a diet of 100-octane fuel becomes imperative. One serious drawback for touring use is the omission of the fan, without which the radiator soon boils in standstill traffic jams. Trumpet-shaped inlet pipes replace the air-cleaners and separate tail pipes take exhaust gases from the middle and outer pairs of cylinders. The test car was fitted with 1¼-in. S.U. carburetters in place of the normal 1⅛-in. components. This modification, which is probably more useful at high than at low speeds, is unfortunately no longer available.

The 4.55 : 1 rear axle ratio is lower than standard. A close-ratio gearbox giving overall ratios in the indirect gears of 6.14, 9.05 and 13.67 : 1 which was also fitted on the car supplied for test has been discontinued. Normal indirect ratios with the 4.55 : 1 axle would be 5.53, 9.30 and 14.21 : 1.

Fast and accelerative in a straight line, the modified Sprite is also an extremely roadworthy sports car. Without sacrifice of the quick steering which is one of the normal Sprite's

PERFORMANCE

(See text for note on parts no longer available)

	Normal Sprite (The Motor Road Test, May 21, 1958)	Modified Sprite
Instruments		
Speedometer at 30 m.p.h.	3% fast	12% fast
Speedometer at 60 m.p.h.	5% fast	13% fast
Distance recorder	2% fast	7% fast
Acceleration in top gear		
10–30 m.p.h.	13.7 sec.	12.2 sec.
20–40 m.p.h.	12.6 sec.	10.4 sec.
30–50 m.p.h.	12.6 sec.	11.7 sec.
40–60 m.p.h.	14.4 sec.	13.9 sec.
50–70 m.p.h.	18.5 sec.	13.2 sec.
60–80 m.p.h.	—	19.1 sec.
Acceleration from standstill*		
0–30 m.p.h.	5.1 sec.	5.0 sec.
0–50 m.p.h.	13.7 sec.	11.6 sec.
0–70 m.p.h.	31.1 sec.	24.0 sec.
Standing quarter-mile	21.8 sec.	20.7 sec.
Maximum speed	82.9 m.p.h.	91.6 m.p.h.
Fuel consumption		
At constant 30 m.p.h.	52.5 m.p.g.	47.0 m.p.g.
At constant 50 m.p.h.	53.5 m.p.g.	45.5 m.p.g.
At constant 70 m.p.h.	36.0 m.p.g.	37.5 m.p.g.
Overall fuel consumption	33.6 m.p.g.	30.5 m.p.g.
Brakes from 30 m.p.h.		

Normal	Modified
0.97g with 90 lb. pressure.	1.0g with 140 lb. pressure.
0.75g with 75 lb. pressure.	0.96g with 96 lb. pressure.
0.49g with 50 lb. pressure.	0.67g with 75 lb. pressure.
0.22g with 25 lb. pressure.	0.47g with 50 lb. pressure.
	0.30g with 25 lb. pressure.

*Using close-ratio gearbox no longer available.

pleasantest features, the fitting of a front anti-roll bar and possibly the wider track resulting from knock-off Rudge hubs have produced a more stable car with slight but consistent understeer. The modifications include stronger valves on both front and rear dampers, improving the already excellent road-holding at some cost in riding comfort.

With the extra weight of wire wheels, disc front brakes, larger rear drums and a shapely reinforced plastic hard-top, but lightened of its front bumper, the car weighed-in unladen at about ½ cwt. heavier than its normal counterpart, a weight which the new brakes cope with most easily and reassuringly; stopping is stable even from high speed on a wet road. As an alternative and less costly conversion it is possible to have wire wheels with the existing drum brakes.

All the modifications listed here are carried out after purchase, in order to avoid a heavy increase in purchase tax which would be payable if the costs were included in the price of a complete new car. For the complete set of extras (excluding those which do not relate directly to performance or road-worthiness) the total to be added to the Sprite's £631 11s. British price is just over £166, plus charges for fitting.

CONVERSION BY ITEMS

Engine	£	s.	d.
Pistons for 9.3:1 compression ratio	9	10	0
Camshaft	6	0	0
Distributor	5	10	0
Valve springs		15	4
1¼-in. carburetters	no longer available		
Modifying and polishing cylinder head	10	0	0
Dual exhaust system	11	0	0
Transmission			
Close-ratio gearbox	no longer available		
4.55:1 rear axle	23	0	0
Chassis			
Wire wheel and disc brake set	89	0	0
Stronger front and rear damper valves	3	0	0
Front anti-roll bar	8	10	0
Body			
Hardtop with sliding windows	46	10	0
Quick action filler cap	2	4	0

Rudge hubs make the front and rear tracks noticeably wider without altering the suspension, to which a front anti-roll bar is added. Girling disc front brakes are matched by larger drums on the rear wheels.

SPRITELY AND SPRITELIER

An assessment of the standard Austin Healey Sprite and an Alexander Sprite

DURING 1958 the Austin Motor Co., in conjunction with Donald Healey, has brought sports car ownership within reach of a vast new section of the motoring public. With the relaxation of hire purchase restrictions the open air fan is no longer forced to consider a series of rather doubtful second-hand bargains—"never raced or rallied, old boy"—most of which have a very considerable taste for petrol. Instead he can invest in a new vehicle which, with reasonable care and attention, should be no more expensive to run than a small saloon car and is, above all, exceptionally safe, requiring extreme provocation to out-perform its roadholding.

Conventional in design, and using many components of the Austin A35 and Morris Minor 1000 in a chassis/body of unitary construction, the Sprite appeals on account of its handling qualities, its manoeuverability and its lively performance—the latter obtained more as a result of low weight and frontal area than of high power output. It is great fun to drive, particularly in open trim, and has an endearing quality of which both driver and passenger seem quickly to become aware. It can be used far more effectively on busy roads than some of the more normal (and much more expensive) British sports cars and, although not particularly fast, completed an afternoon journey from London to Norwich far more quickly than several genuine 100 mph cars under the same conditions.

One of the reasons why this should be the case is obviously the feeling of confidence which the Sprite imparts, even on initial acquaintance. It is an easy car to drive, particularly for anyone accustomed to quick, positive steering, and it responds to brisk driving in a most heartening manner. Initially there is a tendency to accuse the Sprite of oversteer, or more precisely of roll-oversteer—the result of rather soft front suspension—which is noticed far more in the first few miles than when one is really used to the car. Anyway the body lean never assumes alarming proportions and rear wheel adhesion is maintained far longer than the driver has any right to expect. For this the rear suspension layout, technically one of the car's most interesting features, deserves considerable praise.

As on certain pre-war Austin sports cars, the live axle is mounted on quarter-elliptic springs, controlled by piston-type shock absorbers, and located by trailing arms. The tail can be *made* to slide by determined driving, but does so in a completely predictable manner, and even in the wet there is a tremendous safety margin before all adhesion is lost, while Sprite-owners of more sedate disposition can drive far and fast under all conditions without any fear of tail-end twitch.

Raising the front bodywork—in itself no light task—completely exposes engine, front suspension, steering gear and all accessories for servicing, and this is particularly appreciated on the Alexanderised car, where the under-bonnet space becomes a little crowded. And one soon learns not to step back to admire one's work without ducking to avoid the forward edges of the wings!

Despite appearances, the Sprite accommodates six foot five quite easily, and the seats are extremely comfortable although the cushions are not always adequately secured in their frames. The layout and operation of the pedals is excellent and the remote control gear-lever provides a quick change, so much so that it is not difficult to beat the syncromesh. First gear is extremely low for such a light car, and second and third are rather distant—a deficiency even more noticeable on the Alexander Sprite than on the standard model. Alternative intermediate ratios in the region of 12.5, 8.0 and 5.5 to 1 to replace the present 15.31, 10.02 and 5.96 to 1—direct drive is ideal at 4.22 to 1—would undoubtedly increase the car's potential for competition, as well as giving it an even more "sporting" character for road use. The brakes are adequate for the performance in standard trim, but the purist will object to the "fly-on." rather than "fly-off" type of handbrake.

The instruments, including water temperature and oil pressure gauges, but not ammeter, are well placed. Among the optional extras is a tachometer, reading to 6,000 rpm; it is hardly necessary on the standard car and on two examples tested the needle fluctuated rather wildly at around 5,000 rpm. However, the engine with its lead indium bearings and sturdy crankshaft, will run up to 6,000 rpm without protest, so the tachometer may be considered more of a concession to sporting taste than a mechanical necessity.

In addition to its journey over a test route to Norfolk the standard Sprite was driven as quickly as conditions permitted round the lanes of Romney Marsh, and it is on such roads—of the type often chosen for rallies—that the car is most appreciated. Kept in third gear for long periods, and rarely attaining more than 60 mph, the Sprite nevertheless covered the ground amazingly quickly, a sign of its surefootedness being the passenger's complete calm—except when a lorry tried to run us down on the only long straight for several miles—and the infrequency with which she needed to have recourse to the grab handle.

During a number of late evening journeys the efficiency of the Smith's heating and demisting unit was much appreciated, and even with the hood down it is possible to keep feet and legs warm, while enjoying the exhilaration (and visibility) of an open car.

A maximum speed of around 80 mph is by no means exceptional in this day and age, and for those who like the Sprite but consider it should go faster an Alexander

The live rear axle of the Sprite is suspended on quarter-elliptic springs and located by trailing arms.

conversion, produced by Alexander Engineering Co., Ltd., Haddenham, Bucks, is the obvious answer.

Distinguished by paint flashes along the body-sides, special wheel discs and Alexander emblems at front and rear, the Alexander Sprite has undergone very considerable engine modification. The chief source of extra power and rpm is the high flow efficiency cylinder head. A compression ratio of 9.4 to 1 has been obtained by the fitting of special pistons. The Alexander head also incorporates exhaust valves of K.E. 965 steel and inlet valves of silichrome steel. At the "bottom end" the flywheel has been lightened and balanced and the crankshaft and connecting rods have been balanced.

A resonance-type inlet manifold is used, flexibly mounted to the cylinder head and fitted with two 1½ inch SU carburetters which are supplied from a cold air pressure box. The exhaust manifolding is also modified, and incorporates a full flow centre port adaptor, but the standard silencer and tailpipe are retained. It is

ride. As it stands, however, the Alexander Sprite can be steered round appreciable bends at a speed in excess of the terminal velocity of the standard car without any deviation from the chosen line, and will return A to B averages of more than a mile a minute with ease. A journey from Aylesbury to Gravesend—through central London—on a Tuesday evening was completed in 1¾ hours, while the return trip, starting at 6.15 pm on a Sunday, occupied ten minutes less; Westminster Bridge to Aylesbury Market Square took just one hour.

Thus it has none of the limitations occasionally experienced on cars with engine-only conversions, and gives the keen driver the advantage of improved acceleration and increased rpm with absolutely no snags. The power unit has an unburstable feel, even after several miles at more than 6,000 rpm, and fuel consumption at any given speed is obviously less than on the standard car, due to the increased efficiency imparted by the conversion. All-in-all, there is something very attractive about a

The horn is deplorable, and is more liable to be received with derision than to act as a proper warning device. In addition, on one test car the horn developed a short in the steering wheel boss—which caused it to operate feebly and intermittently until it was completely disconnected, while on another it ceased to work at all. An ideal Christmas present for any Sprite owner would be a pair of foolproof, wind-tone horns.

So far no really satisfactory hood has been made, for the original type, with tenex fasteners along the top of the windscreen, was not waterproof and the later one, which fits into a slotted extension of the windscreen frame, twice lifted at around 80 mph—an alarming experience.

Lack of attention to detail is also seen in the method of attaching the headlamp rims; adjustment of the lamps at the onset of fog proved a very long job, even for Alf Francis. The lamps themselves provide a very adequate beam. Protruding from the bonnet top like eyes on long stalks, they also help the driver to place the car

Engine compartment of the Alexander Sprite

The Alexander Sprite in competition trim

also possible to obtain a Stage One engine conversion, to the above specification but without the cold air box or attention to the bottom end. At a later date a special camshaft will be available. The conversion is intended for use with premium rather than super grade fuels.

The result is a much more freely revving engine, which lifts the car's performance on to a different plane in terms of both acceleration and maximum speed. For competition work a plastic "aero-screen" can be supplied, and in this trim the converted Sprite is just capable of 100 mph, at which speed the tachometer needle is getting round towards the headlamp beam warning light; even with the normal windscreen and hood fitted it will reach over 90 mph.

The enhanced performance is matched by very much more powerful braking, the increased pedal effort required by the harder, fade-free linings being counteracted by a Lockheed suspended vacuum-type booster. At low speeds some care is needed to avoid locking the brakes, but at 80 mph or more the knowledge that swift and progressive retardation is available is most reassuring. In this respect the Alexander Sprite now "feels" much better than when originally tried, some months ago, with small windscreen and standard brakes.

It is a measure of the quality of the basic design that no suspension modifications have been deemed necessary, although an anti-roll bar might help to stiffen the front end and provide a completely even

car in which, on a clear road, it is possible to use the throttle pedal almost with abandon; the results, in terms of speed with security are most gratifying.

In enthusing over the performance of these cars, and particularly the Alexander-converted example, one is apt to overlook some of the detail features which can cause annoyance in the cold light of dawn. The Sprite is, quite naturally, trimmed to economy standards. No one is going to object to rubber floor covering and plastic trim, but unfortunately the latter stops at the rear wheel arches, and luggage is consigned to completely untrimmed space where it tends to get mixed up with spare wheel, tools and electrical wiring for the various rear lights. However, it is wonderful to have so much luggage space in a sports car and the keen type could no doubt fit out the rear compartment to his own requirements.

accurately on tortuous roads.

The most distressing feature of all, however, is the way in which the Sprite rattles on poorly-surfaced roads. This is partly due to the way in which tools and other items are stowed, uninsulated, in the luggage space, and partly to the fit of body panels—particularly the bonnet.

On the open road, however, it is easy to tolerate a few rattles, an uncertain hood (take it down altogether) and an ineffective horn; after all, they can all be put right at very little expense. For going about one's business with pleasure in the British Isles it would be difficult to choose a more rewarding vehicle—certainly when initial outlay and economy of operation are taken into account; anyway, for a short period when I had three cars in my garage, or rather under the nearest street lamp, I did all my travelling in the Alexander Sprite—it gets you that way.   D.P.

PERFORMANCE DETAILS

		Standard Sprite in full road trim	Alexander Sprite in full road trim	Alexander Sprite with aero screen
Acceleration				
0—30 mph		5.4 seconds	4.6 seconds	4.2 seconds
0—50 mph		13.0 seconds	10.8 seconds	9.4 seconds
0—70 mph		33.8 seconds	22.0 seconds	19.2 seconds
Standing ¼ mile		21.0 seconds	19.6 seconds	19.2 seconds
Maximum speed				
mean		80 mph	89 mph	98 mph
Best one-way time		82 mph	92 mph	100 mph
Overall Fuel Consumption		32 mpg	29 mpg	—

ROAD TEST
Supercharged Sprite

ALL the way from Scotch Corner to Boroughbridge the little Sprite cruised at over 6000 rpm—95 mph. Traffic was light, and, except when roundabouts impeded progress, its speed rarely dropped below 90 mph. At Boroughbridge, having done 188 miles in 3½ hours, I stopped to check the effect of this flogging on the car. The oil level was just as it had been at Edinburgh. The header tank was still full and petrol consumption worked out at just over 100 miles on every four gallons of petrol.

This, of course, was no ordinary Sprite, but a supercharged one supplied by the Donald Healey Motor Co., Ltd., of Warwick and fitted with a Shorrock supercharger. Bolting-on the supercharger to the otherwise standard Sprite engine increases the maximum power output from 42.5 hp at 5000 rpm to 68 hp at 5700 rpm; the relative torque figures are 52.5 lb ft at 3300 rpm and 64.8 lb ft at 3,000 rpm. Other modifications on the test car included the Healey disc brake/wire wheel conversion (the front discs being supported by 8 inch drums), an anti-roll bar and competition shock absorbers.

A more thorough test than is sometimes possible was given to this combination by driving from London to the Isle of Skye via Warrington, Lancaster, Carlisle, Glasgow and Fort William, exploring most of the island's varied roads, and returning southwards by way of the Highlands, Edinburgh, A68 and A1. In a total of 1700 miles it proved to be an ideal means of covering 300 or more miles in a day (on the return trip it did Edinburgh-Aylesbury in 7½ hours) and its general behaviour throughout this time was an absolute revelation.

By comparison with the standard car the performance of the supercharged Sprite is on an altogether different plane, and its road-holding could hardly be faulted, except perhaps on fast Ess-bends where a stiffer anti-roll bar might have helped on the change from one lock to the other. The slight "roll-oversteer" of the standard Sprite is completely eliminated, however, and this—together with the positive rack-and-pinion steering, results in handling qualities which are almost up to sports/racing standards. The modified brakes are well up to the increased

performance, and the front disc/rear drum set-up seems ideally suited to this comparatively light car, additional advantages being the provision of moderate pedal pressure at all times and a really adequate hand-brake.

As to performance itself, the fitting of the Shorrock supercharger completely transforms the car. Acceleration times through the gears are improved by more than 100 per cent in some cases, and at the same time the engine is smoother and more flexible than the standard unit. Maximum speed is increased by some 20 per cent, even with the normal hood and sidescreens fitted, and it seems almost certain that the smoother contours of a hard-top would make this a true 100 mph car.

Such considerations are of far less importance, however, than the more practical aspects of the car's performance, particularly its remarkable "liveliness" in traffic. From any sort of check the Supercharged Sprite will accelerate back to a cruising speed not far short of its maximum in an incredibly short time. Even in top gear it will go from 30—80 mph quicker than some 1½-litre sports cars. And the engine of the test car was so smooth at all speeds that I suspected it of being specially prepared and balanced, although I was assured that this was not the case.

The supercharger installation on the Sprite, illustrated below, consists of a Type C/75/B Shorrock eccentric-rotor-type compressor—suitable for all BMC 'A' series engines and distributed in the British Isles by the Donald Healey Motor Co, Ltd—together with a 1½in SU horizontal carburetter mounted on a replacement inlet manifold. Drive is by "V" belts in combination with a special crankshaft pulley, and maximum boost is 7 lb per square inch. Automatic lubrication is achieved by means of a metering valve built into the supercharger and

connected with a special tapping into the engine oil pressure line. All these components, together with supercharger mounting brackets, studs and bolts, are included in the price of £69 17s. Fitting is quite straightforward, the only alterations required being the removal of the existing manifold and replacement of the crankshaft pulley. Alternatively, the Donald Healey Motor Company will fit the supercharger to the Sprite, or any BMC 'A'-series engined car, for £10.

One of the chief advantages of the eccentric rotor-type supercharger is that it affords both high mechanical efficiency and reliability due to there being no actual contact between the vanes and the outer casing. Both of these features were demonstrated during the recent BMC record runs in Utah, when an A-series-engined car fitted with a Type C/75/B supercharger covered 146.95 miles in one hour and did 1000 miles at an average of 138.55 mph. These runs, in addition to gaining world-wide publicity, also acted as a final proving for the "blown" power unit, and the availability of a supercharged Sprite was announced during the second week of the Earls Court Motor Show.

PERFORMANCE DATA

	Standard Sprite	Supercharged Sprite
Acceleration		
0—50 mph	13.0	8.2
0—60 mph	21.2	10.8
0—70 mph	33.8	14.8
Standing start ¼ mile	21.0	18.4
Mean Maximum speed	80 mph	96 mph
Overall fuel consumption	32 mpg	27 mpg

With many conversions it is necessary to make certain concessions in the interest of higher performance or improved roadholding, but the supercharged Sprite gave absolutely no grounds for criticism by comparison with the standard car. The engine was much more flexible, always started easily and showed never a trace of temperament. The ride, although firm, was no less comfortable than in the standard model, and both driver and passenger appreciated the marked reduction in roll. The disc brake/wire wheel conversion, although dearer than the supercharger, also proved its worth not only by slowing the car abruptly whenever necessary, but also by imparting the comforting feeling that, however steep the descent, whatever the hazard, the Sprite would always be able to stop.

Fully converted, then, the Sprite is in an altogether different class from the standard version (and would generally be placed in a higher capacity class for competition purposes) and becomes one of the quickest cars on the road. It is also one of the most enjoyable to drive, and extremely practical in that its large, if rather austere "boot" will carry a surprising amount of luggage. For Sprite-owners who object to being left at the lights, or anyone who wants a really good, safe, small sports car, this could well be the answer.

DAVID PHIPPS.

Under the bonnet, the Shorrock supercharger, anti-roll bar, disc brakes and wire wheels.

The Autocar ROAD TESTS 1752

Austin-Healey Sprite Hardtop

Most of the exterior brightwork is chromium plated, but the new Weathershields sidescreens have a polished metal frame

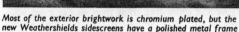

WITH its enviable position as the cheapest British production sports two-seater, the Austin-Healey Sprite would not have to be particularly outstanding to enjoy a keen following. Very good it is, though—and it offers so many attractive features in its design, construction and behaviour on the road, that it is easy to understand how it has become so popular in the short time since its introduction in June last year. Now, useful improvements have been made for the comfort of its occupants and for the car's utility as an all-weather vehicle in winter and summer. Thus, it is available in detachable hardtop form, and the flimsy sidescreens are replaced (on the hardtop version) by an improved design. Our Road Test of the earlier Sprite appeared in *The Autocar* of 20 June 1958.

Constructed of resin-bonded glass fibre, with a large wrap-round rear window of Perspex, the hardtop is not heavy, and it was found possible to fit or remove it single-handed. Its fittings are ingenious, and even without previous experience it was a simple matter, taking only two minutes, to remove it. At the front it is secured to the windscreen top rail by two "crocodile" clips, released by raising their chrome handles, which lie flush with the hardtop in grooves. The back is secured by two bolts and wing nuts, locating in slots beside the seats. It was only for replacement of the hardtop that assistance was appreciated, to ensure that the rear securing bolts did not scratch the paintwork, or the shiny metal rail which surrounds the driving compartment to the rear of the facia.

The hardtop may be added retrospectively to existing Sprites without any modifications to the car, since its securing bolts fit into the normal hood-stay slots. In this case the hardtop—as supplied by the Donald Healey Motor Company—costs £46 10s including sliding sidescreens of slightly different construction. This price shows a reduction in comparison with the listed price of £49 11s 8d when the hardtop is ordered with the new car. The explanation given by B.M.C. for this discrepancy is that full purchase tax is not charged on an accessory ordered after delivery; so buyers will benefit if they purchase the hardtop as an afterthought.

A first-class fit results with the hardtop in position, and draughts are eliminated almost completely. There is no leakage in heavy rain, but a considerable noise increase is noticed at speed, in comparison with the open or the hood-up conditions. Exhaust boom and wind roar combine to make the car decidedly noisy at more than 60 m.p.h. which, although forgivable on a sports car, will perhaps be unwelcome to the class of motorist who will specify the hardtop for protection against the elements.

Engine noise contributes to this above about 65 m.p.h., but at lower speeds it is unobtrusive. The engine is exceptionally willing to rev.; the driver wishing to obtain the best from the car takes advantage of this, and finds that on a fast run the rev. counter spends much of the time above the 4,000 r.p.m. mark. Throughout the range, and particularly at low speeds, it is noticeably smooth. However, it lacks torque until it is revving fairly freely. Starting is immediate, the choke being necessary only for a cold start and for the first minute or two of running to prevent hesitation and misfiring. The warm-up is slow.

The overall consumption of just over 40 m.p.g. is extremely creditable, including, as it does, considerable use in London traffic and consistent hard driving. It is only in the most unfavourable conditions that the worst figure of 36 m.p.g. is achieved; most owners will readily obtain up to 45 m.p.g.

Well-placed within natural reach of the driver's left hand, the gear lever is remarkably light and precise to operate. The synchromesh is not easily beaten even in the fastest movements of the lever. In these respects the gear box earns praise, but the choice of ratios is less satisfactory. Second gear in particular is too low, and the maximum speed difference between bottom and second gears is only 12 m.p.h. Third gear could also be higher—for a car of this character a readily usable maximum of at least 60 m.p.h. should be available in this ratio.

In relation to the Sprite tested last year, the acceleration is comparable, and shows a slight gain at the higher

Removal of the hardtop or the hood to the fully open condition takes only two minutes. The hood and its supports stow neatly out of sight

Austin-Healey
Sprite Hardtop . . .

With the hood up, the flexible wrap-round rear window allows an unobstructed view when the car is being manœuvred. The sidescreens have been removed for this view

speeds. This suggests that the hardtop shape offers less wind resistance than the hood—borne out by an increase of 5 m.p.h. in the best top gear maximum speed. If the Sprite is considered more as an open two-seater than as an out-and-out sports car—which is perhaps a more pertinent description of it—the acceleration may be considered quite adequate.

Clutch operation is smooth, and the pedal pressure is light. Although there is little pedal travel, the take-up is not abrupt, and there is no clutch spin even under full-throttle standing starts.

On first acquaintance with the Sprite the remarkably positive rack-and-pinion steering comes almost as a surprise, particularly to anyone accustomed to the more "woolly" steering layouts which are fitted to many cars of less sporting character. If the driver clings too rigidly to the wheel his own involuntary movement caused by the motion of the car is sufficient to affect the directional stability. A sensitive and gentle hold on the wheel gives the best control, and the complete lack of free play is appreciated. As the car is driven the steering is appreciated more and more; it

Quite an effort is required to raise the bonnet and front-wings unit, but when it is up, self-locking stays hold it securely and accessibility of all components is unusually good. It is only when working on the engine for some time that a higher locking position for the bonnet, or forward hingeing, would be appreciated

remains light and quite free from road shocks even when rough surfaces are taken fast. It is relatively high-geared, and on the open road almost imperceptible movements of the wheel are adequate to hold the car straight. Perhaps because of this precise steering, the slight tail wander which results from the quarter-elliptic rear springs is noticed more than it would be otherwise. The slight changes of direction which occur are easily corrected, however, and the car is little affected by cross-winds. At low speeds the steering remains light, and the car's good lock makes manœuvring easy.

Average British road surfaces do not show up weaknesses in the suspension, but when the Sprite is driven at all fast on rough or unmade roads there is a great deal of firm, almost violent, vertical movement. It seems that the wheel travel permitted by the suspension is too restricted for bad surfaces, and the rear suspension in particular bottoms unduly readily. A shortcoming of this kind is not a serious fault on such a car, however, and for normal road work a commendably level and well-damped ride is provided.

Among the best features of the Sprite is its extremely high standard of cornering. In hard cornering on an uneven surface there is a tendency for the back of the car to "hop out," giving a momentary oversteer situation. When this occurs the car's movement as a whole is so small, and its recovery so quick, that the driver has no need to compensate with the steering. The balance of the Sprite on cornering is near perfect, and this is the sort of car on which the driver may easily get out of trouble after he has grossly misjudged the speed at which a given corner may be taken. In these extremes the very slight tendency to oversteer helps the driver, and is in no way vicious or progressive. Thus, on dry roads the limit of adhesion leaves a considerable margin of safety at the highest speeds at which the car is likely to be driven, and in the wet one may still make violent manœuvres without too much apprehension about surface conditions. Heavy application of the brakes on wet roads will lock the wheels, and it is also possible in these conditions to provoke wheelspin in the lower gears, but liberties may still be taken with the Sprite without any feeling of lack of control.

Dependable brakes add to the overall safety factor, and the hand brake, with readily accessible lever to the left of the transmission tunnel, will hold the car firmly on a 1 in 3 gradient. Reference to the data panel shows that the maximum deceleration figures are not as high as one might expect; they are influenced by the need to avoid wheel lock, which occurs fairly readily during heavy brake applications, even on dry roads. In normal use, however, the brakes are well up to the job of stopping the car from its around 70 m.p.h. cruising speeds, and prolonged spells of hard driving do not cause fade.

Good all-round visibility, little reduced by the hardtop, is a feature of the Sprite. The windscreen wipers are self-parking, and they clean a large area of the screen. Although the driver feels—and is—very low on the road, so that the wheels of a bus or lorry tower above him, his view is un-obstructed. To the front, a little of the bonnet, and the tops of the head lamp bodies, are visible from the driving seat. Rearward visibility also is good, but the interior mirror is mounted so near to facia level as to be of little use. It scarcely satisfies the demands of the Construction and Use regulations, and during the later stages of the Road Test it had to be replaced by a suction-mounted mirror attached to the windscreen.

For tall drivers some modification to the seat mounting would probably be helpful, to lower their eye-level and prevent the car from seeming rather beetle-browed. The fore-and-aft seat adjustment is adequate for the longest legs, and there is space for the driver's left foot off the clutch, resting lightly on the dip-switch. There is also sufficient space to the right of the driving seat for the driver to sit comfortably without finding that his elbow is nudging against the door.

An accessory fitted to the test car was the fresh-air heater, which has a powerful delivery and warms the car quickly after a night in the open. A facia control is pressed to admit air to the heating element. Distribution is controlled by hinged flaps on each side of the heater unit. To demist the windscreen only, both flaps are closed. At low speeds, when there is little ram effect, a fan may be brought into action by turning the facia knob to the right; the fan may be switched on only when the air control is pressed fully home. In warm weather the delivery of hot water to the element can be switched off by a tap under the bonnet, so that the heater may be used to admit unheated fresh air when required.

Reference was made earlier to the ingenious design of the new hardtop, but the folding hood of the Sprite also has been improved; considerable thought has gone into the new design, and this is one of the easiest sports car hoods to manipulate. The hood detaches altogether from its stays, the main supports of which fit into slots at each side of the seats. The rear hood rail engages with two shaped chrome hooks, and there are Lift-the-dot fastenings around the quarters. At the windscreen the hood clips over the top rail, and is secured by two press-stud fasteners.

Hood tightness is ensured by spring loading in the vertical supports of the framework, and to simplify the business of erecting the hood the springs can be compressed and locked, and then released after it has been secured. Little more than a minute is needed to fit or remove the hood; and when it is removed its stays fold behind the seats, and the material stows away in a wallet provided with toolkit.

Further improvement on the new Sprite is offered by the Weathershields sidescreens which, unfortunately, are standard only with the hardtop. On non-hardtop models there is an extra charge of £3 15s plus £1 11s 3d tax, and the cost is higher still if they are not specified at delivery—some allowance being included in the price for the saving on the standard screens.

They have a rigid, bright metal frame which is surrounded by rubber strips to ensure a reasonable seal when the hard-top or the hood is in position. The windows are of Perspex, and the rear section is arranged to slide forward; that on the test car was extremely stiff on the passenger side. The sidescreens fasten to the door by two large screws which can be undone readily, using a coin as a screwdriver. Access to the car from outside is gained by sliding forward one of the windows and reaching in to the small handle protruding forward from the latch. There is, of course, no way of locking the Sprite, and as there is no lockable boot or facia compartment, the owner must take a chance with any possessions left in the car.

Interior comfort owes much to the well-designed seats, which provide good support in the right places and extend fairly well under the thighs. In cornering, the driver and passenger are firmly located laterally. A touch of austerity is given by the simple interior fittings and furnishings. The uncluttered facia layout is somewhat plain. Floor mats are of moulded, ribbed rubber. The interior of the hardtop is not covered, and has the appearance of unfinished glass fibre. Full width, open door pockets are provided on each side, and generous accommodation for luggage is available to the rear of the seats. Stowage is difficult, however, and if small odd-

The interior layout and finish is plain but neat. The steering wheel is small enough not to obstruct forward visibility, and all controls come conveniently to hand. Provision is made for addition of a radio

ments find their way to the back of the luggage space the owner must crawl in to locate them. The most worth-while improvement which could now be made to the Sprite would be the provision of a separate luggage compartment with exterior lockable lid. A small grab handle is provided on the left of the facia for the passenger.

Steady readings are given by the speedometer and the optional extra rev counter—a unit which one might expect to be standard on such a car. There is a thermometer and oil-pressure gauge, but no ammeter—a reasonable omission. The gauge for the six-gallon fuel tank is fairly accurate. For a small car, the toolkit of the Sprite is unusually generous—including a simple jack, wheel-nut spanner, and a few hand tools. The jack lifts either side of the car, and it engages with an unobtrusive slot in the door sill, which is vertically below the windscreen, and covered by a rubber plug when not in use. There is no provision for a starting handle; there are no ashtrays on the car, and no reversing lamp is fitted. Such economies are reasonable with the Sprite, and form part of the general policy of keeping the price to a highly competitive minimum. In view of this it was a mild surprise to find under the bonnet an extra stay

The hardtop seats on rubber and fits snugly, leaving little space for draughts to enter the interior. The amber winking indicator lamps at the rear are protected only by the standard equipment overriders

Austin-Healey Sprite Hardtop . . .

near the radiator—in addition to the double rear self-locking stays—for holding the bonnet in the open position. This does not provide any extra lift to the open bonnet, and there is little use for it. Prospective buyers are reminded that the front bumper and overriders are also listed as optional extra equipment. Without them, the side lamps in particular would be very vulnerable.

In its new improved form the Austin-Healey Sprite is even better value than before, and continued popularity may be expected for it. The combination of first-class roadholding and steering, and good brakes, in a car of not startling all-out performance, makes the Sprite potentially extremely safe. Although more adequate protection against the elements is now available on the standard car, the option of the hardtop will no doubt appeal to many—in particular to those who must park their car in the open through the winter months.

AUSTIN-HEALEY SPRITE HARDTOP

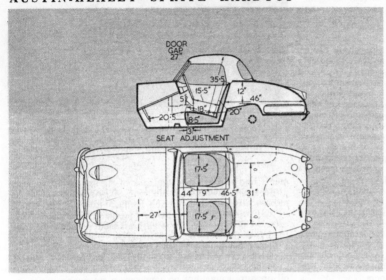

Scale ⅛in to 1ft. Driving seat in central position. Cushions uncompressed.

DATA

PRICE (basic), with hood, sidescreens, rear overriders, spare wheel and tyre, £445.
British purchase tax, £186 10s 10d.
Total (in Great Britain), £631 10s 10d.

Extras:	Basic			U.K. Tax		
	£	s	d	£	s	d
Radio	£18	0	0	£7	10	0
Heater	£13	17	6	£5	15	8
Hardtop	£35	0	0	£14	11	8
Rev. counter ..	£3	0	0	£1	5	0
Tonneau cover	£4	0	0	£1	13	4
Front bumper and overriders	£4	0	0	£1	13	4

ENGINE: Capacity, 948 c.c. (57.82 cu in).
Number of cylinders, 4.
Bore and stroke, 62.9 × 76.2mm (2.478 × 3.0in).
Valve gear, o.h.v., pushrods.
Compression ratio, 8.3 to 1.
B.h.p. (net) 42.5 at 5,500 r.p.m. (B.h.p. per ton laden 52.1).
Torque, 52lb ft at 3,200 r.p.m.
M.p.h. per 1,000 r.p.m. in top gear, 15.4.

WEIGHT: (with 5 gals fuel), 13.31 cwt (1,491lb).
Weight distribution (per cent): F, 54; R, 46.
Laden as tested, 16.31 cwt (1,827lb).
Lb per c.c. (laden), 1.92.

BRAKES: Type, Lockheed, two-leading shoe (front), leading and trailing (rear).
Method of operation, hydraulic.
Drum dimensions: F, 7in diameter; 1¼in wide. R, 7in diameter; 1¼in wide.
Lining area: F, 30.6 sq in; R, 30.6 sq in (75.2 sq in per ton laden).

TYRES: 5.20–13in Dunlop four-ply tubeless.
Pressures (lb sq in): F, 18; R, 20 (normal).

TANK CAPACITY: 6 Imp. gallons.
Oil sump, 6 pints.
Cooling system, 10 pints.

DIMENSIONS: Wheelbase, 6ft 8in.
Track: F, 3ft 9.75in; R, 3ft 8.75in.
Length (overall), 11ft 5.25in.
Width, 4ft 5in.
Height, 4ft 1.75in.
Ground clearance, 5in.
Frontal area, 13.3 sq ft (approximately).

ELECTRICAL SYSTEM: 12-volt; 38 ampère-hour battery.
Head lamps, double dip; 42-36 watt bulbs.

SUSPENSION: Front, independent, coil springs and wishbones. Rear, quarter elliptic leaf springs with radius arms.

PERFORMANCE

ACCELERATION TIMES (mean):

Speed range,	Gear Ratios and Time in Sec.			
M.p.h.	4.22 to 1	5.96 to 1	10.02 to 1	15.31 to 1
10—30	—	8.7	5.1	—
20—40 ..	11.8	8.3	—	—
30—50 ..	11.9	8.7	—	—
40—60 ..	15.1	—	—	—
50—70 ..	19.2	—	—	—

From rest through gears to:

30 m.p.h. ..	..	6.0	sec.
40 ,,	..	10.2	,,
50 ,,	..	14.9	,,
60 ,,	..	23.7	,,
70 ,,	..	33.4	,,

Standing quarter mile 22.3 sec.

MAXIMUM SPEEDS ON GEARS:

Gear		M.p.h.	K.p.h.
Top ..	(mean)	84.1	135.2
	(best)	86.0	138.4
3rd ..	.. ..	58.0	93.3
2nd ..	.. ..	35.0	56.3
1st ..	.. ..	23.0	37.0

TRACTIVE EFFORT (by Tapley meter):

		Pull (lb per ton)	Equivalent gradient
Top ..	..	225	1 in 9.9
Third ..	..	315	1 in 7.0
Second..	..	490	1 in 4.5

BRAKES (at 30 m.p.h. in neutral):

Pedal load in lb.	Retardation	Equiv. stopping distance in ft.
25	0.21g	144
50	0.37g	82
75	0.77g	39

FUEL CONSUMPTION (at steady speeds):

Direct top

30 m.p.h.		58.8 m.p.g.
40 ,,		55.9 ,,
50 ,,		51.3 ,,
60 ,,		44.9 ,,
70 ,,		38.4 ,,

Overall fuel consumption for 1,452 miles, 40.3 m.p.g. (7.02 litres per 100 km.).
Approximate normal range 38-46 m.p.g. (7.4-6.1 litres per 100 km.).
Fuel: Premium grade.

TEST CONDITIONS: Weather: Dry, still. Air temperature, 53 deg. F.
Model described in *The Autocar* of 23 May 1958.

STEERING: Turning circle:
Between kerbs, L, 31ft 0.5in; R, 30ft 1in.
Between walls, L, 32ft 4.0in; R, 31ft 4.5in.
Turns of steering wheel from lock to lock, 2.3.

SPEEDOMETER CORRECTION: M.P.H.

Car speedometer ..	10	20	30	40	50	60	70	80
True speed	10	19	28	38	48	57	67	77

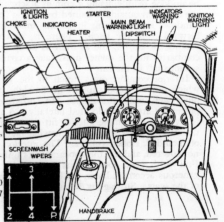

As well as driving numerous borrowed versions, the author has run two red Sprites, the first one, MCF 149, here seen at a Silverstone club meeting, being modified for racing. The present car, YOL 267, has merely been personalized for comfortable everyday road work.

MOTORING FOR FUN

CASE HISTORY
OF A SPRITE

By J. W. Anstice Brown

The Small, Practical Austin-Healey, Used for Business and Pleasure, Provides Fun with Economy and Few Disadvantages

BEING a simple optimist by nature it has always been a source of wonder to me that it is only trouble that is reputed to come " in battalions." My feelings on this subject have been given substance of late by the number of examples of The British Motor Corporation's smallest sports car that seem to have positively overwhelmed me. I have raced Sprites, road-tested standard Sprites, tuned Sprites, used a Sprite as transport and yet perhaps the greatest compliment that can be paid to them all is that having owned one more or less from the day on which they were announced I still find no regret in stepping out of a very large majority of the road-test cars that it is my lot to drive and insinuating my six-foot-two back into my current version of this little car which, even in this present age, manages to possess that fast-vanishing asset, character.

Ownership of one of these cars started for me when I asked Marcus Chambers of the B.M.C. competitions department one Friday what the chances were of a Sprite on the following Monday so that I could enter it in an Irish road race to be held in three weeks time. They were, he assured me, quite definitely nil, but miracles do happen and once again the optimist was in luck and a car was ready for collection not on the Monday I had requested but on the one after that, leaving very little time for preparation before we set sail for the Emerald Isle. With help from many friends, Speedwell modifications were hastily added. the headlights brutally chiseled off, tubes put into the tyres, and harder Mintex brake linings fitted, all in the space of four days during which the hours of 9 to 5 were booked by less agreeable activities than fiddling with sports cars. Much to the amazement of one and all the race provided the first win for a Sprite.

More important, however, is the fact that the car was used for 8,000 miles during which it competed in sprints and races, and served as normal transport without even a decoke. With the exception of three coils which it devoured most avidly, nothing required replacement, and when it was sold, so far as I could tell, only new tyres were needed.

The realization that I should have to spend another £200 on the car to make it compete on level terms with those which were then appearing in the hands of other competitors, on top of the £800 that I reckoned the car had already cost in modified

form, decided me to part with it and race something which required less in the way of modification, and this I did. However, the necessity of a car in my present occupation presented the opportunity of running another Sprite, merely as bread and butter transport, but naturally deriving what pleasure I could from the fact that it was a sports car and also suffering any attendant disadvantages of running an open two-seater all the year round.

After a very much longer wait than was required for the first car, the second one arrived and was almost identical to the first, before it had been turned into a racer. Minor and much appreciated modifications were the repositioning of the coil and a new method of hood fastening at the front which, unlike the system employed on the previous car, actually does keep out rain and flies, the weather protection now being as good as could be desired. Apart from this and the registration number, however, it might be the same car, a fair indication that not much development of the design has proved necessary once it reached the production stage. The colour is red with red interior, as before.

This machine has now covered nearly 17,000 miles, shows very little signs of wear, and, as previously stated, there is still pleasure in making a journey in it. However, there is no clearer example of the inability to please all of the people all of the time than the motorcar and although I feel that the advantages of running a sports car on the road outweigh the disadvantages, it must be admitted that the disadvantages are there. The principal one is getting into the driving compartment, which makes the Sprite a car in which I would rather travel 50 miles than go shopping, entry and exit being difficult, although once inside there is a surprising amount of room. Equally, carrying oddments is not made simple by the lack of an outside opening for the boot. However, it must be said that, carefully packed. a vast amount of luggage can be carried and it is possible to carry three people in the car, with the hood up, over considerable distances in a reasonably comfortable manner.

Quarter elliptic rear springs (the front suspension is A35) definitely have advantages for the man who motors briskly as

CASE HISTORY OF A SPRITE

The hood is now completely watertight, unlike the one on the earlier car. The original number plate which made lifting the heavy bonnet even more difficult has been replaced by the stick-on variety which fits between the headlamps which are powerful enough to allow full performance to be used at night.

The name on the back is all that gives a clue to the casual observer of the car's identity, so effective is the disguise provided by the Ashley Laminates hardtop. It is held in place by four small bolts and can be removed in well under ten minutes when the occasion demands.

of some sort is obtainable at any hour of the day or night, the range of stations being wide. This particular set is remarkably free from interference, the M1 bridges being one of the few things that affect its performance.

Whilst on the subject of extras, a few words about those fitted to the car may be of interest. A car, as well as being a means of transport, is also something personal and as such a certain type of motorist, amongst which I must include myself, revolts against owning just another mass-produced car similar in most respects to his neighbours. Unlike that protagonist of the performance-modified car for road use, Mr. Pomeroy, I go to the other extreme, believing that it is better to keep the mechanism as standard as possible and to use what is there fully for a longer time and as a result I am averse to any engine alterations which must accelerate wear and slightly affect reliability in the long run. Therefore, the only changes around the engine department are the fitting of platinum-pointed plugs in place of the normal ones which were reducing performance after 10,000 miles (the platinium ones are as new after 6,000-odd miles) and the replacement of the heater tap by a water valve controlled from the driving compartment, thus enabling either

anyone who has experienced axle tramp on a Morris Minor and then sampled a Sprite will testify. The suspension is, however, firm in the interests of handling, and a passenger not used to sports cars pronounced it one of the most uncomfortable rides he had ever experienced, but this is, of course, purely a matter of personal opinion as I myself far prefer this firmness to the soggy seasick-making feel of a softly sprung saloon. Less endearing is the tendency of the rear suspension to bottom on certain uneven road surfaces and the work that has been imposed upon it has produced the car's only real failure in that the offside front and rear road springs require replacing after 14,000 miles. It must, however, be admitted that little consideration has been shown to it when rough surfaces were encountered on the road. Curiously, however, the previous car, which was frequently overloaded with excess passengers and suffered the rigours of racing, showed no sign of developing this trouble.

The really noisy sports car is great fun on a short journey but for everyday use quietness is desirable for many reasons. The exhaust note of the Sprite is little different from that of a saloon and the engine is turbine-like in its smoothness and lack of mechanical clatter. The car is, in fact, only noisier than a saloon in respect of a few rattles emanating from the back (tool kit, spare wheel, etc., which could easily be eliminated should an owner so desire) and in the matter of wind roar, although this is less great when the hardtop is in place and could no doubt be reduced still further by the addition of sliding sidescreens (these have, incidentally, recently been standardized to replace the one-piece type on production Sprites). Although this noise is sufficient to make conversation tiring on a long run at speed, a Pye TCR2000 push-button wireless has been fitted and is found to work admirably, it even being possible to listen to plays when driving fast whilst music

Under-bonnet changes from standard are few, consisting of platinum pointed plugs and a water valve for the heater fitted at the rear of the cylinder head. There is a tendency to bang one's head on the bonnet when working on the engine and the battery is not easy to service, but otherwise accessibility is good.

CASE HISTORY OF A SPRITE

Without exception the author has never found a car with a better-planned interior. The pedals allow heel and toe retardation, there is a resting place for the clutch foot, the steering wheel is well placed and all the dashboard controls fall readily to hand. Extras are the heater and water valve, wireless, rev. counter, hidden interior light and the invaluable windscreen-washer.

hot or cold air to be obtained from the heater (which operates excellently but does fill the car with fumes in traffic) without stopping and delving under the bonnet. A rev. counter (an optional extra) and an interior light have been added. The latter is easily fitted under the rail at the top of the dashboard and is a very useful minor improvement which could, one feels, easily be incorporated at the factory. The major alteration, a recent one, is the fitting of a removable hardtop which was announced at the Racing Car Show by Ashley Laminates, specialists in glass fibre bodywork who, as well as producing their own shells, make bodies for Team Lotus. It is no small praise to say that one of the principal advantages of the hardtop is in the change which it effects in the appearance of the Sprite; this is so much so from the back that, when the car is parked, people have walked round to the front to discover what make it is. Draught reduction is a practical asset as is the parcel shelf by the rear window, although if it were covered in non-slip material of some sort it would be even more useful. Rear vision by way of the rear view mirror is vastly improved, but this is paid for by side blind spots which can be a nuisance at road junctions.

Lack of front bumpers and the use of stick-on front numbers further distinguish the car and complete the few alterations from standard; the only other addition that would, I feel, be worth while is a radiator blind (Sprites are, for some reason, very slow to warm up) and, were I a smoker, an ashtray, very necessary in a car where you cannot open the windows.

The road behaviour of the Sprite has been fully covered in *The Motor* road test, which appeared when it was announced, so most of its road characteristics should be well known, and the following details do not cover all facets of performance. Starting from cold the choke, which cannot be locked in

position, must be used for a considerable distance and performance is not good till the engine is warm. Thereafter the little engine is most willing and is not worried by high r.p.m., developing its power fairly high up the rev. range and feeling happier than when being slogged. The gearchange has been criticized in some quarters as being stiff to operate, but I have always found it extremely light and pleasant to use, this being true of all examples that I have driven. From approximately 60 m.p.h. on the overrun a strange transmission noise is evident but the previous car also made this sound and it has produced no ill effects so I have grown used to it, as one does for instance, to the jingle of the starting handle of one of the car's distant predecessors—the Austin Ruby.

Roadholding is of a very high order, although the vehicle, being very light and having sensitive steering, can reach the point of no return rather quickly if severely provoked. Oversteer is prominent and when cornering quickly the technique is to unwind the lock a fraction before the corner really ends and this will produce a smooth change of direction. In the wet the roadholding is quite exceptional although my previous car was somewhat better than the present one, due, I suspect, to the fact that its wheels had been balanced. Recommended pressure for the tyres is 18 p.s.i., but I find that 24 p.s.i. front and 26 p.s.i. rear suits me better and complete lack of tyre squeal at these pressures is a frequent point of complimentary comment from passengers.

On borrowing the car for a day or two, a member of *The Motor* staff remarked that if he drove it to work every day in place of his six-seater saloon he would arrive in a far better temper each morning, and this nippiness is one of the great advantages of owning this type of car. Light weight and a reasonable amount of power make it easy to gain that vital first few yards in the traffic-lights Grand Prix and the small overall size of the car makes it possible to wriggle into gaps where limousines fear to tread. This, and appearance, can, however, annoy the frustrated saloon-car driver and it is not possible to get away with some of the cheeky manœuvres which would pass unnoticed in a more ordinary machine without provoking angry hooting. A psychiatrist could no doubt tell me why. *Continued*

There is plenty of boot space although it is not as accessible as might be, and the position of the spare wheel, just visible, means that it must be kept reasonably clean.

CASE HISTORY OF A SPRITE

Six foot two of author emphasize the low build of the Sprite even when the roofline is raised by the hardtop. Once inside, there is plenty of room.

The Sprite being higher geared than the A35, for instance, which uses the same engine, nippiness around town is not coupled with fussiness on the open road and even the length of the Motorway is quite bearable at a cruising speed around a genuine 70 m.p.h. whilst on main roads it is possible to average 55 m.p.h. when traffic density is low.

There is little sign of wear anywhere, a passenger recently remarking that the Sprite still had the taut feel of a new car. A pint of oil is usually required every 2,000 miles, just as a change is due anyway, the car actually seeming to have a greater appetite for water, another somewhat inexplicable Sprite characteristic. Petrol is consumed at the very reasonable rate of 35.9 m.p.g., although this has shown a tendency to rise slightly of late and checks with a compression tester indicate that a decoke would not be out of place, which probably accounts for the increased thirst. The tubeless tyres have behaved well and will, I feel, last until over 20,000 miles are completed without incorporating the spare which is stored in such a manner that it is desirable to keep it clean and therefore not use it if possible. Thereafter a set of Michelin "X" will be fitted in order to gain experience of how these somewhat controversial tyres behave over a considerable mileage. Brake linings are wearing and will require replacement ere long but otherwise I do not envisage any major replacements. The dust from the linings, incidentally, cannot escape, and it pays to remove the drums and blow this out every 5,000 miles.

Minor ills have been a shattered windscreen, replaced by a laminated one which promptly cracked, a burst water hose, failure of both stoplights and one slow puncture. Starting with very little chrome there is not much to go rusty and the paintwork has stood up to City use very well, only a few chips having been knocked off the bumperless (another extra) front by flying stones. The driver's seat shows slight signs of use whilst the passenger's is as new. The floor mats, which never fitted anyway, are tearing and are one of the few parts which do not do the rest of the car credit.

A point which struck me when a colleague recently tested his everyday transport and reported on it was the discrepancy between the top end figures which he obtained and those of a similar model we had recently road-tested, and it is interesting to note a similar drop in performance in the Sprite figures. In this case the widely varying weather conditions and the different test venues account for some of the differences and the need for decarbonization also has effect. As a matter of interest it is, however, my intention to discover how much must be done to bring the car back to full performance and report thereon. The increase in speed when the hard top is in position is commendable.

Here, then, is a car which has provided me with thoroughly efficient and reliable transport and, at the cost of a few, in my opinion, quite minor disadvantages of the type associated with the refined modern sports car, far more fun and far less frustration than I could ever have obtained from a saloon.

AUSTIN-HEALEY SPRITE COMPARATIVE TESTS

"The Motor" Road Test, 1958	1959 Sprite after approx. 17,000 miles

Weather

Warm and dry with moderate breeze. (Temperature 70°—74°F.; Barometer 30.2—30.4 in. Hg.)	Wet with 10 to 34 m.p.h. wind. (Temperature 42°—44°F.; Barometer 29.4—29.2 in. Hg.)

Kerb Weight

12¾ cwt.	13¾ cwt.

Maximum Speeds

Mean of 4 opposite ¼-mile runs:		Mean lap of banked track:	
Open	—	Open	73.1 m.p.h.
Hood erect	82.9 m.p.h.	Hood erect	77.3 m.p.h.
Hardtop	—	Hardtop	79.1 m.p.h.
Best ¼ mile:		Best ¼ mile:	
Open	—	Open	76.3 m.p.h.
Hood erect	86.5 m.p.h.	Hood erect	79.6 m.p.h.
Hardtop	—	Hardtop	82.9 m.p.h.

Acceleration times on upper ratios

M.p.h.	top sec.	3rd sec.	top sec.	3rd sec.
10–30	13.7	8.6	13.5	8.4
20–40	12.6	7.7	12.1	7.5
30–50	12.6	8.6	13.7	8.6
40–60	14.4	11.4	19.2	—

Steady speed fuel consumption

	m.p.h.	m.p.g.	m.p.g.
At constant	30	52.5	46.5
At constant	40	54.5	45.4
At constant	50	53.5	41.0
At constant	60	38.0	40.0
At constant	70	36.0	32.6

Hill Climbing—at sustained steady speeds

Max. gradient on top gear—1 in 11.7 (Tapley 190 lb./ton)	1 in 12.7 (Tapley 176 lb./ton)	
Max. gradient on 3rd gear—1 in 7.5 (Tapley 295 lb./ton)	1 in 8.4 (Tapley 264 lb./ton)	
Max. gradient on 2nd gear—1 in 4.5 (Tapley 485 lb./ton)	1 in 5.1 (Tapley 429 lb./ton)	

Instruments

Speedometer at 30 m.p.h.	3% fast	6.3% fast
Speedometer at 60 m.p.h.	5% fast	7.3% fast
Distance recorder	2% fast	2.5% fast

Compression Pressures
(On 1959 Sprite only)
Cyls. 1 to 4 respectively—
At 1,200 miles: 150; 153; 148; 140. (lb./sq. in.)
At 16,750 miles: 127; 125; 122; 120. (lb./sq. in.)

SPRITE & MIDGET

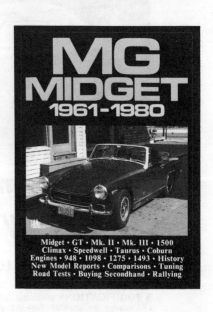

AUSTIN HEALEY SPRITE 1958-1971

Some 32 articles lead us through Sprite development from the introduction of the 'bug-eye' in 1958. There are 11 road tests a 'spot check', a road research report, a comparison with the Honda S800 and a Used Car Classic rundown. Models covered include the MkI, MkII, MkIII, MkIV, the Sebring and cars prepared by Warwick, Gaston and Alexander.
100 Large Pages.

AUSTIN HEALEY 'FROGEYE' SPRITE Collection No. 1. (1958-1961)

A total of 23 stories drawn from the US, Australia and the UK make up this book. They include 5 road tests, 2 used car reports, 3 articles on rebuilding, history, and cover a supercharged model plus the one Sammy Davis drove for over 120,000 miles.
70 Large Pages.

MG MIDGET 1961-1980

Fifteen road tests are included in the 33 stories that lead us through the development of the last of the MG Midgets. Other pieces include a comparison test vs. a Spitfire, articles on rallying, history, new model reports, tuning and an excellent guide to buying a secondhand car. Models covered include the Mk.I, Mk.II, Mk. III and the 1500.
100 Large Pages.

These soft-bound volumes in the 'Brooklands Books' series consist of reprints of original road test reports and other stories that appeared in leading motoring journals during the periods concerned.

The following factory workshop manuals, parts catalogues and owners handbooks are currently available for Sprite and Midget owners.

Part No.
50312	Sprite Mk1 Workshop Manual
X023	Complete Official 948cc and 1098cc Sprite/Midget Workshop Manual
X027	Complete Official 1275cc Sprite/Midget Workshop Manual
AKM 0036	Sprite Mk3 and 4 and Midget Mk2 & 3 Parts Catalogue
AKD 1909A	1961 Midget Parts Catalogue — Owners Edition
97H 1583A	Sprite Mk1 Owners Handbook
AKM 3229	Midget Mk2 Owners Handbook

From specialist booksellers or, in case of difficulty, direct from the distributors:
BROOKLANDS BOOK DISTRIBUTION, 'HOLMERISE', SEVEN HILLS ROAD, COBHAM, SURREY KT11 1ES, ENGLAND. Telephone: Cobham (09326) 5051
MOTORBOOKS INTERNATIONAL, OSCEOLA, WISCONSIN 54020, USA.
Telephone: 715 294 3345 & 800 826 6600

The Ashley Laminates bodywork on this extremely potent Austin-Healey Sprite leaves the Sprite grille unchanged but beneficially alters the headlamp layout. Note the wider track of the car resulting from the wire-wheel conversion.

A 100 m.p.h. Sprite – by Gaston

A Highly-tuned Austin-Healey with Ashley Bodywork

MODIFICATIONS available from one source or another for the popular little Austin-Healey are fast becoming legion and vary from mild tune-up kits to complete body, engine, and suspension alterations which turn the car into a G.T. machine. Such a vehicle is the Ashley Laminates bodied car, with tuning by Paddy Gaston, that was shown at the Racing Car Show and was submitted to us for test on the Monday after it closed.

Paddy Gaston is well known for his successful racing exploits with a Sprite and he offers the benefit of his experience to other owners by selling a variety of tuning aids. The car tested had a very large number of these modifications, but cars are tuned to individual customers' wishes so the specification can be varied at will. The engine had, in this case, been fully developed and bored out .060 in. to increase the capacity to 994 c.c.

Flat-top racing pistons are fitted in place of the concave-crown ones normally used and the cylinder head is highly modified, including larger inlet valves, double valve springs and modified valve guides. Larger S.U. carburetters are fitted to a special inlet manifold and a fabricated exhaust system further improves gasflow. Pushrods, rockers and base tappets are lightened and the racing camshaft runs in special bearings. The flywheel is lightened and a nine-spring clutch used. Modifications are also made to the oil and water pumps and a high-pressure electric fuel pump replaces the mechanical one. The engine is, of course, balanced. These and various other minor alterations raise the power output from 43 b.h.p. at 5,200 r.p.m. to 70 b.h.p. at 6,500.

Chassis modifications include an anti-roll bar at the front and stiffer shock absorbers, the rear suspension being left as standard. A knock-on wire-wheel conversion incorporating disc brakes at the front has, as well as its obvious features, the effect of increasing track. Dunlop racing covers were fitted to the wheels and a 4.22 rear axle ratio used although there are various options and a ZF differential is also available.

Bodywork alterations by Ashley Laminates comprised a glass-fibre removable hard top and a restyled forward-hinging bonnet made in the same material. Internally, Gaston modifications include cutting away a section of the bodywork immediately behind the

seats, thus allowing luggage to be stowed more easily or a child to be carried. The interior is now furnished with carpets in place of rubber mats and a wood-rimmed steering wheel and a special rev. counter fitted. More comfortable seats, upholstered in leather, are also available but were not fitted to the test car.

All this costs a considerable amount of money, particularly when the low initial cost of the Sprite is taken as a yardstick, but it is true to say that the car is so transformed as to make it almost a separate entity from the standard vehicle. The performance has been improved greatly and the car is the fastest Sprite that we have ever driven. Although the tune of the engine was

Improved accessibility for a very non-standard engine. Detail changes are the electric fuel pump and the larger-than-standard brake-fluid reservoir. Special coil, distributor and Champion N3 sparking plugs are less obvious.

PERFORMANCE DATA: GASTON MODIFIED SPRITE

	"The Motor" Road Test No. 15/58	Gaston Sprite
Test Conditions	Temperature 70-74°F. Barometer 30.2-30.4 in. Hg. Dry with moderate wind	Temperature 35-36°F. Barometer 29.3-29.2 in. Hg. Wet with light wind
Weight		
Kerb weight (unladen but with oil, coolant and fuel for approx. 50 miles)	12¾ cwt.	12½ cwt.
Front/rear distribution of kerb weight	55/45	50/50
Weight laden as tested	16 cwt.	16¼ cwt.
Maximile Speed (timed ¼-mile after 1 mile accelerating from rest)		
Mean of opposite runs	81 1 m.p.h.	97.8 m.p.h.
Best time equals	83.3 m.p.h.	101.1 m.p.h.
3rd Gear Acceleration		
10-30 m.p.h.	8.6 secs.	13.6 secs.
20-40 m.p.h.	7.7 secs.	12.6 secs.
30-50 m.p.h.	8.6 secs.	11.6 secs.
40-60 m.p.h.	11.4 secs.	7.7 secs.
50-70 m.p.h.	—	7.4 secs.
Acceleration from Standstill		
0-30 m.p.h.	5.1 secs.	3.6 secs.
0-40 m.p.h.	8.5 secs.	5.5 secs.
0-50 m.p.h.	13.7 secs.	7.7 secs.
0-60 m.p.h.	20.5 secs.	11.5 secs.
0-70 m.p.h.	31.1 secs.	15.5 secs.
Standing ¼-mile	21.8 secs.	17.8 secs.
Fuel Consumption		
At steady 30 m.p.h.	52.5 m.p.g.	44.5 m.p.g.
At steady 50 m.p.h.	53.5 m.p.g.	43.5 m.p.g.
At steady 70 m.p.h.	36.0 m.p.g.	37.0 m.p.g.
At steady 80 m.p.h.	—	32.5 m.p.g.
Overall consumption	33.6 m.p.g. for 1,696 miles	31.1 m.p.g. for 482 miles

Brakes from 30 m.p.h. (Figures for standard car shown in italics.)

Retardation		Stopping distance		Pedal pressure
..	*0.97 g*	..	*31 ft.*	90 lb.
0.8 g	*0.75 g*	37½ ft.	*40 ft.*	75 lb.
0.73 g	*0.49 g*	41 ft.	*61½ ft.*	50 lb.
0.49 g	*0.22 g*	61½ ft.	*137 ft.*	25 lb.

Price. Cost of Standard Sprite anc modifications to bring to the same stand rd as tested; £975.

Items obtainable individually:

70 b.h.p. engine, on exchange	£180
Disc brake wire-wheel conversion	£81 (less fitting).
ZF differential	£62.10s.
Anti-roll bar	£7
De luxe seats	£12
Interior modification and carpeting	£15
Ashley Laminates Hardtop and Bonnet	£80

Addresses: J. H. Gaston and Co., Ltd., Albany Park Service Station 215 Richmond Road, Kingston-upon-Thames. Ashlcy Laminates Ltd., Bush Fair, Harlow, Essex.

A 100 m.p.h. Sprite

Carpeting the interior gives this G.T. Sprite a far more luxurious appearance whilst the functional layout of the instruments and controls which is such a pleasing feature of the standard car remains almost unaltered.

said to be more suited to racing than ordinary road work and a slightly less radical unit is advised for everyday use, it was remarkably smooth and quiet, only the exhaust and carburetter intakes producing rather more noise than might be desired. The camshaft did not start producing power at much below 3,500 r.p.m., although it was possible to drop below this figure without any effect save that acceleration was less rapid. In the higher rev range there was an enormous improvement which carried on until a limit of something slightly over 7,000 r.p.m. was reached. The only signs of temperament were a tendency to run on and slight pinking even on 100 octane fuel. Although the fan had been removed the water temperature actually remained lower than on a standard car, which was probably due to the improved airflow through the radiator core, thanks to the ducting at the front of the special bonnet.

The increase in maximum permitted r.p.m. had the effect of making the rather wide gap between second and third gears less noticeable when motoring hard, but for competition close-ratio gears would naturally be fitted. Similarly, the 4.22 rear axle does not give maximum acceleration and when this is coupled with our standard test load a standing start quarter-mile covered in 17.8 sec. is admirable, as is the car's ability to reach over 100 m.p.h. in the more favourable of two directions after one mile accelerating from rest compared with 83.3 m.p.h. best for a standard car. When we took performance figures the carburetters were in need of adjustment, which was later made, in order to give reasonable low-speed pulling power, and did not allow representative acceleration figures to be taken in top gear. Similarly braking figures could probably have been improved had there been sufficient time to adjust the front/rear braking ratio to stop the rear wheels locking prematurely, but this was the price that had to be paid for obtaining the car for test at very short notice, and is no reflection on its preparation. The pedal pressures required were low for disc brakes.

Turning to the ride and handling qualities of the car, the latter had been improved at the expense of the former. The Sprite in standard trim gives a firm ride and when on racing tyres, which are designed with one end only in view, this characteristic is even more pronounced. Steering which is normally exceptionally light has become slightly, but not unpleasantly, heavier and some kick back is evident whilst vibration is felt through the wheel at high speeds over certain surfaces. On the credit side is the complete stability of the car at around its maximum speed and high cornering power on dry roads. For normal road use, however, most customers would prefer ordinary tyres and rely on the suspension modifications for improvement.

Interior Layout

The bodywork alterations have several practical advantages as well as making the car more pleasing in appearance. Its improved aerodynamic shape is responsible for some of the increase in performance and lack of wind noise compared with a normal Sprite with soft top. The sliding side screens that have now been standardized also help in the matter of silence, so a customer who is prepared to have a less "efficient" exhaust system and carburetter air cleaners would have a remarkably quiet car. The bonnet, thanks to its repositioned headlights, gives a completely different aspect from the driving seat, giving a clearer view of the road immediately ahead. Due to the flexible nature of the glass fibre it does however tend to shake at high speed. Hinging forwards it offers a vast improvement in accessibility, allowing such items as the battery, and brake and clutch master cylinders to be serviced more easily than on the standard bodied car.

The hard top provides far more room inside than a hood and makes the interior warmer and completely waterproof. Vision is reduced slightly to each side at the rear, there being blind spots between the back of the side screens and the large rear window. The interior of the hard top is flock sprayed and the whole is held in place by two nuts and bolts at the front and two at the rear, making it a simple matter to convert the car back to an open one.

Carpeting on the floor, boot and in the door pockets makes the car more snug, whilst cutting away a section of the upper part of the body behind the rear seats provides more room. The alloy beading fitted at this point was rather sharp at the edges. The three-spoke wood-rimmed steering wheel tended to obscure the instruments, which were as standard except for a rev counter which coped with the higher r.p.m. obtainable. The horn is now operated by a flip switch on the dash.

Those motorists who are attracted to the Sprite by virtue of its extremely low initial price are probably in no position to spend money of this order on their car, but for those who want a machine for competition or desire a remarkably accelerative car with excellent top speed without the clumsiness and heavy fuel consumption almost inevitably associated with larger vehicles, the Gaston G.T. Sprite is a very attractive proposition.

Supercharged Sprite with wire wheels

European road test of supercharged A-H Sprite

By David Phipps

One of the cheapest and undoubtedly one of the simplest ways of radically increasing the performance of the BMC 'A' series engine is to fit a Shorrock supercharger. By this means the power output of the Austin Healey Sprite can be raised from 42. bhp at 5000 rpm to 68 bhp at 5700 rpm at a cost of $225. No internal modifications of the engine are necessary, and the fitting of the supercharger should be well within the compass of most Sprite owners. A further advantage is that, at a later date, the car can either be sold complete with blower or restored to standard trim, the supercharger being retained for use on another car.

Due largely to its long-term effects on the reliability and fuel consumption of certain pre-war engines, supercharging is regarded with suspicion in some circles, but 2000 miles in a Shorrock-blown Sprite revealed absolutely no disadvantages other than a 15 per cent increase in fuel consumption in return for a reduction of over 100 per cent in the time required to accelerate from a standstill to 70 mph and a 20 per cent improvement

in maximum speed. And as the supercharged Sprite reached 96 mph with the normal hood and sidescreens fitted, it seems almost certain that the smoother contours of a hard top would make it a genuine 100 mph car.

The supercharger installation on the Sprite consists of a Type C/75/B Shorrock eccentric-rotor-type compressor — suitable for all BMC 'A' series engines — together with a 1½ inch SU horizontal carburettor mounted on a replacement inlet manifold. Drive is by "V" belts in combination with a special crankshaft pulley, and maximum boost is 7 lb. per square inch. Automatic lubrication is achieved by means of a metering valve built into the supercharger and connected with special tapping into the engine oil pressure line. All these components, together with supercharger mounting brackets, studs and bolts, are included in the price of $225. Fitting is quite straightforward, the only alteration required being the removal of the existing manifold and replacement of the crankshaft pulley.

One of the chief advantages of the eccentric rotor-type supercharger is that it affords both high mechanical

efficiency and reliability as there is no actual contact between the vanes and the outer casing. Both of these features were demonstrated during the recent BMC record runs in Utah, when an A-series-engined car fitted with a Type C/75/B supercharger covered 146.95 miles in one hour and did 1000 miles at an average of 138.55 mph.

On the road the increased performance of the blown engine is achieved without any loss of smoothness. In fact, due to a torque increase from 52.5 ft. at 3300 rpm to 64.8 lb. ft. at 3000 rpm, this unit is even more flexible than the standard one. Its greatest appeal, however, lies in its willingness to rev freely up to 6000 rpm in the intermediate gears, rushing the Sprite away from traffic delays in a way which few other small cars can match. It requires no specialized driving technique, no keeping the revs up, keeping the plugs clean or slipping the clutch, you just press down your right foot and go.

The test car was fitted with a number of extras, all desirable if not essential on a car of this performance, including disc brakes at the front, (together with 8 inch rear drums), competition shock absorbers and an anti-roll bar. Wire wheels, which are an essential adjunct to the fitting of disc brakes, also give the car a more sporting appearance. The disc brake wire wheel conversion is, however, rather expensive approximately $200.00 — $250.000, cheaper alternatives being a change of lining material or the fitting of 8 inch front drums.

Regarding the suspension modifications, the anti-roll bar counteracts the roll oversteer of the standard car (posibly at some expense in front tire wear) and the competition shocks eliminate the slight pitching experienced on some surfaces with normal suspension. The ride is a little firmer than standard but few owners are likely to complain about this, particularly as the modifications bring the handling almost up to sports racing standards.

Austin Motor Co. (Canada) Ltd. do not import supercharged Sprites. They import factory Sprites and it is up to the owner to take it from there.

The only people we know of in Canada who import and fit the Shorrock supercharger are Shelton-Mansell Motors who advise that would-be supercharged Sprite owners be prepared for a wait of 6-8 weeks between ordering and delivery for their Sprite all nicely souped up.

If there are any other dealers who do this conversion we would be happy to print their name and address.

SPECIFICATIONS

PRICE: $2110 in Canada
BODY STYLE: Open two-seater
ENGINE: 4 cylinder in line, OHV, Shorrock C/75/B Supercharger
BRAKE H.P.: 68 at 5700 rpm
BORE/STROKE: 62.9 mm x 76.2 mm
DISPLACEMENT: 948 cc
MAX TORQUE: 64.8 lb. ft. at 3000 rpm
COMPRESSION RATIO: 8.3 to 1
CARBURETOR: One S.U. 1½ inch horizontal
FUEL PUMP: Mechanical
CLUTCH: 6¼ inch single dry plate
IGNITION & ELECTRICAL SYSTEM: Lucas battery & coil
GEAR RATIOS: 1st 15.31, 2nd 10.02, 3rd 5.96, 4th 4.22
DRIVE: Rear wheel drive, gearbox in unit with engine
SUSPENSION: Front: double wishbone & coil springs; Rear: live axle & quarter elliptic springs.
*BRAKES: 7 inch front brakes, 7 inch rear drums
STEERING: Rack and Pinion, 2⅓ turns lock to lock, Turning circle 31 ft. 6 in.
GENERAL DIMENSIONS: Wheelbase 6 ft. 8 in. Ground clearance 5 in., Track; front 45¾ in., rear 44¾ in.
OVERALL DIMENSIONS: Length 11 ft. 5¼ in., width 4 ft. 5 in., Height 49¾ in.
WEIGHT: 1456 lb. dry
FUEL TANK: 6 imperial gallons
OIL CAPACITY: 7 pints (3½ quarts)

Supercharged Sprite showing blower installation, anti-roll bar, disc brakes and wire wheels.

TIMES

0 - 30 mph— 4.0 seconds	0 - 40 mph— 5.8 seconds
0 - 50 mph— 8.2 seconds	0 - 60 mph—11.4 seconds
Maximum speed 96 mph	Fuel Consumption 27 mpg

*Brakes listed here are stock, however with the increased power larger brakes are essential. Test car had 8½" discs f. 8" drums r.

SPRITE TEST

(Continued from page 85)

hampered by the thick pillars of the new, curved screen which are abetted by the extra metal necessary to frame the hinging quarter panels.

All the Mk. III's controls are well placed for easy operation, including the window winders. The handbrake is mounted on the passenger's side of the tunnel and there is not much space between it and the seat cushion, but enough, nevertheless.

Since the switch to baulk-ring, BMC gearboxes have improved no end. The Sprite's stubby little lever is just where it should be, although unusually high. The movements from one cog to another are short and precise, but synchromesh in first would be a real advantage for town motoring.

On the Road

Hot or cold the engine is an instant starter, but you need to be patient and an adept choke twiddler to keep the engine operating sanely during the longish warm-up period.

Running on a 9:1 compression ratio, the engine will accept supergrade petrol without pinging, but sometimes runs-on in a rather alarming manner. Apparently it does not like pottering through town in Saturday morning traffic, for we fouled a plug under these conditions. It cleared itself after a short burst of rapid running.

Power in the Mk. III has been increased from 55 b.h.p. (net) at 5500 r.p.m. to 59 at 5750 revs by using the MG 1100 (Morris 1100 shape, MG badges and hot engine) cylinder head and revised induction and exhaust systems. Torque is fractionally better and remains at 3250 r.p.m., so the Sprite is still not a strong puller at long revs.

In the cause of making this wildly undersquare engine — stroke is almost 20mm. longer than the bore — stronger, the crankshaft has been stiffened and the three main bearings have been increased in width from 1¾in. to 2in.

The engine likes to be worked and gets very sweet up around the 4000 rev mark, spins rapidly to 6000 which we used as the outside limit.

It's a swift enough motor car, but it's not a ball of fire by any stretch of the imagination. At 15.4 m.p.h. per 1000 revs in top, you need to spin the engine fairly hard continuously to maintain a good cruising speed on the open road, but this is something the car does not seem to mind.

No one really seems to know why BMC changed the Sprite's longstanding and unique quarter-elliptic back springs (if you are starting to feel nostalgic, try to remember how they used to squeak and groan) for conventional semi-elliptics. But, quite frankly, I find it very hard to detect any practical difference between the two systems on the road.

However, there was far more tyre scream under hard cornering — and most of it seemed to be coming from the back — than I can recollect in earlier Sprites, but the handling remained basically neutral all the way and was less inclined to do unexpected things.

When the car runs over uneven ground halfway through a corner the tail dances out, just as it did on the earlier models. In general, though, the car seemed to behave much better on dirt roads than its predecessors.

If this alteration has done anything significant it has made the ride a little better. That's about all.

The disc/drum braking system needs a fair push on the pedal, but there is ample retardation available all the time. The rack-and-pinion steering points the car with the accuracy of a scalpel and responds to a gentle touch.

You pay a price when you get these good features in an inexpensive car for the Sprite could be better put together.

But this is the young enthusiasts' introduction to better motoring—and putting up with noise and tracing ailments is a part of the initiation.

Road Research Report: AUSTIN-HEALEY SPRITE

► If you've passed the P-R-N-D-L stage of driving and are interested in sports cars, there's probably no better starting place than an Austin-Healey Sprite. It is far and away the cheapest sports car that is readily available with nationwide service and parts distribution to back it. It has the further advantage that it is a genuine sports car and not a four-wheel motorcycle. Whatever you learn about sports cars while apprenticed to a Sprite will serve you in good stead when you graduate to something larger and faster.

While no car will ever be a genuine successor to the MG TC, the Sprite comes the closest and that is how it should be. After all, Donald Healey designed it by exactly the same principles that had governed the MG Car Company, namely, to build a good sports car to a sensible price by clever, simple design and, wherever possible, components already proven by and tooled up for existing sedans within the parent company.

COCKPIT CAPERS

Because the Sprite has an integral body-frame, the cockpit is far more spacious than the car's size would indicate. The doors are good-sized but access is made somewhat awkward because the door-latch's pin can catch on your coat pocket (and will if you don't watch out). The bucket seats, the real kind with simply curved wrap-around backs that are hardly upholstered at all, get a good grip on you and won't let you fall out. The seat cushions, while not overstuffed, were comfortable enough. They would have been better if they'd been tilted up at the front. We found we kept hitching ourselves back in the seat every few minutes.

All the controls are well placed, especially the stubby little shift lever which sprouts from the deeply curved metal transmission cover. One of those old-fashioned suction-cup-style ash trays would be a useful accessory for someone to revive; it would stick easily to that bulge and be handy to both driver and passenger. The starter pull seemed awkward, being nearly in front of the passenger, because the choke was also to the right of the steering column (and with too tight a spring to stay out by itself).

With an only 80-inch wheelbase and springs stiff enough for sporting driving through the bends, the Sprite has an understandably jiggly ride. On long undulating dips, the effect is that of a small sailboat in a following sea. Spring rates, for the technically minded, are 71 pounds per inch front and 98 rear.

Though short on ride comfort, the little Sprite's roadholding is as tenacious as its tires allow. The car is very low to the ground so it rolls but little and doesn't transfer too much weight to the usually overworked ouside tires. Combine this with its quick-as-a-wink steering and the Sprite is sheer joy to tool through ess-bends on smooth, lightly-traveled roads.

Being a small car, it's natural that its living quarters should be a bit on the cramped side. Most of our staff always left the seat in the fully-rearward position and its range is only 3 inches.

WEATHERPROOFING

In this respect the Sprite is a far cry indeed from the TC and TD. True, it has side-curtains rather than roll-up windows, but they have sliding panes which permit hand signaling from the inside (and door opening from the out). Made of plastic, these panes scratch quickly and become difficult to see through unless cared for with loving tenderness and soft, clean rags. They slide reluctantly in felt-lined aluminum frames which clamp to the doors with knurled nuts. In a sleet storm, of course, you may be temporarily locked out since the door handles are only on the inside. (Unfasten the top's nearby buttons and reach way in.) A following wind will drive rain in through the gap but in practice this is no problem as the rain water runs down the front, fixed pane onto the body-contour surface of the door, then seeps under the fabric draft-excluder which surrounds the aluminum frame.

When the Sprite was introduced the folding top attached across the top of the windshield with a row of "lift the dot" fasteners. Since the fabric itself was un-stiffened, it tended to develop a severe case of gaposis between the "dots" and the interior was considered to be rather a shower. Now redesigned, the front edge of the top is reinforced and hooks over a narrow flange all across the front, having but two fasteners, one at each corner.

When the top and the side curtains are in place, Sprite riders, snug in their draft-free quarters, have

another advantage over the old-timers: that very standard option, the $50 heater/defroster. It's a simple device; there's only one switch, either twist for blower-on or pull for ducts-open (through the heater, of course), plus the two small flaps above the transmission tunnel which, if closed, direct all the air on the windshield. Open, the warm air blows right on your ankles. When the temperature is in the twenties, you start getting warm air within a couple of blocks even though the engine is still demanding a rich mixture.

In summertime, Sprites are a rarity among front-engined sports cars in that the cockpit *can* be kept cool and well ventilated. The same fresh air duct which warms you in winter is used but the hot water from the engine is, of course, turned off by an under-hood tap.

FOLDING THE TOP

In fine old British sports car tradition, hiding the "rain-rag", an unfair euphemism these days, is a time-consuming chore. It's easiest to describe the process by telling how the top is erected first.

We've mentioned the flange across the upper edge of the windshield. There are also two hooks on the rear deck and a half-dozen fasteners. After all these items are hooked up, the spring-loaded tensioners (!) in the tubular steel, hoop-like framework are released, popping the center portion of the top up to its full height. Removing the top is, as the owner's manual details, merely "a reversal of the above steps."

After the fabric top with the wide rear window is rolled up and stowed behind the seats, the "hoop" is lifted out and the forward-reaching "zig-zags" are collapsed. Then the whole assembly is turned around and inserted in a second pair of holes, low down near the floor, and pressed under the rear lip of the cockpit edge. A small leather strap retains it there, out of the way.

It may be a struggle, but what joy it is to drive in the open air again. For us, the Sprite was the first open car after too many weeks of snow and cold and over-heated buildings and claustrophobic cars. Of course we left the heater on full-bore and the side-screens were in place, and boy, did our noses and ears get red, but we loved every moment of it. There were a few well-wrapped people in stuffy sedans who may have stared but that just made us enjoy it more.

Logic-minded types may balk at paying more for a Sprite than an equivalently hopped-up sedan such as a Minor or 850 which carries twice as many people and does other such useful tasks, but what use is logic against the appeal of the open air and the open road? Perhaps you do have to be nuts to want to drive around with the top down and catch pneumonia, but if it happens you *are* nuts that way, it's hard to see what keeps you from buying a Sprite.

LIDLESS TRUNK

Both seats fold forward to give access to the luggage space. To stiffen the integral body-frame structure and to economize, there is no external lid. Although it's hardly easy to get at, Sprite owners soon become adept at reaching in there. They learn several valuable lessons. There is a great deal of room there, probably twice as much as you'd have if there were a proper trunk with a floor over the spare tire. You should avoid hurling sturdy suitcases in with excessive vigor, otherwise you may make an inside-out dent! For that reason and because the trunk is so irregularly shaped, soft canvas tote bags are the preferred luggage pieces, no matter how big or small. It is also an excellent idea to wipe off the spare before replacing it.

LIGHT, QUICK STEERING

One of the favorite delights of sports car owners is their car's agility, its ability to change course instantly or to swerve abruptly to avoid an unexpected obstacle. The Sprite has this in spades. Its steering is the quickest we've ever tested on our 400-foot Test Circle. At 50 mph indicated, the limit of adhesion, the one-eighth of a turn of lock required (45°) is less than many cars require at only 10 mph. In fact, it is equal to the amount of free play allowed by some states in their vehicle inspection criteria!

Nearly all driving can be done without removing your hands from a fixed position on the rim. Because the Sprite's overall dimensions are so small, the car is thus exceedingly nimble in traffic. In highway maneuvers there is no delay; you turn the wheel and the Sprite turns right now. For those accustomed to slower steering (it's only 2½ turns lock to lock for a 30-foot turning circle), the Sprite seems a little "nervous" and takes some getting used to. On icy roads and on the race track, this is especially true, as extensive swinging of the arms is just what the doctor didn't order.

Because of this quickness, if you grip the wheel too firmly, the very motions of your body as the car reacts to bumps in the road will affect the steering. If you take care to hold the rim very lightly, letting it jiggle through your hands when the bumps feed back, your Sprite will maintain a steadier course and hold the road better on bumpy bends. A gentle grip also discourages over-controlling.

CIRCLE TESTING

While the Test Circle's steady-state results indicate a very mildly understeering car, transient conditions such as entering a turn or abruptly straightening out indicate that there is very little in-built directional stability. When you toss her into a turn violently, the Sprite's tail end may snap around to embarrass you. While the quick steering is an asset beyond doubt in giving you the means to recover from the resultant sideslip, we are inclined to believe that its too-quick-ness is what tempts or leads you to over-control in the first place. The optional anti-roll bar ($34 — a bit steep) will have the dynamic effect of slowing the steering and increasing the understeer. It would also reduce the tendency to lift the inside rear wheel when accelerating out of a tight turn.

While we hesitate to say that the Sprite's steering is too quick, we certainly wouldn't want to drive on *(Text continued on page **46** data overleaf)*

For a lot of sportiness with the minimum of fuss and bother at your local bank, the Sprite's charms are proving irresistible to more and more Americans. Demand exceeds supply, even after three years.

Sprite's lidless trunk is unusual enough but how about these bumper guards without bumpers?

PHOTOGRAPHY: CHITTENDEN

Handwork with portable grinder to heart-shaped combustion chambers is unmentioned in Tuning Booklet but it's a useful move for good gas flow.

Hold it, cowboy! Final oversteer is induced only by overcontrolling. Basic Sprite handling is good enough to permit increases in horsepower.

Out of a vast array of options, official and not, there's nothing quite like a $603 wire wheel/disc brake kit to make Sprites sit up and grin.

Road Research Report: AUSTIN-HEALEY SPRITE

Importer:

Hambro Automotive Corp.
27 West 57th Street
New York 19, N. Y.

Number of U. S. dealers: 580
Planned annual production: 18,000
Dollar value of spare parts in U. S.: $5,000,000

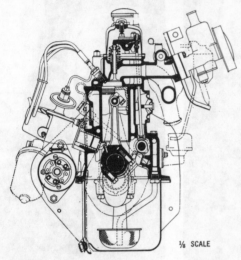

⅛ SCALE

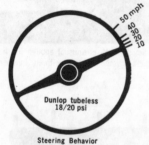

Dunlop tubeless
18/20 psi

Steering Behavior

Wheel position to
maintain 400-foot circle
at speeds indicated.

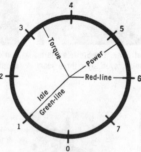

Engine Flexibility
RPM in thousands

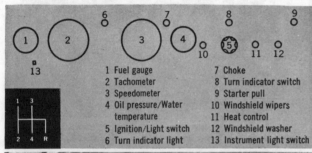

1 Fuel gauge
2 Tachometer
3 Speedometer
4 Oil pressure/Water temperature
5 Ignition/Light switch
6 Turn indicator light
7 Choke
8 Turn indicator switch
9 Starter pull
10 Windshield wipers
11 Heat control
12 Windshield washer
13 Instrument light switch

PRICES:

Basic Price	$1795
Options fitted on all cars imported:	
Heater/defroster	50
Tachometer	30
Windshield washer	15
Total	1890
Other options fitted on test car:	
Tonneau cover	35
White sidewall tires	30
Dealer preparation	35
Total price of car, as tested	$1955 at New York
Factory option:	
Stage V engine, prepared by Donald Healey, ordered as original equipment	380
Other options, available only through local dealers:	
Hardtop	$ 225
Quick-action filler cap	15
Lockable filler cap	7
Wire wheel and disc brake conversion kit	603
8-in front brake drum kit	56
Anti-roll bar	34
Stiff shock valves (set)	17
Stiff front springs	17
Stiff rear springs	36
Light steel flywheel	142
Close-ratio gearbox (see drive train specs below)	290
Parts to convert normal gearbox	66
5.38 ring and pinion set	27
5.38 complete assembly	75
4.55 ring and pinion set	20
4.55 complete assembly	75
3.73 ring and pinion set	29
3.73 complete assembly	80
9.3 piston set (std., .010, .030)	49
Set of piston rings for above	8
Camshaft (.315-in lift)	32
Set of inner valve springs & collars	11
Distributor	37
Front manifold	11
Exhaust pipe	7
Muffler	8
Clips for above	2
Dual exhaust system	21
Thermostat blanking sleeve	1
Large capacity oil pan	40
Oil cooler kit	110
Pair of 1¼-in S U carbs	77
Manifold for above	30
Polished cylinder head assembly	158

OPERATING SCHEDULE:

Fuel recommended	Regular
Mileage	32-35 mpg
Range on 7.2-gallon tank	230-250 miles
Oils recommended	SAE 30 or 20W/30; below freezing, 20W; below 10° F., 10W. (SAE 10W/30 is also approved.)
Crankcase capacity	3.6 quarts (4.2 with filter change)
Change at intervals of	3000 miles (filter at 6000 miles)
Number of grease fittings	12
Lubrication interval	1000 miles
Most frequent maintenance, interval recommended: Refill transmission, rear axle; oil water pump; grease front hubs—6000 miles.	

ENGINE: (BMC "A" series)

Displacement	57.9 cu in, 948 cc
Dimensions	Four cyl, 2.48 in bore, 3.00 in stroke
Valve gear	pushrod operated, vertical overhead valves, stamped rockers
Compression ratio	8.3 to one
Power (SAE)	48 bhp @ 5200 rpm
Torque	52 lb-ft @ 3300 rpm
Usable range of engine speeds	1000-6000 rpm
Corrected piston speed @ 5200 rpm	2360 fpm

CHASSIS:

Wheelbase	80.0 in
Tread	F 45.8, R 44.8 in
Length	113.3 in
Ground clearance	5.0 in
Suspension: F, ind., coil spring, wishbone and control arm; R, rigid axle, trailing quarter-elliptic leaf springs and control arm.	
Turns, lock to lock	2½
Turning circle diameter between curbs	30 ft
Tire and rim size	5.20 x 13, 15 x 4J
Pressures recommended	F 18, R 20 psi
Brakes; type, swept area	7 in drums, 110 sq in
Curb weight (full tank)	1480 lbs
Percentage on driving wheels	47%

DRIVE TRAIN: (BMC "A" series)

Gear	Synchro?	Ratio	Step	Overall	Mph per 1000 rpm
Rev	No	4.66		19.69	—3.3
1st	No	3.63	—	15.32	4.3
2nd	Yes	2.37	53%	10.02	6.5
3rd	Yes	1.41	68%	5.96	10.9
4th	Yes	1.00	41%	4.22	15.4
Optional close-ratio gearbox:					
Rev	No	4.11		17.39	—3.8
1st	No	3.20		13.51	4.8
2nd	Yes	1.92	67%	8.09	8.1
3rd	Yes	1.36	41%	5.72	11.4
4th	Yes	1.00	36%	4.22	15.4

Final Drive Ratios: 4.22 to one standard; 3.73, 4.55 and 5.38 to one optional.

AUSTIN-HEALEY SPRITE

SCALE: EACH SQUARE ON DRAWING
REPRESENTS ONE SQUARE FOOT

C A R · and · D R I V E R

T · E · FORNANDER

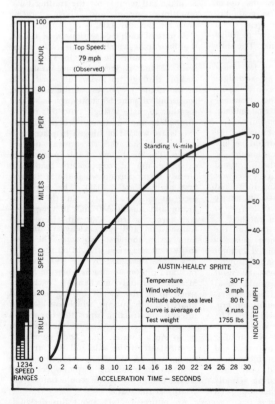

Top Speed:
79 mph
(Observed)

Standing ¼-mile

AUSTIN-HEALEY SPRITE

Temperature	30°F
Wind velocity	3 mph
Altitude above sea level	80 ft
Curve is average of	4 runs
Test weight	1755 lbs

1234
SPEED
RANGES

ACCELERATION TIME — SECONDS

ROAD RESEARCH REPORT: AUSTIN-HEALEY SPRITE

Continued from page 42

public roads with steering any quicker. The least movement of your hands changes the Sprite's course, which becomes noticeable if you throw a quick shift in the middle of a fast bend. Yet the steering forces are always very moderate indeed, a factor perhaps in the Sprite's extensive popularity with women.

NIGHT DRIVING

The Sprite's headlights are at full legal height, as any stylist will quickly remind you. American sealed-beam units are used on cars shipped over here and they are easily adequate to the Sprite's performance. The high beam indicator is at the bottom of the speedo dial, and doesn't annoy you at night, but the turn indicator light is much too bright and gets you right in the eyes. Why a smaller bulb isn't used here is beyond our comprehension. We found that a small piece of masking tape placed over it at dusk when we first turned on the lights was an eye-saving trick that paid dividends in destroying dazzle later on.

ENGINE PERFORMANCE

Our test was performed in winterlike weather so we had excellent opportunity to check the Sprite's cold-start characteristics. Even with the temperature down to 20° F, it would start promptly and run steadily provided you pulled the choke knob all the way out. However, even with a piece of cardboard covering three-fourths of the radiator, continued use of the choke was required for at least the first mile and the water temperature needle wouldn't move for one or two more.

The importers recommend premium gas so we used that for our acceleration runs but for normal driving we found that regular gave no trouble at all. No adjustments were made to the carburetors or ignition during the test.

Though the idle and "green-line" speeds are a bit on the high side at 1000 rpm for both, the Sprite engine doesn't act up or behave fussily in any way. A pint of oil was used, but only after the always tiresome (for the engine) acceleration runs. In fact, other than for photography, the only reason the hood was lifted was to show someone how it was done. Our only concern was with the oil pressure gauge which consistently read about 45 psi instead of the specified "60 or higher."

Like the brakes, the clutch is operated hydraulically. The clutch itself is tiny, only 6¼ inches in diameter, so the forces are quite low. Perhaps there was some stickiness in our clutch cylinder; we could certainly feel that some force was needed, yet the mechanism seemed devoid of "feel."

ACCESS TO THE ENGINE

What the Sprite misses in the way of a trunk lid it more than makes up for with engine access. The entire front body structure opens up, exposing both engine and front suspension. To keep everything else reasonably clean there are two very spartan-looking sub-fenders. The hood is unlatched by reaching behind the license plate on the front bumper below the grille and twisting the tee-handle with the left hand while releasing a safety catch with the right. Then you take a firm grip (and a deep breath) and lift the heavy structure up until the telescoping struts engage their ratchets.

Everything under the hood is then exposed for checking or adjusting, but there are two drawbacks. If it's been raining, then there is a good chance that, as you bend awkwardly under the nose (it's such a small car, even when the nose is up, it's low), you'll get water dripped on you by the upraised body. The other is that tall people will find it awkward to bend that low. Since the fender sides come up too, your access is limited mainly to the front where the under edge of the nose hangs low enough to make it awkward to avoid touching it with your back.

The dipstick is back between plugs #2 and #3 and lies quite close to the warmth of the cylinder head, but not, fortunately, anywhere near the exhaust manifold. It's hard to see the hole in the block to replace it because you stand so far away.

The "electrics" and the suspension's grease fittings are unusually easy to reach. In the case of the latter, the most important nine of the 12 total fittings on the car can be lubricated by the owner at home without aid of a hoist. It's better though to lube suspension bushes with the car's weight off its wheels so the grease can flow where the load is greatest, so use of the car's jack is recommended if money-saving greasing-at-home appeals to you.

TRANSMISSION

The ubiquitous BMC A-series gearbox (cars using it range from Lotus to Austin A40) has four forward speeds, the upper three being synchronized. The gears are indifferently spaced as second gear could usefully be moved much closer to third without getting too far from first. The shift is very stiff when it's new, but by the time you're ready to trade the car in for a new one it's as smooth as silk and a real delight to use. The synchromeshes are easily beaten, especially when the near-new shifting mechanism is so tight that smooth, delicate shifts are nearly impossible.

While it is true that eventually the mechanism does wear in, it would be fine if the manufacturing process could be sharpened up so that gear-shifting could be a pleasure right from the very day you drive away. If we were trading in an old Sprite for a new one, we'd have the service department swap transmissions for us so we wouldn't have to break in another.

With standard 4.22 to one gears in the rear axle, the Sprite is almost perfectly geared for top speed. We achieved 79 mph with the soft top and side curtains in place; with the hardtop's smoothness, 80 itself should be possible. If so, it would be at exactly 5200 rpm, the speed of peak power.

If tip-top speed isn't your main concern, there are alternative ratios available. The 3.73 to one gearset would cut the acceleration, increase the amount of gear-shifting necessary and reduce the engine revs and noise while cruising. If a *vast* increase in power were made, then and only then would this big change in gearing actually result in the theoretically higher top speed one expects with a "longer" gear.

For better acceleration, there are two "shorter" gearsets available, 4.55 and 5.38. The former would be fun around town, yet still usable on the open road, being only 8% shorter than the stock 4.22 set. The latter is strictly for racing on short, twisty circuits or scaring the opposition in gymkhanas. Its red line (6000 rpm) would come up at only 72½ mph, and discretion would be in order to avoid blowing up your engine by literally over-revving in top gear.

On the other hand, over-revving will not be a problem with the 4.55s, as 80 mph, if you could achieve it, would equal 5600 rpm, past the power peak but short of the red-line. Of course, a long down-hill grade might tempt you . . . .

CONSTRUCTION

The outstanding technical feature of the Sprite is the use of integral body-frame design with an open two-seater body. Generally this technique is used on coupes and sedans where the roof and windshield posts play an important stress-carrying part in making up a stiff, box-like structure with which to replace the separate frame. As usual with such designs, the welded assembly of sheet metal stampings looks in many places just like a series of box-section members.

The Sprite's suspension mounts are joined to one another by two U-shaped arrays; that is, the front cross-member caps a small U which passes each side of the engine and gearbox (also carrying them) and runs into a median cross member below the driver's knees. This cross-member extends the full width of the car, serving as a suitable jacking point, complete with sockets. Near its extremities, under the door sill, a pair of box-sections run aft, sprouting upward just as they end to make tall mounts for the trailing quarter-elliptic springs and, above, locating arms for the rear axle.

A part of each box-section is, of course, the floor pan which extends fully across the car, enclosing the propellor shaft. (The front U-joint is greased from inside the cockpit through an awkwardly small hole in the tunnel.) The rest of the sub-frame, consisting of some 50 stampings, is welded together to make a single unit; this is then shipped to another factory where all body panels are welded or hinged in place.

So much for the sheet-metal side of things. The machinery of the Sprite makes extensive use of components that were already in production when the Sprite was first built (March, 1958). The engine is used in single-carb style in the Morris Minor and Austin A40 and, in very modified form, in the 850 mini-twins. The transmission and rear axle gears are the same as in the first two cars. The front suspension was taken straight off the Austin A35, since succeeded by the A40, and the rack and pinion steering is from the Morris Minor. The only mechanical "exclusive" seems to be the use of trailing arms and quarter-elliptic springs, which are ideal for integral construction since the box-section suspension reinforcements to the floor can be so much shorter. Only body panels are required aft of the axle and they are self-supporting. A drawback evidently is the difficulty in obtaining ample wheel travel for we found the Sprite would bottom out readily at the rear.

An impressive fact about this design is that after three years of production the only serious modification has been in the method of attaching the top to the windshield frame, and that was made shortly after introduction.

OWNER'S TIPS

In checking with friends and relations who own and drive Sprites we came up with a surprisingly short list of tips, which again testifies to the basic soundness of the original layout.

One is to apply glycerin, graphite or, if they aren't available, Vaseline to the felt slides of the sliding pane sidescreens. They will then work smoothly and more easily.

As to getting under the hood, one earnest recommendation is always to set the auxiliary hood stay (the one which folds across the front of the radiator) rather than trusting wholeheartedly to the telescopic self-latching props on each side. If that heavy hood drops on you accidentally, you'll be stuck for the day.

While you're under there checking the oil, it might be a good idea to check the tightness of the two bolts mounting the oil filter to the block.

If you have trouble with overheating on hot summer days, you'll find that moving your front license plate down or to one side will allow lots more air to the radiator.

In the wintertime when you need to use the choke for so long, you can out-fox its overly strong return spring by putting a nickel (5¢) edgewise between the knob and the dash. If you're the type that has a "church-key" on your keychain, it has just the right width too. (But you need a long keychain.)

About the stiff gear change, the universal advice is this: the more you use it, the faster it'll break in. But be careful with your brute strength, as too violent an effort will overload and "beat" the synchromesh cones.

Finally, there is the matter of clutch adjustment. There should always be 5/32-inch free play at the pedal itself. The normal adjustment is at the pedal end of the pushrod to the master cylinder. If you have used up all the adjustment there, lengthen the fixed-length pushrod to the slave cylinder by welding on a piece of screw stock, using trial and error to get the right length by cutting or grinding off some of the extension.

OPTIONS GALORE

Most any sort of person is likely to buy a Sprite; what makes the Sprite so charming is that it can be "arranged" to suit the individual, personal desires of any of them. You may keep it virtually stock as the center couple in the photo on pages 58-59 have done; you may fit it with every conceivable device for rallying as the pair on the left are about to, or you may use it as your foundation for going racing on a limited budget as the group on the right intend. The factory offers a wide range of options and what they don't offer, somebody else does. Marion Weber's firm, who lent us all those items in the left foreground, is a leader among the many specialists in the latter sort of thing. What they offer is well advertised (in C/D, of course) so we will dwell only on those items which, though offered by the factory, are harder to find out about.

STURDY ENGINE

If auto factories have learned anything from hot-rodders, it's that a given engine may be rearranged to have any one of several characters. It may be a sweet, docile and unnoticed powerplant for little old ladies or a fire-breathing, defiance-screaming packet of power for a racing car or anywhere in between; in every case with appropriate smoothness and reliability. The Sprite's engine is a good example of a half-way point in such a range. The Sprite's manufacturers, the British Motor Corporation, certainly utilize this system and their A-series engine is a marvelously versatile unit. The Sprite version of it with 48 SAE bhp or 43 net is only a moderate boost from the basic Morris version's 37 (net).

At the other end of the scale is the Formula Junior version, such as powered Charlie Kolb's championship Elva last year. It is rated at over 70 bhp SAE.

Few Sprite owners may want *that* specialized an engine under their hood, but if they're interested in more than stock output, the best dollar's worth of option they can get is part number AKD1021A. That's the Sprite Special Tuning booklet which lists all the options available and describes how to group the engine ones for varying increases of power. They list five stages; in terms of net horsepower (i.e., with accessories) they increase the peak output by 2, 4, 7, 9 and 11 or 12 bhp respectively, with the speed going up to about 5800 rpm.

A .315-inch lift competition camshaft jumps the overlap from a mild 15° to a still hardly hair-raising 37°. If you want every last revolution before valve bounce (and who doesn't?), a set of inner valve springs raises the red-line to 7000 rpm.

While the engine parts may seem rather limited, the booklet describes in great detail how to achieve the five stages of performance. Of course it's not merely a matter of installing parts; considerable careful hand reworking must be done to the cylinder head.

PERFORMANCE OPTIONS

Don't get carried away by the Tuning Booklet's list of 86 items because you cannot get each and every one of them here in the States. At this writing, Hambro does carry 25 of the 86, seven of them under different part numbers. Better yet, they also list 15 items that *aren't* in the booklet. Everything they have is shown on page 62, though we have condensed the array somewhat.

As we go to press, we have been informed that a simpler disc brake conversion is being introduced by the Donald Healey Motor Co., Ltd. of Warwick, England. For $126 plus shipping and duty, you get two Lockheed discs and calipers for the front wheels. Order direct, not through channels.

The close-ratio gearbox may be bought over the counter or you can rebuild your own by buying only the parts you need. Either way, it's an option we recommend. To give a comparison, the Drive Train specs include the figures for the close-ratio box below the standard one. If you're serious about road-racing, nothing will improve your "skill" as suddenly and impressively, unless it's the stiffening group of suspension parts (anti-roll bar, stiff springs and stiff valves for your shocks). It was used on the now-famous Sebring Sprites (along with a few other well-chosen items

— namely everything on Hambro's list) and it turns a complete fun car into a serious piece of racing iron. Flat cornering, we mean *flat*, an engagingly snarling engine up front with a sharp, crackling exhaust just behind you, and if you top it off with a handsome wood-rimmed steering wheel, well, you might as well be Fangio. Such a car is a long way indeed from the docile car you buy off the showroom floor, but that's a distance the Sprite can easily reach. As our lead photo indicates, it's only one of the directions you can choose, for the Sprite is a truly sound foundation for economically building your very own, thoroughly personalized sports car. If you prefer a bread-and-butter Sprite to one with jam, you'll still find it tasty. —C/D

MOTOR week ending September 5 1964

77▶

The gearchange should be crisp but on early cars the synchromesh may not work properly, or at all. On later examples an improved design gives no trouble. The Mk. II has close ratios.

Gear lever chatter is caused by a "tired" spring under the ball end of the lever where a Nylon pad is fitted. Rattles at the rear usually come from worn-through felts on the brake rods.

First and reverse gears may be quite noisy, which is in order, and there is no need to be alarmed by a fearful creaking when moving over bumps which seems to fill the whole car.

This emanates—the only really suitable word—from the rear spring attachments and regular greasing, preferably with a molybdenum-base grease, is the cure. Note that the spring safety eye can also cause some of the noise.

The rear axle and prop shaft are tough and if they are worn then the odds are that the rest of the car is pretty well "on the way".

● General

For the best handling, tyre pressures should have a 2 lb. differential, the higher pressure being at the rear—22/24 is suggested but stick to the 2 lb. difference even if other pressures are used.

Such a car is normally driven rapidly so an engine life of 50,000 miles must be regarded as average. All spares are available as are handbooks (4s.), workshop manual (27s. 6d.), spare parts list (16s. 6d.) and, for the Mk. I only—although, obviously, much will apply to the early Mk. II—a tuning manual dealing with various stages of tune (3s.). These should be ordered from Austin dealers.

Tuning specialists include: Donald Healey Motor Co., Warwick; The Healey Centre, Leighton Buzzard; and John Sprinzel, Lancaster Gate Mews, London, W.2.

WITH the introduction of their Austin-Healey Sprite in May, 1958, the British Motor Corporation no doubt had young people mainly in mind as customers. An open two-seater, small and economical to run, its initial cost was kept low and its good handling qualities quickly earned it a name for safety.

In standard form the performance was insufficient perhaps to justify the name sports car but the sporting character of the car was obvious. Latent possibilities in engine power and handling soon encouraged enthusiasts to tune and otherwise improve Sprites until they could enter national and international competitions with marked success. In rallies, tuned Sprites have proved true successors to the M.G. Midgets and Austin Seven specials of earlier days. Donald Healey's plans have been fully justified by the array of awards in sporting events during the last three years, and good commercial judgment on the part of the manufacturers has also been confirmed by the popularity of the Sprite in export markets.

Now the familiar, rather pert-looking Sprite is to be replaced by an improved and completely rebodied Mark II version which not only has a more svelte appearance but better acceleration, slightly higher top speed and much greater convenience for everyday use. The total home market price of the new model will be barely £10 more than the model superseded.

The most obvious changes for the Mark II Sprite are the completely restyled bonnet and grille, squared up and rather reminiscent of those of its attractive close relative, the Innocenti 950, assembled in Italy. The headlamps are incorporated in the wings. At the rear the bodywork provides a reasonably large boot with lid, and increased stowage space behind the seats. The restyling includes squared off wheel arches and vestigial fins, rounded off by moulded lamp covers.

Reflecting the ever-increasing weight of opinion in favour of safety belts, the body shell of the car has been modified to provide anchorages for seat belts of an approved type.

When the Sprite was originally conceived, the intention was to fair the headlamps into the combined bonnet and wing structure. Unfortunately, late in the development stage it was discovered that the designed height of the lamps did not comply with certain American state laws. Various schemes to retract the lamps into the bonnet top were considered but rejected on the score of unreliability and cost; the alternative, which was adopted,

Austin-Healey
SPRITE
Mark II ◀ ····

RESTYLED BODY

MORE POWER

Left: Plenty of accessible space is provided in the new, separate boot. The spare wheel is retained by a setscrew. Below: Added space behind the seats could be used either for luggage or for accommodating a child. On top of the wheel arches can be seen the safety belt attachment points

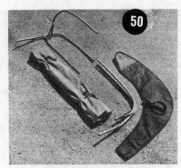

The hood is much easier to erect than this picture of the component parts suggests. The boomerang-shaped protective bag normally holds the hoodsticks

Austin-Healey
SPRITE II...

was to mount the lamps in their now familiar " pop-eyed" position.

Although there were initial misgivings about this, the sterling qualities of the little car made so many friends for it that this slightly unusual appearance soon became accepted as a characteristic. Certainly they were good lamps to drive behind, and were easily removed for sporting events.

On the Mark II car the whole front end and bonnet structure has been re-engineered, and the front wings now form a welded-on extension of the scuttle, tied together at their forward ends by a horizontal pressed panel and the front vertical panel incorporating the radiator grille. The new hinged bonnet gives good access to the engine and its accessories; only the front suspension will be more difficult to approach, although not more so than with other conventional cars.

On the original Sprite, the rear body panel was a stressed member, joining the rear wheel arches of the car. While this was a light and strong solution from an engineering point of view, it made access to the luggage space beneath it difficult because the spare wheel and any baggage had to be inserted between the backs of the seats and the front edge of the panel. In the course of the car's life there have been frequent demands for a more convenient means of loading luggage. In the Mark II Sprite an 8in. wide panel with internal bracing does the load-bearing duty of the original rear panel, and a boot lid is provided for access to the luggage space. Additionally, the cockpit length

has been increased by almost a foot, so that there is now a space behind the seats for more baggage or even a small child.

Although the length of the car appears greater because of the new front wing and headlamp treatment, in fact it is no more than before. The body improvements have brought an increase in all-up weight of 59lb, the maker's total weight being 1,525lb as compared with 1,466lb. Compensating for this, the maximum power of the engine has been increased from 42.5 b.h.p. net to 46.5 b.h.p. at 5,500 r.p.m., and the point of maximum torque is lowered from 3,300 r.p.m. to 2,750 r.p.m.

This increase in power follows four detail changes in engine design: flat-

topped, solid-skirt pistons with three compression rings and one oil control ring replace the older concave top split-skirt type; a redesigned camshaft gives a longer inlet valve opening time; inlet valve diameters are increased from 1·095in. to 1·156in., and twin 1¼in. S.U. HS2 carburettors replace the original 1⅛in. ones. An innovation is the provision of twin air filters of Cooper paper element type which have cold air intakes.

Lowering the point of maximum engine torque has made it possible to close-up the gearbox ratios, bottom gear now being 13·5 to 1 instead of 15·32; second gear is raised from 10·02 to 8·08 to 1, and third gear from 5·96 to 5·73 to 1. The rear axle ratio and top gear remain unchanged. With the new ratios and higher engine revolutions, maximum speed in third gear exceeds 60 m.p.h. and in second 40 m.p.h.

No changes have been made to the Sprite's suspension. At the front coil springs are used, in conjunction with pressed steel wishbones below and with the damper arms forming the upper links. At the back are 15-leaf quarter elliptics, with blades 1·75in. wide, which serve also to locate the rigid axle laterally. Parallel with the springs are longi-

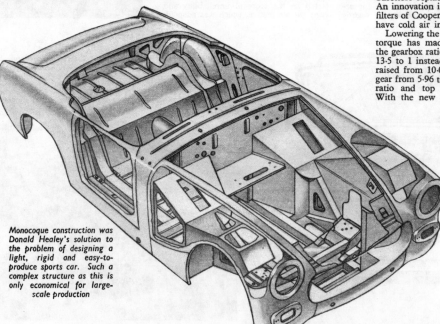

Monocoque construction was Donald Healey's solution to the problem of designing a light, rigid and easy-to-produce sports car. Such a complex structure as this is only economical for large-scale production

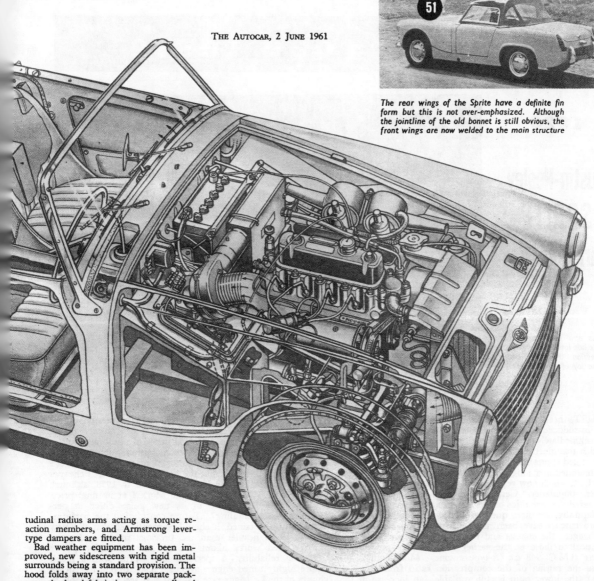

51

The rear wings of the Sprite have a definite fin form but this is not over-emphasized. Although the jointline of the old bonnet is still obvious, the front wings are now welded to the main structure

tudinal radius arms acting as torque re-action members, and Armstrong lever-type dampers are fitted.

Bad weather equipment has been im-proved, new sidescreens with rigid metal surrounds being a standard provision. The hood folds away into two separate pack-ages, the hood fabric into a neat roll and the hood sticks into a protective case. Both items normally are stowed in the boot.

Minor changes to the interior appoint-ments make for greater convenience in use. For example, on the instrument panel toggle lever switches replace the push-pull type, and the high beam warn-ing light is fitted into the speedometer instead of being located separately in the

facia or in the optional rev. counter. Sealed beam headlamps are also a stan-dard fitting.

In keeping with previous policy, the basic model will be offered at as low a price as possible—£641 9s 2d, inclusive of £189 9s 2d purchase tax. The de luxe version, with heater-demister unit, bumpers, overriders, adjustable passenger

seat, revolution counter and screenwasher, costs approximately £14 more, the exact price being £655 12s 6d. The range of extras is listed on page 885.

With its much better layout and appear-ance, and its enhanced performance, the Sprite should make a very favourable impression on overseas markets, for which all initial production will be reserved.

SPECIFICATION

ENGINE

No. of cylinders	...	4 in line
Bore and stroke	...	62·94 x 76·2mm (2·48 x 3·0in.)
Displacement	...	948 c.c. (57·8 cu. in.)
Valve position and op-eration	...	Overhead, pushrods and rockers
Compression ratio	...	9 to 1
Max. b.h.p. (gross)	...	49·8 at 5,500 r.p.m.
Max. b.h.p. (net)	...	46·5 at 5,500 r.p.m.
Max. b.m.e.p. (net)	...	138 p.s.i. at 2,750 r.p.m.
Max. torque (net)	...	53 lb. ft. at 2,750 r.p.m.
Carburettors	...	Two S.U., type HS2
Fuel pump	...	AC-Delco mechanical
Tank capacity	...	6 Imp. gallons (27 litres)
Sump capacity	...	6·5 pints (3·7 litres)
Oil filter	...	Full flow
Cooling system	...	Pump, fan and thermostat
Battery	...	12 volt, 43 amp. hr.

TRANSMISSION

Clutch	...	Single dry plate 6·25in. dia.
Gearbox	...	Four speeds, synchromesh on 2nd, 3rd and top; central control
Overall gear ratios	...	Top 4·22; 3rd 5·73; 2nd 8·08; 1st 13·50; reverse 17·36 to 1.
Final drive	...	Hypoid; ratio 4·22 to 1

PERFORMANCE DATA

Top gear m.p.h. per 1,000 r.p.m.	...	15·37
Torque lb. ft. per cu. in. engine capacity	...	0·92
Brake surface area swept by linings	...	110 sq. in.
Weight distribution	...	F. 52·7 per cent; R. 47·3 per cent.
Kerb weight	...	1,525lb, 13½ cwt (692 Kg.)

1823

Austin-Healey
SPRITE
Mark II de Luxe

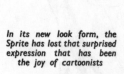

In its new look form, the Sprite has lost that surprised expression that has been the joy of cartoonists

JUST three years ago the British Motor Corporation introduced the Austin-Healey Sprite; it was welcomed immediately as the first effort since the 'thirties by a British manufacturer to market a small, quantity-produced, low-priced sports car. Its continued success has shown that the manufacturer judged his market correctly, but the Sprite Mark II, which now replaces it, seems likely to enjoy a still wider popularity. Certain improvements have greatly increased the amenities of this hitherto rather stark little car.

Naturally, the first question likely to be asked is what improvements have been made. Basically the car remains unchanged, the chassis and mechanical components being identical to those of the earlier model. The power unit is the B.M.C. 948 c.c. A-type engine. Modifications include the raising of the compression ratio from 8·3:1 to 9·0:1 (the lower ratio is still available), an increase in the inlet valve diameter and the adoption of double valve springs; the camshaft and ignition distributor are also new. Air cleaners of a different pattern are fitted to the twin S.U. carburettors which have been increased in size from 1⅛in. to 1¼in. These changes have so altered the power curve that the engine now develops 46·5 b.h.p. nett at 5,500 r.p.m. instead of 42·5 b.h.p. at 5,200 r.p.m. A detailed description with drawing appears on page 873.

More important, however, than the increased power output are the changes that have been made to the bodywork. It is, in fact, an entirely new body shape. The very fact that several firms are selling differently styled bonnets for the Mark I car—as it will now be called in retrospect—shows that hitherto for reasons of either æsthetics or efficiency, not everyone liked the shape of the old Sprite. Gone now are the bulbous headlamps protruding above the bonnet, and no longer does the whole front body assembly hinge upwards for access to the engine and forward chassis components. The bonnet lid now consists of a small panel, the headlamps are faired into the wings, and the radiator grille has become squarer and larger.

Behind the passenger compartment, which is the same size as before, the tail has become less rounded and—most important of all—a locking exterior lid has been provided for the luggage boot. All of the main dimensions on the Mark II Sprite are about the same as its predecessor.

The Autocar received for test a de luxe version of the new Sprite; in this form it costs about £14 more than the standard model, but has several items of additional equipment—a rev counter, windscreen washers, bumpers and overriders, and fore-and-aft adjustment on the passenger's seat. It is noteworthy that the luxury model is £13 cheaper than the Mark I when it first appeared in 1958, although costing some £23 more than the Mark I at its final price.

How does the Sprite in its new guise differ in performance and handling? Before considering the performance figures obtained, it should be mentioned that this new car is 59 lb heavier than the previous model. Also, no owner need worry about the increase in engine power affecting reliability—a special-bodied Sprite with a much more highly tuned engine averaged 85·62 m.p.h. for the 24 hours of the Le Mans race last year. It seems reasonable to contrast the Mark II directly with its forerunner, since many potential owners will be particularly interested in such a comparison. The results of *The Autocar's* Road Test of a hard-top model in November 1959 make a suitable yardstick. They are, however, not directly comparable since the

Strapped against the front wall of the boot are bags containing the tools, the hood and its frame. The spare wheel is secured to the floor

Mark II Sprite has a close-ratio gearbox as standard; it was previously available only as an optional extra. This gearbox has higher ratios for first, second and third, and the maximum speeds in the indirects for the Mark I and the Mark II respectively are: 23-28 m.p.h., 35-46 m.p.h., 58-68 m.p.h. The increase in outright maximum speed is purely fractional but the standing start acceleration figures are greatly improved. From a standstill the new car covers the quarter-mile in 21·8sec as compared with 22·3sec, and 60 m.p.h. can now be reached in 19·8sec—3·9sec less. There is a parallel saving in time up to 70 m.p.h. This level of performance continues until around the 75 m.p.h. mark, after which it falls away and above 80 m.p.h. speed is gained rather slowly.

Although the standing start figures are thus appreciably better than those previously recorded, a similar improvement could not be shown on the 20 m.p.h. interval speed figures in the individual gears. A combination of greater weight and higher gearing in the indirects increases the necessity to make considerable use of the gearbox to keep the engine speed within the high power range, if the best performance is to be obtained. This does not imply, however, that the engine is intractable and, indeed, it pulls as willingly as ever at low crankshaft speeds, and seems smoother than the units fitted to some earlier Sprites.

All the listed performance figures were taken with the hard top in position. When a maximum speed run was made with the car open but with the sidescreens in place the fastest speed attained was reduced by over 6 m.p.h.

As well as the slight increase in weight there has been a small change in its distribution. There is proportionally less weight on the front wheels than previously. This has not appreciably altered the handling characteristics of the car, although it has probably aggravated the tendency of the rear wheels to steer the car when cornering. It is characteristic of this type of suspension that the flattening of the outer rear spring and the arching of the inner one bring the axle out of line with the chassis and create a mild oversteer. As the car is straightened after a corner the reverse effect is also noticed.

Softer Ride

Nearly everyone who drove the car thought that the springing felt softer than previously, although according to the makers no changes have been made.

Perhaps the additional weight reacting against the springs, results in a slightly greater suspension movement. As might be expected, however, the ride can still definitely be described as firm and the car handles best on smooth roads. Cornering on rough surfaces causes the rear wheels to bounce outwards and the rear axle struck its bump stops rather too easily on rough roads.

Although the above remarks might give the impression that the car did not handle particularly well, in fact it could be thrown about with almost complete abandon. One of the greatest assets while treating it in this way is the very direct and sensitive steering with which the suspension's peculiarities can soon be countered. On the test car the rack and pinion mechanism of the steering was a little sticky due to its built-in friction damping, but this is merely because it was new. Experience with other cars having this type of steering gear has shown that it will loosen up perfectly after a few thousand miles have been covered. Accordingly, on the test there was practically no self-centring.

There is no doubt that the new gear ratios have improved the versatility of the car—this particular box, however, was not a good example of its kind. The selector lever was easy to move when the oil was cold but became rather stiff when it warmed up. Synchromesh, on the upper three ratios, was only beaten by the fastest changes. First gear was not always very easy to engage when the car was stationary. The unit was noisy in all gears—especially on the overrun.

It is almost impossible to get something for nothing, and hand in hand with the improved performance goes an increase in petrol consumption. The overall figure for the 1,086 miles of the test was 33·2 m.p.g. and three pints of oil were added to the engine. A hard cross-country run

of over 100 miles with the car open resulted in 28·7 m.p.g. and the best return observed, when 50 m.p.h. was rarely exceeded, was over 43 m.p.g. Running costs have also been increased since the manufacturers now insist that 100-octane fuel be used with this 9 : 1 compression ratio engine. When checking the fuel consumption rate at constant speeds the figure at 30 m.p.h. was found to be no better than at 40 m.p.h.—presumably a result of the carburettor needles that provide a relatively rich mixture at low speeds for clean pick-up. When in a hurry on a long journey one had to replenish the six-gallon petrol tank with irritating frequency.

Most main road bends can be rounded by the Sprite at its natural cruising speed, and it is on minor roads that the brakes receive most punishment. For ordinary road use the effectiveness of these brakes must be related to the car's acceleration; it was only when using full performance on twisty roads that any signs of fade became evident. For check braking the pedal pressure seems a little high, and from near-maximum speed the brakes feel less effective than the figures would seem to indicate. In fact the retardation figures are outstandingly good. A proper fore-and-aft balance of weight must partly account for the maximum figure of 0·98g obtained. The handbrake lever is mounted to the left of the transmission tunnel and held the car on a

To enter the car the Perspex window is slipped forward and the interior handle operated. The wheel trims are an optional extra

Once inside, the interior of the Sprite is surprisingly roomy. The radio mounted below the passengers' grab handle is most useful when waiting in traffic jams. It is difficult to hear when on the move

The Autocar, 2 June 1961

Austin-Healey Sprite Mark II . . .

The last few inches of the exhaust pipe are chromed. A lockable petrol filler cap is an optional extra. The handbook gives detailed instructions for folding the hood to avoid damage

1-in-3 test hill without being pulled to the ast notch. The car could not move off from this incline.

For the price, the standard of finish and bodywork detail is high and there was almost complete freedom from rattles. An irritating one was made by the side-screen flapping against the windscreen when the car was open. The bonnet lid of this car vibrated at any speed, but inspection showed that a slight modification or re-positioning of the rubber stops would probably cure this. Without doubt one of the greatest improvements is the alteration of the boot for external access—a feature that everyone has clamoured for since the Sprite was first introduced. That the car now has a completely lockable compartment greatly increases its potential for touring abroad. On the floor of the boot is the spare wheel, but this does not occupy an excessive amount of room, and the capacity is good for such a small car.

There is space for a little extra luggage behind the seats and here it was also found possible to seat two small children. For maps, torches and other miscellaneous items the door pockets are extremely commodious.

Except behind the seats, where it is carpeted, the floor of the passenger compartment is covered with rubber matting. The side-screens are well made and have neat sliding Perspex panes. They are not as rigid as they might be and with the hardtop in place the right-hand one was inclined to lean out when the car was moving fast. The basic car is sold with a Vynide hood which is mounted over a tubular frame. This frame is spring-loaded in its sockets so that the hood can be fitted without straining and then be stretched taut by releasing the spring. At the second attempt one person managed to unpack the hood from the boot and fit it completely in under four minutes. Removing it takes a similar length of time.

Both the hardtop and the tonneau cover are extras. The hardtop was worn during most of the test and made the interior both snug and draughtproof. It is even easier to fit and dismount than the hood and is light enough for one person to handle, although a woman would probably be grateful for assistance. Provided with the tonneau cover is a rail to prevent luggage slipping off the shelf.

As would be expected the amount of noise varied according to whether the car was open or closed, with hood or hardtop. It is at its noisiest with the hardtop mounted but one could overcome this by lining the glassfibre interior. Mark I Sprite owners will feel perfectly at home in the cockpit of the latest model; the facia layout and driving control positions remain almost identical. Main differences are the independent switch for the head and side lamps (away from the ignition switch) and the fitting of a high beam tell-tale light in the speedometer face. All the instruments are simple and easy to read.

Well Placed Controls

Particularly praiseworthy in such a small car is the layout of the pedals, and the heel-and-toe technique can be performed without need to twist the ankle to any awkward angle. Twice during the test the throttles stuck open for no apparent reason. There is plenty of room to rest the left foot off the clutch pedal. The foot-operated dip-switch is easy to find, but it is surprising how often, with a relatively low-powered sports car, the need to dip and to change gear coincide. Illumination from the headlamps, which are the latest sealed-beam type, is such that they impose no limitation on fast night driving.

To open the bonnet a toggle below the facia is pulled; when open the new lid gives access only to the engine. Items needing frequent checking can be reached without difficulty. Light struts hold the boot and bonnet lids open. Particularly good on this car was the fresh air heater and ventilator which provided large quantities of hot or cold air as required. Flaps either side of the transmission cover directed the airstream to the screen or interior. The temperature could be regulated very accurately but it was impossible to stop the air flow completely, the control on the facia apparently needing adjustment.

The car is offered in a cheap basic form and a large list of optional extras is available—nearly all of them were fitted to the car on test. Individual owners can select those that best suit their pocket and purpose, but the heater and tonneau are almost indispensable, and the hardtop can be particularly recommended. A cigar lighter is very useful in an open car and the twin horns could always be heard. B.M.C.-approved accessories in this car were the combined

With the new bonnet lid, inspection of the battery has been made an easier task. As well as the main bonnet release, there is a safety hook which fastens in the loop at the bottom right corner of the picture

lap-straps and diagonal belts, but the anchorage points for these are now fitted on all Sprites.

Visibility when the car is open is good. With the hardtop or hood in position, however, even a person of medium stature found difficulty in seeing much to the side. The mirror was mounted too low for a reasonable view through the hardtop rear window.

A rather meagre tool kit is provided with the Sprite—especially since this is the type of car that many owners like to tinker with. Servicing requirements are moderate—there are 12 greasing points, and a number of other places requiring lubrication every 1,000 miles.

It would appear that many of the criticisms—certainly most of the complaints mentioned in previous *Autocar* Road Tests of the Sprite—have been remedied with the introduction of the Mark II. It does everything its predecessor did with a little more refinement—it is, therefore, a very worthy successor.

AUSTIN·HEALEY SPRITE II

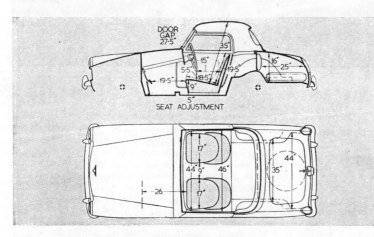

Scale ¼in to 1ft. Driving seat in central position. Cushions uncompressed.

PERFORMANCE

ACCELERATION TIMES (mean):

Speed range, m.p.h.	4·22 to 1	5·8 to 1	8·08 to 1	13·5 to 1
10—30	—	9·8	6·2	—
20—40	14·4	8·9	6·1	—
30—50	14·2	9·5	—	—
40—60	16·6	11·3	—	—
50—70	19·2	—	—	—
60—80	31·7	—	—	—

From rest through gears to:

30 m.p.h.	..	5·7 sec.
40 "	..	9·0 "
50 "	..	13·8 "
60 "	..	19·8 "
70 "	..	29·4 "
80 "	..	51·8 "

Standing quarter mile 21·8 sec.

MAXIMUM SPEEDS ON GEARS

Gear		m.p.h.	k.p.h.
Top	(mean)	85·3	137·3
	(best)	85·5	137·6
3rd	.. ..	68	109
2nd	.. ..	46	74
1st	.. ..	28	45

TRACTIVE EFFORT (by Tapley meter):

	Pull (lb per ton)	Equivalent gradient
Top	.. 195	1 in 11·4
Third	.. 280	1 in 7·9
Second	.. 370	1 in 6·0

SPEEDOMETER CORRECTION: M.P.H.

Car speedometer	.. ..	10	20	30	40	50	60	70	80	90
True speed	.. ..	10	19	29	38	47	56	66	75	84

BRAKES (at 30 m.p.h. in neutral):

Pedal load in lb.	Retardation	Equiv. stopping distance in ft.
25	0·14g	216
50	0·36g	84
75	0·64g	47
100	0·88g	34
110	0·98g	30·9

FUEL CONSUMPTION (at steady speeds in top gear):

30 m.p.h.	50·0 m.p.g.
40 "	51·3 "
50 "	46·0 "
60 "	39·2 "
70 "	35·6 "

Overall fuel consumption for 1,086 miles, 33·2 m.p.g. (8·5 litres per 100 km.).
Approximate normal range 28-45 m.p.g. (10·1-6·3 litres per 100 km.).
Fuel: Super Premium.

TEST CONDITIONS: Weather: Dry and sunny. No wind.
Air temperature, 60 deg. F.
Model described 2 June, 1961.

STEERING: Turning circle:
Between kerbs, R, 30ft 0in.; L, 30ft 9in.
Between walls, R, 31ft 4·5in.; L, 32ft 1·5in.
Turns of steering wheel from lock to lock, 2·25.

DATA

PRICE (basic), with open two-seater body, £462.
British purchase tax, £193 12s 6d.
Total (in Great Britain), £655 12s 6d.
Extras, inc. p.t.:
  Radio £29 7s 11d.
  Heater £17.
  Hardtop £49 11s 8d.
  Laminated windscreen £3 17s 11d.
  Cigar lighter £1 11s 2d.
  Locking petrol cap 17s 9d.
  Tonneau cover, rail, and bag, £6 7s 6d.
  Wheel discs £15 17s 9d.
  Twin horns £1 11s 2d.

ENGINE: Capacity, 948 c.c. (57·9 cu. in.).
Number of cylinders, 4.
Bore and stroke, 62·9 × 76·2 mm (2·478 × 3·00in.).
Valve gear, overhead, pushrods.
Compression ratio, 9·0 to 1.
B.h.p. (net) 46·5 at 5,500 r.p.m. (b.h.p. per ton laden 55·5).
Torque, 53 lb ft at 2,750 r.p.m.
M.p.h. per 1,000 r.p.m. in top gear, 15·37.

WEIGHT (with 5 gal fuel): 13·75 cwt (1,540 lb).
Weight distribution (per cent): F, 51·4; R, 48·6.
Laden as tested, 16·75 cwt (1,876 lb).
Lb per c.c. (laden), 1·97.

BRAKES: Type, Lockheed hydraulic.
Drum diameter and lining width: F and R, 7in. diameter; 1·25 in. wide.
Total swept area: F and R, 110 sq. in. (131 sq. in. per ton laden).

TYRES: 5.20—13in.
Pressures (p.s.i.): F, 18; R, 20 (normal). F, 20; R, 22 (fast driving).

TANK CAPACITY: 6 Imperial gallons.
Oil sump, 6·5 pints.
Cooling system, 10 pints.

DIMENSIONS: Wheelbase, 6ft 8in.
Track: F, 3ft 9·75in.; R, 3ft 8·75in.
Length (overall), 11ft 4in.
Width, 4ft 5in.
Height, 4ft 1·75in.
Ground clearance, 7in.
Frontal area, 13·3 sq. ft. (approximately).
Capacity of luggage space: 11·5 cu. ft. (approximately).

ELECTRICAL SYSTEM: 12-volt; 43 ampère-hour battery.
Headlamps: 42 watt bulbs.

SUSPENSION: Front, coil springs and wishbones, lever-type dampers.
Rear, live axle, quarter elliptic leaf springs and radius arms, lever-type dampers.

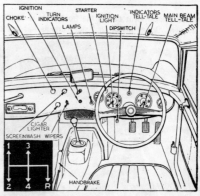

With a new look, new power and new gearing, the Sprite has come of age. It's more expensive than before but it's more fun and more automobile too.

AUSTIN-HEALEY SPRITE II

► There's a new Sprite in town! May 31st is the official introduction date for a face-lifted, repowered Mark II edition of the world's best-loved sports car. It's a grown-up car with a grown-up price, and as such we believe it's the first move in a BMC plan to upgrade its whole series of sports cars and introduce a new, cheaper MG Midget (SCI, June, 1960) at the bottom of the ladder.

In basic frame design, suspension, handling and braking, the Sprite II is identical to the car we Road-Researched in C/D of last April. This Road Test will thus deal only with the changes.

The whole front end has been restyled in a much more conventional idiom that certainly makes the Sprite look more like an automobile. It's still based on the old sheet metal distribution, as you can see from the retention of the old hood parting lines along the sides. The new hood is ordinary alligator-type with a single central latch in front and a very long supporting stay on the left side. The hood latch control is a knob under the dash lettered with a large "B", for "bonnet." Unless you miss the ready access to the front suspension, you'll find the new hood opening doesn't significantly affect service ease. The fuel pump is one of the few engine accessories that's nearly vanished behind the sheet metal curtain.

More rugged in design, the front bumper is also more solidly braced to the platform frame by virtue of being placed closer to it. A reduction in front overhang has made possible a lengthening of the rear, and an increase in luggage capacity, while actually reducing overall length. (C/D's RRR figure was accidentally two feet short, should have read 137.3 inches for the original Sprite.)

Revolutionary is the inclusion of an external trunk lid with a lockable latch, worked by a different key than the ignition. It opens onto a remarkably roomy (technically 11½ cubic feet) compartment with the spare lying flat on the floor. There's a new bulkhead separating the cockpit from the trunk, and to this is strapped a big padded case that holds the collapsed top bows and prevents them from rattling.

On the cockpit side, the new bulkhead forms the back of a carpet-trimmed compartment that's opened up at the top by cutting back the rear edge of the cockpit. This new volume is tremendously useful for extra baggage, temporary stowage of packages or cameras, or even laterally-installed children. When the top's up it's a handy integral part of the interior. When the top's down it can be kept available by leaving off the tonneau cover, and when the cover is installed it's kept firm right up to the seat backs by a two-piece bow that's inserted in the top sockets. On our test car the two bow pieces wouldn't readily telescope together; sawing a slot in the female piece solved that.

Basically the interior is unchanged but the dashboard controls have been rearranged. Gone is the headlight knob around the ignition, replaced by a three-position toggle

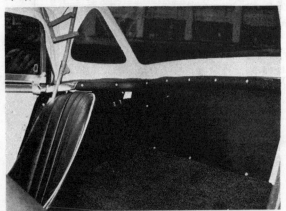

New carpeted compartment behind the front seats is very handy with the top up, as here. Design of top and side curtains has not been changed.

New hood arrangement is wide, light and easy. Engine changes include use of larger Coopers air cleaners in place of original wire-mesh type,

switch. A matching toggle now controls the windshield wipers. Heater and windshield control knobs were moved up to the top row, where the choke and starter pulls have swapped positions. A clockwise twist of the choke now locks it in any position. A subtle change is the use of a horn that's still the same raffish razzberry but with a richer, deeper tone. Its voice is changing too!

The Sprite II's BMC A-Series engine has been pepped up in many areas, using up several stages in the tuning manual. Flat instead of cupped-crown pistons increase the compression ratio to the point where we tentatively recommend Premium instead of Regular gas for best performance. Better breathing accrues from a new cam with more generous timing, valves enlarged in diameter by 1/16 inch, a smoother exhaust manifold and the use of 1¼-inch instead of 1⅛-inch twin S.U. carburetors. As-installed power is now 46.5 bhp against 43 before; our SAE figure of 52 bhp is estimated. Peak power speed is up to 5500 from 5200 rpm, and though peak torque is practically the same as before, it now comes in much lower at 2750 instead of 3300 rpm. The new engine is strong and smooth through its whole range, being if anything more tractable at low speeds than its predecessor.

New power is mated to new gearing. The figures given indicate it's virtually the same gearbox as the close-ratio unit described in our Sprite RRR, and it's a honey. With just a little more power available to pull them, the new higher indirect cogs are beautifully spaced. In particular second gear, which was all through at 39 mph before, now soars enthusiastically to 48. None of our readers will mind that the Sprite no longer starts easily from rest in second!

Performance is not significantly better than that of the old Sprite, but the acceleration curve is a little steeper up to 50

Short strut on left supports the new lockable trunk lid. The tool kit, with the jack, is strapped to the forward wall with top bow container.

mph and the quarter-mile time is cut by 0.6 second. Since frontal area is unchanged, top speed is increased by 5 mph. Early BMC releases stated that brake shoe width had been increased from 1¼ to 1¾ inches, to match the higher speed, but a check of our test car's binders showed that no change had been made. Thus this was either a typo or a last-minute technical decision.

In style, roominess and performance the Sprite II today is everything the MG TD was ten years ago. It does it on much less gas and, even without accounting for the shrinkage of the dollar, it costs less to buy. Thanks very much, BMC, for a tremendously enjoyable car, and for an improved Sprite that really is improved.

—C/D

ROAD TEST:

AUSTIN-HEALEY SPRITE II

Price as tested: $1995

Importer: Hambro Automotive Corp.
27 West 57th Street
New York 19, N.Y.

ENGINE: (BMC A-Series)

Displacement	57.9 cu in, 948 cc
Dimensions	Four cyl, 2.48 in bore, 3.00 in stroke
Valve gear	pushrod-operated vertical overhead valves
Compression ratio	9.0 to one
Power (SAE)	52 bhp @ 5500 rpm
Torque	52.5 lb-ft @ 2750 rpm
Usable range of engine speeds	900-6000 rpm
Corrected piston speed @ 5500 rpm	2500 fpm
Fuel recommended	Premium
Mileage	30-33 mpg
Range on 7.2 gallon tank	215-235 miles

CHASSIS:

Wheelbase	80.0 in
Tread	F 45.8, R 44.8 in
Length	136 in
Ground clearance	5.0 in
Suspension:	F, ind., coil spring, wishbone and control arm; R, rigid axle, trailing quarter-elliptic leaf springs and control arm.
Turns, lock to lock	2 1/3
Turning circle diameter between curbs	30½ ft
Tire and rim size	5.20 x 13, 15 x 4J
Pressures recommended	F, 18, R 20 psi
Brakes; type, swept area	7 in drums, 110 sq in
Curb weight (full tank)	1500 lbs
Percentage on driving wheels	49%

DRIVE TRAIN: (BMC A-Series)

Gear	Synchro?	Ratio	Step	Overall	Mph per 1000 rpm
Rev	No	4.12		17.40	—3.7
1st	No	3.20		13.51	4.8
			67%		
2nd	Yes	1.92		8.08	8.1
			39%		
3rd	Yes	1.38		5.80	11.2
			38%		
4th	Yes	1.00		4.22	15.4

Final drive ratios: 4.22 to one standard; 3.73, 4.55 and 5.38 to one optional.

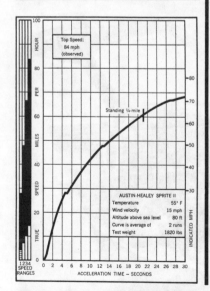

Top Speed: 84 mph (observed)

Standing ¼-mile

AUSTIN-HEALEY SPRITE II
Temperature 55° F
Wind velocity 15 mph
Altitude above sea level 80 ft
Curve is average of 2 runs
Test weight 1820 lbs

HOUR · PER · MILES · SPEED · TRUE

1234 SPEED RANGES

ACCELERATION TIME — SECONDS

INDICATED MPH

Above: The car which was tested competes at an International Silverstone meeting with Australian, Paul Hawkins, at the wheel. Below: Not after the fire . . . but it shows the lengths to which competitors go to remove all surplus weight

SEBRING SPRITE

ALTHOUGH many different conversions of standard production cars come the way of *The Autocar* Road Test staff, few have been so internationally famous in competition motoring as the Austin-Healey Sebring Sprite. This car, perhaps, only just falls within the category of a conversion, since the modifications are extensive enough for it to be regarded as a separate model. Although based on the normal Sprite, it has been built in sufficient numbers for the car to be recognized and homologated as a Grand Tourer by the international authorities.

It is available in a number of different forms, depending on the uses to which the owner wishes to put it. The actual car tested belonged to John Sprinzel and has covered many hundreds of racing miles—some of them with Stirling Moss at the wheel.

Few distinguishable Sprite features remained. The B.M.C. A-type engine had been modified extensively—a formula Junior crankshaft, lightened flywheel, flat-top solid skirt pistons, oversize inlet valves and 11 to 1 compression ratio being among the changes. The fan had been removed, but a full-flow oil cooler helped to keep the temperature down. Mounted immediately behind the driving seat were two S.U. petrol pumps

PERFORMANCE

From rest through gears to:			Sebring Sprite	Mark 2 Sprite
40 m.p.h.	..	..	5·8 sec	9·0 sec
50 ,,	..	..	7·6 ,,	13·8 ,,
60 ,,	..	..	10·8 ,,	19·8 ,,
70 ,,	..	..	14·1 ,,	29·4 ,,
80 ,,	..	..	20·2 ,,	51·8 ,,
90 ,,	..	..	27·8 ,,	—
Standing quarter mile			17·8 sec	21·8 sec
Second Gear				
10—30 m.p.h.	..		5.6 sec	6.2 sec
20—40 ,,	..		4·0 ,,	6·1 ,,
30—50 ,,	..		4·3 ,,	—
Third Gear				
30—50 m.p.h.	..		5·7 sec	9·5 sec
40—60 ,,	..		5·7 ,,	11·3 ,,
50—70 ,,	..		6·5 ,,	—
Top Gear				
40—60 m.p.h.	..		8·6 sec	16·6 sec
50—70 ,,	..		9·5 ,,	19·2 ,,
70—90 ,,	..		14·2 ,,	—
Maximum Speed in Gears				
Gear:				
Top (mean)	100 m.p.h. (7,200 r.p.m.)			85.3 m.p.h.
(best)	100	,,		85·5 ,,
Third ..	73	,,		68 ,,
Second	51	,,		46 ,,
First	31	,,		28 ,,

Modifications under the light-weight bonnet had been carried out in a workman-like style, and accessibility to all components is outstandingly good

SEBRING SPRITE . . .

for supplying the twin 1½in. S.U. carburettors; a nine-spring competition clutch transmitted the torque. A power output of 80 b.h.p. at 7,000 r.p.m. is claimed.

The gearbox was the close-ratio unit now fitted as standard equipment to the Mark II Sprite. Normally the Sebring Sprite has a 4·55 : 1 rear axle ratio, but on the car tested a 4·875 : 1 axle ratio was installed. This was the ratio employed at Brands Hatch, where the car had been racing a few days before it was collected for test. Suspension changes consisted of heavy-duty shock absorbers at the front with an anti-roll bar, and adjustable dampers at the rear. Wire wheels and 5·20—13in. R5 Dunlop covers were fitted. The front drum brakes had been replaced by 8·5in. diameter discs.

The bodywork had been extensively lightened; the bonnet was constructed from glass fibre and an aluminium hardtop of streamlined shape covered the passenger compartment. All the interior trim had been removed, and the battery shifted from under the bonnet to a position just forward of the rear axle. With the spare wheel on board and the 12-gallon fuel tank half-full, the car weighed 11·75 cwt, almost 2 cwt lighter than a standard hardtop Sprite. The weight distribution was almost exactly 50 per cent fore and aft.

First impression after opening the door, which was done by inserting a hand through a small sliding pane in the side-screen and lifting an interior catch, is one of bareness and exposed wiring. The whole of the facia had been removed and the only instruments fitted were an electronic tachometer, an oil pressure gauge, a water thermometer and a petrol gauge. Switches for lamps, ignition, starter and windscreen wiper were mounted on the central console which covered the gearbox and flywheel. Both the road and the rear axle are visible through gaps in the floor on either side of the battery box.

The first thing that one notices as soon as the engine starts, which it always did very easily, is the noise. Even the most hardened extrovert would be embarrassed by the amount of exhaust noise from this car. It is almost impossible to avoid it, however carefully one drives. In town the car was a slight nuisance, as it was inclined to overheat and even the soft plugs started to misfire. It also became very warm in the cockpit and one sat in a mist of Castrol-R fumes—very intoxicating for the diehard enthusiasts. Surprisingly enough, the engine was remarkably tractable, and one could potter along at relatively low engine speeds. Full power from the engine was not available under 5,000 r.p.m., but it then continued right through to 7,000 r.p.m. Rather fierce for road use, the clutch was much as one would have expected on a competition car.

On the open road, if one could submerge the feeling of being anti-social, the car was immense fun to drive. Hard when travelling slowly, the suspension and ride greatly improved with increased speed. The small bucket seats held their occupants

securely. Steering was light, direct and positive, the rack and pinion mechanism being very well run in. Gone was the "darting" feeling experienced with many Sprites and directional stability was excellent. While cornering the good balance of the car made the steering almost completely neutral and gave considerable confidence.

What of the performance? John Sprinzel had asked that the engine speed be limited to 7,200 r.p.m. In practice it was found that the engine started misfiring if this speed were exceeded. With the lower rear axle ratio incorporated it was possible to achieve 7,200 r.p.m. in top gear with remarkable ease, even up a slight incline. This engine speed represented about 100 m.p.h. Acceleration, therefore, not maximum speed, is the interesting feature of this car. In the performance table, the figures obtained are set out alongside those of the recently tested Mark II Sprite. A standing quarter-mile of 17·8sec is extremely fast, as is 0-80 m.p.h. in 20·2sec. In racing trim, with only one person aboard and no road test equipment, these figures naturally would be even better.

The disc brakes fitted on the front of the car are an obvious must for the Sebring Sprite. With these there was never any fade when stopping from high speeds frequently and consecutively.

Total price of the equipment fitted to this car is £650, and there is no reason why the modifications should not be made to a second-hand Sprite. In this case, for just over £1,000 one can have an extremely worth-while racing or rally car to distinguish itself in any international company. Its successes have been widespread and varied, and last year one finished third in the most gruelling of all rallies, the Liège-Rome-Liège, and its name results from regular class victories at Sebring.

The Mosses, brother and sister, sprint across the track to jump into their Sprites at the start of the Sebring four-hour Grand Touring car race earlier this year

AUTOSPORT, AUGUST 31, 1962

JOHN BOLSTER TESTS

A Works-Modified Sprite Mark 2

THE Austin-Healey Sprite, in its Mark II form, is a practical and most attractive little sports car. The Donald Healey Motor Co., Ltd., of the Cape, Warwick, is the parent firm which originates the design of the cars, and this company also specializes in modifying the basic machine. Obviously, the standard model is turned out at a competitive price, but there is considerable scope for the man who can afford de luxe equipment and special tuning.

I have recently had the pleasure of using a fully modified Sprite which had received "the treatment" at Warwick. First of all, an extremely effective fibreglass hard top had been added, plus a pair of lightweight glass fibre bucket seats and a set of fitted carpets. These items cost £52 10s., £18 16s. and £10 respectively.

Then the Healey Sprint Kit had been fitted. This entails enlarging and polishing the ports while lining up the manifolds. Two 1½ ins. SU carburetters and a high-efficiency exhaust system are used. The chassis benefits from an anti-roll bar, heavy-duty front springs, and a set of special damper valves. For the driver's pleasure, a wooden steering wheel is fitted. The complete cost of this Sprint kit is £71.

In addition, the engine tuning had been carried a good deal further. A set of high-compression pistons at £12 12s. was installed, together with a three-quarter-race camshaft and distributor at £19 5s. Larger valves were incorporated, costing 17s. 6d. each for the inlets and £1 3s. for the exhausts. A lightened flywheel at £6 6s. and a nine-spring clutch at £15 10s. were added, plus an oil cooler at £16. An alloy rocker cover with quick-action filler cap completed the engine at £6 6s. Fitting charges would be extra on these items, the work having been carried out to racing standards, with all strategic bolts and nuts drilled and wired. The block was bored .060 in. oversize to bring the capacity up to 995 c.c.

A disc brake and wire wheel kit is a "must" for a little motor of this calibre, at £103. The test car had a 4.55 to 1 axle nose assembly, costing £25. Apart from these few items, "my" Sprite was "absolutely standard, old man"!

From the above specification, it is obvious that the test car was a pretty hot little package. The engine was dead smooth, flashing up to 7,500 r.p.m. at the drop of a hat. Conversely, practically no power was generated under 3,000 r.p.m. and it was advisable to keep below half throttle when coaxing the willing little unit past this critical speed. At 4,000 r.p.m., things were beginning to happen, and in the band between 5,000 and 7,500 r.p.m., the performance was almost beyond belief.

The figures speak for themselves. The 0 to 60 m.p.h. time of 10 seconds is tremendous motoring but the standing quarter-mile in 17.2 secs. is simply breathtaking, 80 m.p.h. coming up in third during this exercise. The acceleration continued strongly in top gear, 90 m.p.h. being seen on any short straight. With a good long run, a timed 100 m.p.h. could be appreciably exceeded.

Driven sensibly, the engine was by no means intractable though it would not suit auntie. I employed the machine as a town carriage on occasion, one oiled plug being the sole penalty for this indignity. The clutch was smooth and the gear change excellent, but while the interior noise level was high, it would be acceptable to the young enthusiasts who would own such a car. I cruised for considerable distances at 6,000 r.p.m. without feeling that I was overdoing it.

The ride, of course, was hard and the seats lacked padding, though they gave excellent lateral location. All this is typical of the small competition car, and would be valued as such by the enthusiastic driver. The usual oversteer had vanished, a completely neutral characteristic being displayed. The

AUTOSPORT, AUGUST 31, 1962

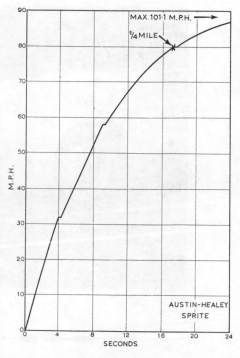

ACCELERATION GRAPH

machine could be cornered very fast, and while it did not encourage one to adopt extreme angles of drift, the roadholding was very satisfactory for hard driving. Bumps could cause a momentary unsticking of the rear end, but a flick of the steering wheel soon subdued that. Severe bumps could force the rear suspension to bottom, but this was exceptional.

The brakes gave me every confidence, and a fat lady who suddenly waddled into the middle of the Watford By-pass evidently had confidence in them too. All four wheels left impressive black lines, the car remaining straight with no hopping or tramp. The steering was sensitive, giving good "feel" on wet roads, at the expense of some kick-back on bumpy surfaces.

There was something very endearing about this little car. It seemed to be so well made, with absolutely no rattles. There were noises, of course, but they were all functional sounds that one expects in a sporting vehicle. The hard top was very neat indeed, the sliding windows fitting satisfactorily with no tendency to open or close themselves. In spite of the low roof line, fully sufficient head room was provided for a tall driver. The driver and passenger were comfortable on a long journey, but though the spare wheel seemed to occupy more than its fair share of the boot, there was extra luggage space behind the seats which I found suitable for the carriage of a large dog.

The Austin-Healey Sprite is a jolly little sports car which adds good looks to its virtues in its Mark II form. When modified at Warwick it becomes a genuine 100 m.p.h. car with formidable acceleration, which can take on almost anything on four wheels up to 2-litres capacity.

SPECIFICATION AND PERFORMANCE DATA

Car Tested: Austin-Healey Sprite Mk. II, price £623 including P.T. For prices of extras see text.

Engine: Four cylinders 64.3 mm. x 76.2 mm. (995 c.c.). Pushrod-operated overhead valves. Compression ratio 10.6 to 1. 68 b.h.p. at 6,500 r.p.m. Twin SU carburetters. Lucas coil and distributor.

Transmission: Special nine-spring single dry plate clutch. Four-speed gearbox with central remote control and synchromesh on upper three gears, ratios 4.55, 6.18, 8.73 and 14.60 to 1. Open propeller shaft. Hypoid rear axle.

Chassis: Punt-type chassis-body structure. Independent front suspension by wishbones and helical springs with torsional anti-roll bar. Rack and pinion steering. Rear axle on quarter-elliptic springs and radius arms. Lever-type hydraulic dampers all round. Disc front and drum rear brakes with hydraulic operation. Knock-on wire wheels fitted 5.20 x 13 ins. tyres.

Equipment: 12-volt lighting and starting. Speedometer. Rev.-counter. Oil pressure, water temperature and fuel gauges, windscreen wipers and washers. Flashing direction indicators.

Dimensions: Wheelbase 6 ft. 8 ins. Track (front) 3 ft. 9¾ ins., (rear) 3 ft. 8¾ ins. Overall length 11 ft. 5¼ ins. Width 4 ft. 5 ins. Turning circle 21 ft. 6 ins. Weight 13 cwt.

Performance: Maximum speed 101.1 m.p.h. Speeds in gears: 3rd 80 m.p.h., 2nd 58 m.p.h., 1st 32 m.p.h. Standing quarter-mile 17.2 secs. Acceleration: 0-30 m.p.h. 3.8 secs., 0-50 m.p.h. 7.8 secs., 0-60 m.p.h. 10 secs., 0-80 m.p.h 17.2 secs.

Fuel Consumption: Driven hard, 27.3 m.p.g.

Although the nose and tail have been drastically changed, there is some similarity to the old Sprite in centre sections.

SPRITE: PRACTICAL FUN FOR LESS THAN £1000

By IAN FRASER *It didn't cost much, but we had plenty of fun . . .*

BY the standards of today it is tempting to regard the Austin Healey Sprite as something less than a sports car if you wish to embrace it in the strictest meaning of the term.

The important thing to remember is that there is an ever-expanding gap between the low cost, moderate performance sports car and the high performance costly model. The difference between the extremes often amounts to a margin of 70 to 100 mph in top speed alone.

And to cap it all off there are a number of sedans around the road these days that can comfortably match sports cars, cubic centimetre for cubic centimetre, in performance. This makes sports cars even harder to define because sedans are getting more sporty in their nature.

However, this is very much inclined to be paperbound theory. As any enthusiast will tell you, there is absolutely no substitute for driving a sports car, regardless of its performance.

The Sprite Mk II is at the more humble end of the scale. It is the only sports car selling for less than £1000 available in Australia, and because of this it is also the most popular.

Success came to the baby Healey in spite of the Mk I's toad-eyed appearance. Its many virtues comfortably outweighed aesthetic appeal and BMC's decision to assemble the cars locally, to keep retail price at a minimum, has paid off handsomely.

Changes were made to Sprite styling in England last year and the ckd packages of this model have only recently arrived for assembly in Sydney. As far as most people are concerned, the Mk II can be regarded as a completely new car. Certainly the psychological attitude of owners is going to change both because of the appearance and the car's more usable concept.

In appearance the Sprite is conventional. The radiator grille is squat and oblong and the headlamps have a normal position on the mudguard extremities with the winker/parkers mounted directly below. The almost flat windscreen is fitted into a frame which can easily be detached from the scuttle, presumably for the benefit of competition drivers who wish to reduce the frontal area of their Sprites. Tail lamp assemblies are fitted in the ends of rear guards. There are sturdy bumpers with over-riders at both ends of the car. Easily recognisable points which assist in establishing identification are the wheel arches and doors, which are virtually the same as the Mk I.

As I see it, that ends the similarities.

The mechanical design of the car is about as straightforward as it could be. The engine and transmission are based on BMC B-series designs, similar to those of the Morris Minor 1000 and the Mini. Front suspension is independent by coil springs. At the rear end the suspension is via a very satisfactory arrangement of quarter elliptic springs and location arms. Construction is unitary — again, one of the very few sports cars in which this method is used, in spite of its rigidity advantages.

In the cockpit there is room for two people, although an extra one can clamor into the space behind which would normally serve as additional luggage space.

The seats themselves are little buckets which, for my 5 ft 11½ in were a little too small and the squabs too vertical for real comfort, but no doubt shorter people would not mind as much and bigger ones may get used to it. Would-be Sprite owners must be prepared to make sacrifices when it comes to driving position. No matter how short the person it would be impossible to get back far enough to achieve the currently favored long arm driving position.

I must admit that this annoyed me at first, but it is something that is not too hard to live with. At the conclusion of our test I felt quite at home. Driving position is not the only thing of which I disapprove. The gear change lever is mounted rather high on its tunnel and in the first and third slots it is all too easy for the driver to slam his knuckles into the dashboard, specially if the ratio is engaged with a rush. The solution lies either in a shorter lever or a smaller knob. The hit or miss distance is only a matter of half an inch or so.

There is no glovebox in the dashboard which is basically only a sheet of pressed metal on which to hang the instruments and switches. In this regard the driver is quite well catered for. There is a tachometer and matching speedo with total and trip distance metres. The fuel gauge is well calibrated and the oil pressure and water temperature dials share the one housing. Winking direction indicators are fitted but do not self cancel. Since they lack audible warning, it is easy enough to miss seeing the flashing green light on the dashboard.

A plunger arrangement on the dash operates the standard equipment windscreen washer — essential because the Sprite's low build allows the screen to catch vast quantities of muddy water splashed up from other cars on wet days. The wipers themselves give as good a sweep as could be expected on the rather shallow screen. There are a couple of blind spots, but that seems to be unavoidable unless three blades are fitted, a la Jaguar E-type.

Other cockpit details include attachment points for safety harness and quite big pockets in the doors for storing all kinds of odds and ends. Come hell or high water the passenger is entitled to a diagonal safety belt to keep his head away from the deadly-looking panic handle on his side, cunningly placed to meet a fast moving head. Panic handles of this type in sports cars should be outlawed along with the wickedly-positioned assist bars taxi owners insist on putting above the front seat squab.

The low sweep of the Sprite's shapely bonnet, combined with the slightly higher mudguards, makes for truly pleasing driving and accurate placement of the car on corners and in traffic.

During most of the test I drove the Sprite with the hood down. Because the seating position is low and body sides high, the car's occupants get good protection from the weather and still have the advantages and pleasures of open motoring. If storm and tempest threaten to overwhelm the spartan motorist, there are two neat sidescreens with sliding Perspex panels and a hood with a big rear window which can be erected. Unfortunately this is not a particularly swift process since the hood bows are separate and require individual attention. When not in use, everything gets packed up and stowed in the boot, thus consuming a fair amount of the available space. The spare wheel fits flat on the boot floor so by the time everything finds its place there is not much space for big suitcases, but if a traveller is prepared to pack his clothes in soft bags and also utilise the space behind the front seats, there is a considerable amount of luggage space — much more, for instance, than the MGA. As I see it, there is enough room for two people to take along most of their requirements for a fortnight's holiday.

Interior trim is not elaborate, nor does one expect it to be. Finish on the car I tested was quite good, but nothing startling, although as production advances it will probably improve.

The luggage boot lid has to be supported by a clip-out stay, which is rather fiddly when you have an armful of parcels — a very cheap price to pay to be

Bold front of the Sprite bears strong resemblance to Italian Innocenti Sprite. Winkers and parkers are combined.

Access to the engine compartment is not as good as it was on Mk I, but is satisfactory nevertheless. Bonnet needs bracing, note distortion.

SPRITE . . . PRACTICAL FOR FUN FOR LESS THAN £1000 . . . continued

able to securely lock valuables away. The fuel filler cap is also lockable, by the way.

Access to the cockpit is okay once you develop a technique and stick to it. Everything falls fairly well to hand once you are inside the car. At first the gear lever seems rather high, but this is again purely a matter of drive adaption. The steering wheel is inclined to hamper access to the starter button which is separate from the ignition switch.

At no stage during the test did I have the slightest difficulty starting the engine, although it was slow to warm up. When it did, however, the temperature remained constant, plus or minus a few degrees, regardless of the circumstances, which often included extended periods of idling in heavy traffic.

Smooth throughout its working rev range, the engine was inclined towards a lumpy idle at 600 rpm, which may be accounted for by the new camshaft in this model. Various other modifications have been made to the Mk II engine in search of more power.

Naturally the gearbox is there to be used and if anything like reasonable results are to be obtained, the only thing that will bring them about is regular changes of ratio. The old model Sprite battled along for several years with a box of difficult ratios. Second, particularly, was frustratingly low, third too far away from it. Learning from past errors (and no doubt taking advantage of the lower range torque) BMC engineers re-hashed the gearbox to make the ratios more sporting. Top remains the same at 4.22 to 1, but third has been raised to 5.72, second jumped up to 8.08 and first to 13.5. The effect of the changes means that second can no longer be used for starting from rest so why BMC did not introduce synchromesh on to first I just would not know. It needs it.

The gearbox ratios are now so well chosen that they are a delight to use through an accurate and positive change mechanism.

Top speed and acceleration are by no means startling by sports car standards but, as the figures show, are comparable with the majority of popular six cylinder sedans. Cruising is nice at around 65 mph at which there is enough acceleration available for easy overtaking. Around about the 4000 rpm mark is comfortable for cruising and well within the suggested rev limit of 5500.

While on the subject of engine performance the staggering economy is worth noting. The figure of **46 mpg**, recorded over 186 miles of suburb and near country roads is nothing short of amazing. The combination of low frontal area and light weight permit the use of very light throttle openings.

On top of this the roadholding is so good that one rarely has to slow for a main road bend, thus it is possible to maintain steady throttle positions.

Of the roadholding little can be said other than

Sprite Mk II has totally different tail to the older model. The boot is lockable, so is the fuel filler. Spare wheel stows on boot floor.

the fact it is outstanding. There is a trace of understeer and when really pushed the rear wheels break first — and very gently.

Steering, by rack and pinion, is light and accurate at all times. At first it is disconcertingly sensitive; a movement of the wheel brings an immediate and positive response, yet out on the open road one is hardly aware of taking corners. You come close to "thinking" the Sprite through bends.

Obviously there is tremendous potential in the handling department — probably much more than the average owner would ever exploit.

Brakes are light and very effective. Discs have not been used and, in the car's standard form, are definitely not necessary. The handbrake, mounted on the passenger's side of the tunnel is unusually powerful, even if it has a rather long action.

Although not everyone will agree, I think this new Sprite is going to give a lot of people, who would not have tolerated the Mk I's compromises, the chance to return to the fun of motoring. That is the important thing about the Sprite. It is damned good fun to drive and immensely usable. It is also the right car for the young enthusiastic motorist in whose hands a more powerful machine would be dangerous. As a second car in a household the Mk II would have few peers since it is economical, light to drive and small enough to park almost anywhere, tremendously safe, and, of course, great fun. What a marvellous chance the Sprite offers to motorists who want to hurl mundane transport right out the window.   #

Instrument panel is neatly arranged, but gear lever is a shade too long, endangers driver's knuckles. Picture was taken from new space behind front seats.

wheels ROAD TEST

TECHNICAL DETAILS
OF THE
AUSTIN HEALEY SPRITE

SPECIFICATIONS

ENGINE:

Cylinders	four in line
Bore and stroke	62.94 by 76.2 mm
Cubic capacity	948 cc
Compression ratio	9 to 1
Valves	pushrod overhead
Carburettor	two SU
Power at rpm	49.8 (gross) at 5500 rpm
Maximum torque	53 ft/lbs at 2750 rpm

TRANSMISSION:

Type	manual
First	13.50
Second	8.08
Third	5.73
Top	4.22
Rear axle	4.22

SUSPENSION:

Front	independent coils
Rear	quarter elliptic springs and radius arms
Shockers	lever type

STEERING:

Type	rack and pinion
Turns, 1 to 1	2.25
Circle	30 ft

BRAKES:

Type	drum

DIMENSIONS:

Wheelbase	6 ft 8 in
Track, front	3 ft 9¾ in
Track, rear	3 ft 8¾ in
Length	11 ft 4 in
Width	4 ft 5 in
Height	4 ft 1¾ in

TYRES:

Size	5.20 by 13

WEIGHT:

Dry	11½ cwt

PERFORMANCE

TOP SPEED:

Fastest run	85.9 mph
Average of all runs	84.3 mph

MAXIMUM SPEED IN GEARS:

First	28 mph
Second	47 mph
Third	68 mph
Top	85.9 mph

ACCELERATION:

Standing Quarter Mile:

Fastest run	21.7 secs
Average of all runs	21.8 secs
0 to 30 mph	5.5 secs
0 to 40 mph	8.8 secs
0 to 50 mph	13.4 secs
0 to 60 mph	18.6 secs
0 to 70 mph	28.2 secs
0 to 80 mph	NA secs
20 to 40 mph	13.3 secs
30 to 50 mph	13.1 secs
40 to 60 mph	15.2 secs

GO-TO-WHOA:

0-60-0 mph	21.4 secs

SPEEDO ERROR:

Indicated	Actual
30 mph	29 mph
40 mph	39 mph
50 mph	48 mph
60 mph	57 mph
70 mph	67 mph
80 mph	NA mph
90 mph	NA mph

FUEL CONSUMPTION:

Cruising speeds	46 mpg
Overall for test	34.5 mpg

MAKE: *Austin-Healey*   TYPE: *Sprite* 1100

MAKERS: *Austin Motor Co. Ltd., Longbridge Works, Birmingham.*

ROAD TEST ● No. 47/62

TEST DATA:

CONDITIONS : *Weather : Cool, dry with 10-15 m.p.h. wind. (Temperature 40°-44° F., Barometer 29.6 in. Hg.) Surface: Dry tarmacadam. Fuel: Premium grade pump petrol (98 Octane Rating by Research Method).*

INSTRUMENTS

Speedometer at 30 m.p.h.	..	..	9% fast
Speedometer at 60 m.p.h.	..	..	6% fast
Speedometer at 90 m.p.h.	..	..	4% fast
Distance Recorder	..	..	1% fast

WEIGHT

Kerb weight (unladen, but with oil, coolant and fuel for approximately 50 miles)		13½ cwt.
Front/rear distribution of kerb weight		54/46
Weight laden as tested	..	17¼ cwt.

MAXIMUM SPEEDS

Mean lap speed around banked circuit 87.8 m.p.h.
Best one-way ¼-mile time equals .. 92.8 m.p.h.
"Maximile " Speed (Timed quarter mile after one mile accelerating from rest.)
Mean of opposite runs .. .. 86.0 m.p.h.
Best one-way time equals .. .. 89.2 m.p.h.

Speed in gears (at 6,000 r.p.m.)

Max. speed in 3rd gear	.. ..	68 m.p.h.
Max. speed in 2nd gear	.. ..	48 m.p.h.
Max. speed in 1st gear	.. ..	29 m.p.h.

FUEL CONSUMPTION

54½ m.p.g. .. at constant 30 m.p.h. on level	
51 m.p.g. .. at constant 40 m.p.h. on level	
44 m.p.g. .. at constant 50 m.p.h. on level	
38½ m.p.g. .. at constant 60 m.p.h. on level	
35½ m.p.g. .. at constant 70 m.p.h. on level	
28 m.p.g. .. at constant 80 m.p.h. on level	
21 m.p.g. at maximum speed of 88 m.p.h.	

Overall Fuel Consumption for 1,422 miles, 45.7 gallons, equals 30.8 m.p.g. (9.17 litres/100 km.)
Touring Fuel Consumption (m.p.g. at steady speed midway between 30 m.p.h. and maximum, less 5% allowance for acceleration) 37.2 m.p.g.
Fuel tank capacity (maker's figure) 6 gallons

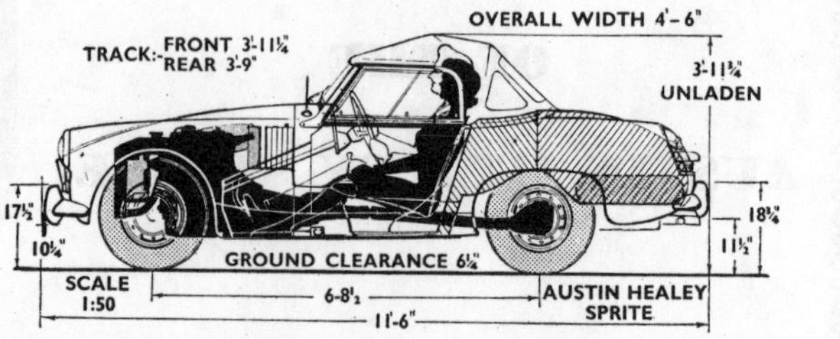

BRAKES from 30 m.p.h.

1.0 g retardation (equivalent to 30 ft. stopping distance) with 95 lb. pedal pressure
0.80 g retardation (equivalent to 37 ft. stopping distance) with 75 lb. pedal pressure
0.56 g retardation (equivalent to 54 ft. stopping distance) with 50 lb. pedal pressure
0.32 g retardation (equivalent to 94 ft. stopping distance) with 25 lb. pedal pressure

ACCELERATION TIMES from standstill

0-30 m.p.h. ..	..	..	..	..	4.4 sec.
0-40 m.p.h. ..	..	..	..	..	7.5 sec.
0-50 m.p.h. ..	..	..	..	..	11.1 sec.
0-60 m.p.h. ..	..	..	..	..	16.6 sec.
0-70 m.p.h. ..	..	..	..	..	25.4 sec.
0-80 m.p.h. ..	..	..	..	..	38.3 sec.
Standing quarter mile ..	..	..			20.9 sec.

ACCELERATION TIMES on upper ratios

	Top gear	3rd gear
10-30 m.p.h.	11.4 sec.	7.3 sec.
20-40 m.p.h.	10.8 sec.	7.0 sec.
30-50 m.p.h.	10.5 sec.	7.3 sec.
40-60 m.p.h.	13.0 sec.	8.6 sec.
50-70 m.p.h.	16.3 sec.	11.9 sec.
60-80 m.p.h.	21.9 sec.	— sec.

STEERING

Turning circle between kerbs:

Left	..	30 ft.
Right ..	..	29¾ ft.

Turns of steering wheel from lock to lock   2

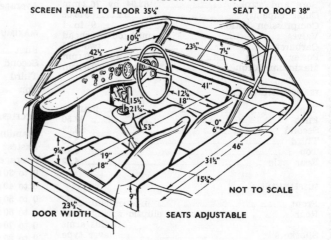

HILL CLIMBING at sustained steady speeds

Max. gradient on top gear	..	..	1 in 10.4 (Tapley 215 lb./ton)
Max. gradient on 3rd gear	..	..	1 in 6.8 (Tapley 325 lb./ton)
Max. gradient on 2nd gear	..	..	1 in 4.8 (Tapley 460 lb./ton)

Specification

Engine

Cylinders	..	..	4
Bore	..	..	64.58 mm.
Stroke	..	..	83.72 mm.
Cubic capacity	..	..	1,098 c.c.
Piston area	..	..	20.3 sq. in.
Valves	..	overhead (pushrods)	
Compression ratio	..	..	8.9/1
Carburetters	..	..	Twin S.U. HS 2
Fuel pump	..	..	AC mechanical
Ignition timing control	..	Centrifugal and vacuum	
Oil filter	Purolator or Tecalemit full-flow		
Maximum power (net)	..	..	55 b.h.p.
at	..	..	5,500 r.p.m.
Piston speed at maximum b.h.p.	3,020 ft./min.		

Transmission

Clutch ..	Borg and Beck 7¼ in. s.d.p.	
Top gear (s/m)	..	4.22
3rd gear (s/m) ..	..	5.73
2nd gear (s/m)	..	8.08
1st gear	..	13.50
Reverse	..	17.36

Propeller shaft ..	Hardy Spicer open
Final drive ..	Hypoid bevel
Top gear m.p.h. at 1,000 r.p.m. ..	15.3
Top gear m.p.h. at 1,000 ft./min. piston speed	27.9

Chassis

Brakes	Lockheed hydraulic, disc front and drum rear
Brake dimensions	8¼ in. discs 7 in. × 1¼ in. drums
Friction areas	46.7 sq. in. of lining area (13.2 front and 33.5 rear) operating on 190 sq. in. rubbed area of discs and drums

Suspension :

Front	Independent by transverse wishbones and coil springs
Rear	Live axle and quarter elliptic leaf springs

Shock absorbers :

Front and rear	Armstrong hydraulic lever type
Steering gear	Rack and pinion
Tyres	5.20-13 Dunlop tubeless

Austin-Healey Sprite 1100

A more comfortable, livelier version of a popular sports car

CHANGES that were made to the Austin-Healey Sprite on the eve of the recent Motor Show received comparatively little publicity at a time when there was heavy pressure of motoring news. Briefly it may be recalled that an increase in engine size from 948 to 1,098 c.c. raised the maximum power from 46.5 to 55 b.h.p. at the same r.p.m. (5,500), that the clutch was enlarged in diameter by one inch, the gearbox acquired the latest baulk ring synchromesh and disc brakes were fitted to the front wheels. These alterations alone have endowed the Sprite with a much better all-round balance of mechanical virtues but in fact development has not stopped here; the latest model is quieter, smoother, better trimmed and equipped, has more comfortable seats and yet it still remains the lowest priced production sports car on the British market.

Latest Developments

ENGINE enlargement has been effected partly by a small increase in bore and partly by a new longer stroke crankshaft very similar to that used in the ADO 16 models. Indeed, the upper part of the engine is virtually identical with that of the M.G. 1100 saloon and except for a narrow range vibration period

Above: Externally there is nothing to distinguish the new 1,100 c.c. Sprite from its predecessor. *Below:* When not in use the hood and its separate folding frame can be removed altogether and stowed in the boot.

at about 4,800 r.p.m. which causes some gearbox chatter, a stiffer crankshaft makes it very smooth all the way up to maximum r.p.m. An orange sector on the rev. counter extends from 5,500 to 6,000 r.p.m. and a red sector from 6,000 to 7,000; in performance testing we treated 6,000 r.p.m. as the limit except for a small excursion into the red to record a 50-70 m.p.h. time in third gear.

This engine has a very long range of handy torque; it pulls strongly from under 20 m.p.h. in top gear and covered the useful 30-50 m.p.h. range in only 10.5 sec. against 13.6 sec. for the previous model. It starts extremely easily and warms up fairly quickly although low-speed pick-up remains very sluggish until a proper running temperature is approached. The heater becomes effective with remarkable rapidity even in very cold weather, delivering large quantities of hot air long before the thermometer needle has moved off its stop. A simple push-pull control regulates the temperature and a quiet fan can be used to boost the air flow at low speeds. However, if this is used in heavy traffic, a fresh air intake mounted low down in the nose very soon fills the cockpit with fumes from the exhaust pipes of vehicles in front.

From outside, the Sprite still has a healthy bark from the exhaust but from inside both exhaust and mechanical noises are more subdued and it seems appreciably quieter and less fussy than previous models. At high speed, however, a dominating wind noise makes conversation very trying at speeds above 60-70 m.p.h. and restricts enjoyment of the radio mainly to town and suburban motoring. Noise apart, however, there is little

In Brief

Price (as tested) £485 plus purchase tax £101 12s. equals £586 12s.	
Capacity	1,098 c.c.
Unladen kerb weight	13½ cwt.
Acceleration:	
20-40 m.p.h. in top gear	10.8 sec.
0-50 m.p.h. through gears	11.1 sec.
Maximum top gear gradient	1 in 10.4
Maximum speed	87.8 m.p.h.
"Maximile" speed	86.0 m.p.h.
Touring fuel consumption	37.2 m.p.g.
Gearing: 15.3 m.p.h. in top gear at 1,000 r.p.m.	

sense of mechanical strain when cruising in the 70-80 m.p.h. region.

A mean maximum speed of 88 m.p.h. was recorded in conditions which were not very favourable with a one-way speed approaching 93 m.p.h. on the downward leg of the circuit. The larger engine has improved the maximile speed much more than the maximum, suggesting that it is now perhaps a little undergeared and that, at 5,700 r.p.m. in top, power has started to fall away. Using the gears acceleration is remarkably good for a 1,100 c.c. car, 50 m.p.h. being reached from rest in 11.1 sec. and the standing start quarter mile completed in 20.9 sec. A clutch which gives a firm positive take-up but which is smooth enough to discourage wheelspin when dropped in at high r.p.m. was a help in recording these excellent figures.

Nearly 30 m.p.h. can be reached in the high bottom gear; a re-start on a 1 in 4 gradient was accomplished easily but a marginal success was recorded on 1 in 3 only by slipping the clutch at high r.p.m. for a considerable distance—an abuse which the previous smaller clutch would not have accepted. The handbrake held the car on these gradients but many drivers will regret that it is not a fly-off type; in the off position it disappears between the seats. The new gearbox has the close well-chosen ratios which first appeared on the 948 c.c. Mk. 2 model and the same smooth, light, positive change but the baulk ring synchromesh is no longer beaten by extremely rapid shifts. First gear is not synchronized and there is some transmission roughness at certain speeds on the overrun. Reverse gear is particularly easy to engage rapidly by a natural movement backwards and towards the driver against a spring gate loading which is quite light—an ideal arrangement for driving tests.

Light, sensitive handling

THE rack and pinion steering is outstanding for quick manoeuvring. With a 30 ft. turning circle, 2¼ turns of the wheel take it from one lock to the other and it is so light that this manoeuvre can be accomplished easily with one hand. There is a certain amount of initial roll on entering a corner which appears to be accompanied by side float of the car on its quarter-elliptic rear springing. This results in a tendency to lurch rather eagerly into a swerve in a manner suggesting strong roll oversteer; in fact, however, once set up for a corner the Sprite stabilizes and sits down very firmly until ultimately the rear wheels begin to break away gently and progressively. A little more air in the back tyres postpones the final breakaway to even higher speeds.

With these characteristics the car can be flicked through a series of fast bends with little more than a few movements of the wrists by a natural and experienced Sprite driver who will probably regard most other cars as sluggish and unresponsive. Heavy-handedness is not compatible with the handling characteristics and a clumsier driver with slower reactions may well regard the steering as over-sensitive.

For a sports car the ride is certainly not harsh or heavily damped and on main roads it is comfortable but the rear suspension has a limited travel so that bad roads soon bring the limiting stops into operation. Sometimes, especially with a light load, a succession of bumps will induce back axle hop and the car will deviate momentarily from its straight course but on corners, when the springs are laterally loaded, this effect is largely suppressed and the rear wheels hold the road very well. The pressed steel chassis structure feels stiff and sturdy and there are very few rattles.

The Sprite has always been notable for a very good driving position and this has now been further improved by seats with much thicker and softer upholstery which still give adequate support against cornering forces and which, although perhaps a little upright, remain comfortable on really long runs. These remarks must be qualified, however, in the case of tall drivers; most people 5 ft. 10 in. tall or more will have the driving seat as far back as it will go and very tall people or those who have particularly long legs may find the steering wheel jammed against their thighs and the pedals difficult to operate. Clutch and brake are well separated but the latter is so close to the side of the body that even a size 8 shoe may be caught between the two. Heel and toe operation of brake and organ type accelerator is easy and straight-forward.

Austin-Healey Sprite 1100

Above: There is little change in the appearance of the enlarged engine and its accessories. Except for the distributor and fuel pump most of the parts are easy to get at. *Above right:* The wide, meshed radiator grille contrasts with the clean, simple lines. *Right:* The boot is the only part of the Sprite that can be kept under lock and key. Although the hinges intrude on the useful vertical height there is room for a large suitcase on top of the spare wheel.

A padded roll along the bottom edge of the dashboard improves the appearance considerably although some drivers thought it made the interior look smaller. Very tall drivers found their left leg in contact with the loudspeaker housing, just out of sight under the facia. The photograph also shows the excellent seats, the handbrake which lies rather inaccessibly in the horizontal "off" position and the carpeted space behind the seats which comfortably houses a carry cot.

The 7 in. drum brakes fitted to previous models had little margin for abnormally fast driving; 8¼ in. discs are now used at the front and these are lighter to use and inspire considerable confidence when stopping really hard from speeds near the maximum.

Improved trim

AT one time the interior of the Sprite was trimmed in somewhat spartan fashion by comparison with its close relative the M.G. Midget but now it is very well padded and fully carpeted. Luggage space in the small but useful lockable boot is supplemented by the space behind the front seats; with these seats moved forward a notch or two it proved possible to carry one extremely uncomfortable adult passenger in this position even with the hood up.

There are no locks on the doors and no exterior handles; in damp frosty weather the sliding plastic side screens froze in their guides and it was then necessary to unbutton part of the hood to reach the inside door catches. At speed these screens tend to pull outwards under wind forces and there are noticeable draughts particularly round the driver's right hand. From the point of view of wind noise and weather proofing they are not to be compared with winding glass windows but they do allow the use of hollowed-out doors which give a great deal of elbow room and have large and extremely useful rigid pockets. There is no facia cubby hole or ash tray.

Visibility is good, a large wrap-round flexible rear window preventing any feeling of being cramped or shut in. A low sloping bonnet gives an excellent close-range view of the road ahead that should be particularly valuable in fog but the mirror tends to cut off the driver's view of the near side wing without giving particularly good rear vision. A larger shallow mirror would give adequate spread in elevation and make better use of the width of the rear window. With the hood down, of course, the all-round view is superb but a back-draught in the open cockpit discouraged much open motoring in the very cold weather which persisted for most of our test. The hood is easy to raise or lower single handed and it is sufficiently well tensioned to prevent much flapping at speed.

It seems a pity that non-cancelling indicators are still fitted although the warning light is a prominent one. A more serious criticism, perhaps, is the small range given by a 6-gallon tank and a fuel consumption in the region of 30 m.p.g. The steady speed m.p.g. figures show that the Sprite is not inherently an extravagant car and it could be driven very economically indeed by anyone who was so minded, but our test staff were more inclined to enjoy its sporting qualities to the full and to drive it as fast as it would go with continual use of the delightful gearbox. Unlike the previous model, the test car did not need 100 octane fuel, there being no trace of pinking on premium grade.

Fundamentally, the Sprite design has changed little since its introduction and not surprisingly it now has rivals which can outshine it in some directions, notably perhaps in rough road performance, but at £586 it now offers even more remarkable value for money than before. Above all it still remains great fun to drive.

Coachwork and Equipment

Starting handle ... ... No	Sun visors ... ... None	Ashtrays ... ... None
Battery mounting On the scuttle under the bonnet	Instruments: Speedometer (with total and decimal	Cigar lighters ... ... Optional extra
Jack ... Bipod screw type with ratchet handle	trip mileage recorders), rev. counter, fuel gauge	Interior lights ... ... None
Jacking points ... Below centre of body	and combined oil pressure/water temperature	Interior heater ... Optional extra fresh air
on either side	gauge	heater and demister
Standard tool kit: Wheel brace, hub cap remover,	Warning lights ... ... Generator, main beam,	Car radio ... ... Optional extra
plug spanner and tommy bar.	direction indicators	Extras available: Radio, heater, tonneau cover,
Exterior lights: 2 headlamps, 2 sidelamps, 2 stop/	Locks:	laminated screen, hard top, cigar lighter, heavy
tail lamps, number plate lamp.	With ignition key ... ... Ignition only	duty tyres, twin horns, luggage carrier, etc.
Number of electrical fuses 2	With other keys ... ... Boot	Upholstery material ... ... PVC
Direction indicators ... Non-cancelling flashers	Glove lockers ... ... None	Floor covering ... ... Carpet
Windscreen wipers ... Twin blade electric	Map pockets ... ... One in each door	Exterior colours standardized 6
Windscreen washers ... Manual pump type	Parcel shelves ... ... None	Alternative body styles ... ... None

Maintenance

Sump ... ... 6½ pints, S.A.E. 30 (summer)	Contact breaker gap ... ... 0.014-0.016 in.	Camber angle ... ... 1°
or 20 (winter)	Sparking plug type ... ... Champion N5	Castor angle ... ... 3°
Gearbox ... ... 2¼ pints, S.A.E. 30	Sparking plug gap ... ... 0.024-0.026 in.	Steering swivel pin inclination... ... 6½°
Rear axle ... 1½ pints, S.A.E. 90 hypoid	Valve timing: Inlet opens 5° before t.d.c. and closes	Tyre pressures:
Steering gear lubricant ... ... S.A.E. 90	45° a.b.d.c.; exhaust opens 51° before b.d.c. and	Front ... ... 18 lb.
Cooling system capacity 10 pints (2 drain taps)	closes 21° a.t.d.c.	Rear ... ... 20 lb.
Chassis lubrication: By grease gun every 3,000 miles	Tappet clearances (hot): Inlet 0.012 in.; exhaust	Brake fluid ... Lockheed (S.A.E. 70 R 3)
to 12 points.	0.012 in.	Battery type and capacity 12-volt 43 amp. hr.
Ignition timing ... ... 5° b.t.d.c.	Front wheel toe-in ... ... 0-⅛ in.	

AUSTIN-HEALEY SPRITE 1100

More under the bonnet, and better to boot

UNLIKE THE U.S. AUTOMOBILE INDUSTRY, most overseas manufacturers produce any given model for several years, with only minor detail changes made each year. Such is the case with British Motors Corporation's Austin-Healey Sprite, although in this case the changes were more than *minor* details and constitute a genuine upgrading of the car.

Briefly, the changes were: An increase in engine displacement from 948 to 1098 cc, which raised the horsepower rating from 46.5 to 55 bhp (still at 5500 rpm); the clutch diameter was increased one inch; baulk ring synchromesh (top 3 gears only) for the transmission; a change in front brakes from drums to discs; new seats which are both reshaped and more thickly padded and the addition of carpeting in the interior to replace the "unborn Gila Monster hide" that came with the original Sprites.

The additional engine displacement was brought about by an increase in bore and a new, longer stroke crankshaft very similar to the ones used in the MG-1100 sedans. In fact, the upper part of the Sprite engine is now almost identical to the MG-1100.

The interior trim on our test car was well detailed and everything seemed to fit, and work, properly. The seat design, in addition to being better looking than before, is also more comfortable and the seats offer good lateral support. The carpeting serves the double function of helping the looks and keeping out some of the road noise. It was the consensus of this office that the Sprite now looks more like a car than a toy—aided by more attention to assembly detail than has been previously shown.

Instrumentation consists of a large-diameter tachometer—red lined at 6000, with an orange warning section from 5500 to 6000 rpm—and matching speedometer set directly in front of the driver; a fuel gauge at the left and a combined oil pressure/water temperature gauge at the right.

In view of current automobile design practice it is surprising that BMC has continued the separate key and starter actuating (most cars now use key-start ignition switches), and even more surprising that it is a pull cable rather than a push button. In further contradiction to the trends, the heater control is a knob similar to the starter knob—but pulls to shut *off*, pushes to bring up cockpit heat.

The steering wheel is set directly in front of the driver (not all the smaller cars have them so placed because of lateral space problems) but the column angles off slightly to the right. This isn't too noticeable and didn't cause any bother. Foot pedals are placed in the spots one would expect to find them and about as close together as possible and still leave room for the large American foot (we've come to the conclusion that British and Italian feet must be smaller than their American counterparts).

All hand controls fall readily to hand—and if one isn't careful, the hand on the shift knob can become battered and bruised from hitting the lower part of the panel on shifts to third. The lower edge of this panel is padded along its full length which prevents permanent damage to knuckles (and passenger's knees) from accidental contact with the edge.

There are still no door locks or outside door handles—it is necessary to reach inside for the handle, which means sliding forward the split side window if the top is up. These sliding perspex side windows, mounted in metal frames, are removable and are far superior to side curtains for both noise and weather protection, but still not as good as roll up windows.

The absence of window winding mechanism in the door does leave room for a hollowed-out area, a necessity if there is to be elbow room in a tiny car, and also helps a great deal in keeping the overall cost of the car down. The side window frames on our test car would not stay in place well because the attaching bolts were too short, so most of the testing was done with the side windows removed. Due to the Sprite's top and side window design, visibility is good even with frames in place and top up—a feature not all convertibles can claim.

Aside from the increased comfort of the seats and the lower noise level, the additional displacement of the engine has added the most pleasure to driving the Sprite because of the extra torque available. Even though 8.5 ft/lb doesn't seem like much increase, it represents 16.2%.

Our top speed runs netted only a fraction more than the 948-cc Sprite II but we believe that a well-broken-in Sprite 1100 should be able to add a few mph to our top speed figures. Even more important to the driver though is the top gear hill climbing and easier passing ability offered by the better torque characteristics throughout the entire range.

The disc brakes in front have contributed a great deal to the safety margin because the former small drums were somewhat marginal when the car was being driven near the maximum. Handling has been unaffected by any of the changes and the Sprite is still one of the most responsive cars on the road.

The steering, rack and pinion, is quick and accurate, although a small amount of road shock is transmitted back to the steering wheel. The Sprite can be driven through a series of fast S bends with only the slightest movement of the wheel and although the tail tends to drift out, from body roll, on entering a curve, it stabilizes almost immediately and gives the feeling of being a completely neutral steering car.

Due to its responsiveness and neutral handling it is an excellent car for the beginning sports car driver; and with the nominal initial cost and good fuel economy it is also ideal for the impecunious.

The ride is severe by comparison with most cars and def-

SPRITE 1100

initely on the stiffish side. Yet, with·two persons aboard, a slight dip or thank-you-ma'm would cause the car to bottom at the rear. The good dampers brought the car back to level with a minimum of vertical oscillation, however.

It was our opinion, at first, that the fuel capacity (7.2 gal) is too limiting, for even with its low fuel consumption the Sprite can safely go just over 200 miles between gas stops. Looking back on our experience in the car, we're not sure we'd want to go more than 200 miles between stops anyway because in spite of the comfortable seats, we found the combination of wind noise and relatively harsh ride tiring.

Luggage space remains unchanged from the Sprite II and its alter ego the MG Midget. Each door contains a map pocket which would do for the usual detritus found in a glove compartment (which the Sprite lacks) with the advan-

tage/disadvantage that it would be difficult for either driver or passenger to reach the compartment on the opposite side. There is room behind the seats for a pretty fair amount of luggage and we've been told that a third person can even ride back there, seated crosswise in the car, but we find this hard to believe and certainly don't recommend it.

The only lockable space on the car is the trunk compartment which holds the spare tire, and top and side curtains when down, and has room for a fairly good sized suitcase.

We have found that Sprite owners are generally unanimous in their praise of the car for daily use and we know several who have put on a large number of miles with very little or no expense above the usual gas, oil and periodic servicing. The biggest and most often heard complaints stem from the annoyance of things coming loose, usually around the cockpit, and from the seemingly incurable oil leaks in the engine.

Be that as it may, we've said it before, and we have to say it again: The Sprite (and Midget) offers more fun per dollar than any car we can name—providing the car is accepted for what it is.

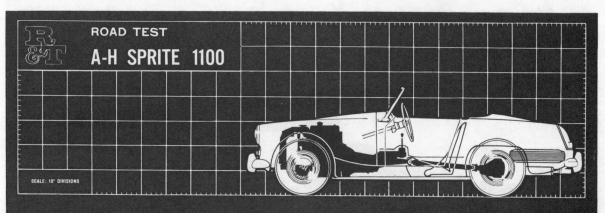

ROAD TEST
A-H SPRITE 1100

SCALE: 10" DIVISIONS

DIMENSIONS

Wheelbase, in. 80.5
Tread, f and r 47.2/45.0
Over-all length, in 138
   width. 54.0
   height. 47.8
   equivalent vol, cu ft . . .206
Frontal area, sq ft. . . .14.3
Ground clearance, in 6.2
Steering ratio, o/a . . . . . . .n s.
   turns, lock to lock. 2.3
   turning circle, ft. 30
Hip room, front. . . . . . . .2 x 16
Hip room, rear. . . . . .n. a.
Pedal to seat back, max . .41.0
Floor to ground. 7.2

CALCULATED DATA

Lb/hp (test wt) 34.2
Cu ft/ton mile. 80.4
Mph/1000 rpm (4th) 15.4
Engine revs/mile. 3900
Piston travel, ft/mile 2140
Rpm @ 2500 ft/min. . . .4550
   equivalent mph 70.0
R&T wear index. 83.5

SPECIFICATIONS

List price. $1985
Curb weight, lb. 1560
Test weight. 1880
   distribution, %. 51/49
Tire size. 5.20-13
Brake swept area. 190
Engine type . . . . . .4-cyl, ohv
Bore & stroke . . . .2.54 x 3.30
Displacement, cc. 1098
   cu in 66.98
Compression ratio. 8.90
Bhp @ rpm. . . . . .55 @ 5500
   equivalent mph. 84.6
Torque, lb-ft . . . .61 @ 2500
   equivalent mph. 38.4

GEAR RATIOS

4th (1.000) 4.22
3rd (1.357) 5.73
2nd (1.918) 8.09
1st (3.222) 13.6

SPEEDOMETER ERROR

30 mph. . . . . .actual, 29.3
60 mph. 57.8

PERFORMANCE

Top speed (5530), mph. 85
Shifts, rpm-mph
3rd (6000). 68
2nd (6000). 48
1st (6050). 29

FUEL CONSUMPTION

Normal range, mpg 30/36

ACCELERATION

0-30 mph, sec 5.4
0-40. . . . . .8.3
0-50. . . . . .12.5
0-60. . . . . .18.3
0-70. . . . . .27.8
0-80. . . . . .42.5
0-100. . . . .
Standing ¼ mile. 20.9
   speed at end 63

TAPLEY DATA

4th, maximum gradient, %. .9.8
3rd. 13.5
2nd. 19.3
Total drag at 60 mph, lb 75

ENGINE SPEED IN GEARS

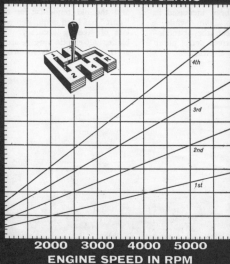

ENGINE SPEED IN RPM

ACCELERATION & COASTING

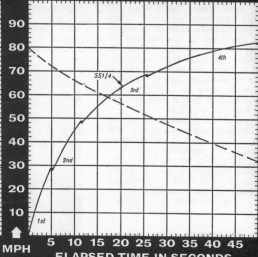

ELAPSED TIME IN SECONDS

NEW ★ MODELS

The M.G. Midget II in standard form and the Austin Healey Sprite III, with optional wire wheels

Austin Healey Sprite Mk. III and

MORE POWER, WIND-UP WINDOWS AND NEW REAR SUSPENSION

LATEST figures released by the British Motor Corporation for Austin-Healey Sprite and M.G. Midget production well exemplify the popularity of British small sports cars. Since 1958, 110,000 of these closely related models have rolled off the production line at Abingdon-on-Thames, helping to make this traditional home of M.G. cars the largest factory in the world devoted to the production of sports cars.

About 85 per cent are exported, mainly to the United States, and it is to satisfy the demand from this market for more creature comforts and to bring the cars into line with the character of the MGB, that the M.G. Midget Mark II and Austin-Healey Sprite Mark III models have been introduced. There has been particular resistance to detachable sidescreens in America, and the rising sales of rivals with wind-up side windows have no doubt encouraged B.M.C. to incorporate this feature in these latest models. At the same time the cockpit layout has been rearranged and restyled, to make it more luxurious and easier to "work" in.

Power output is especially important to enthusiasts, and besides cylinder head and exhaust manifold modifications, which increase maximum power to a genuine 59 b.h.p. (net) at 5,750 r.p.m., a stiffer crankshaft is fitted to reduce vibrations. For these improvements, the modest price increase of £24, including purchase tax, seems well justified.

Modifications to the cockpit layout have made both models into refined roadsters with a high standard of finish. Seat trim style is unchanged

Extra power from the engine has been obtained by increasing the size of the inlet valves by 0·06in. and by modifying and reshaping the siamesed inlet tracts to reduce the "uvula" which separates the ports. At the same time, the compression ratio has been raised to 9 to 1, although an 8·3 to 1 compression ratio engine is available for countries with low octane petrol.

A new cast-iron, four-branch exhaust manifold, similar in shape to that of the MGB, has been adopted to replace the older type inherited from the Austin A.35. The new manifold eliminates the double bend in the down pipe and is responsible for one of the extra horsepower of the latest engine. Crankshaft main journals have been increased in size from 1·87in. to 2·0in., while a minor change has been the abandonment of the engine driven petrol pump in favour of an S.U. electric unit.

Rear suspension has been completely revised by the adoption of half-elliptic leaf springs. It has always been a problem to make quarter-elliptic springs of the old design with a combination of low rate and sufficient lateral rigidity to locate the back axle accurately. Moreover, the whole weight of the rear of the car was carried on an anchorage point only 4in. long, requiring long, heavy channel section stiffeners to spread the loads through to the structure. The result was always a compromise resulting in a hard ride and undue roll stiffness at the rear, with a consequent tendency for the car to be very sensitive on steering.

The new springs give a better ride, and the old tendency for the car to "dart" has been eliminated without any loss of steering accuracy. The four-blade, half-elliptic springs are anchored at the forward ends in brackets, and

Neat and practical, the new instrument panel has the two main dials angled inwards slightly

PRICES	Basic	Total
	£	(inc. P.T.)
		£ s d
M.G. Midget Mk. II	505	610 15 5
Austin-Healey		
Sprite Mk. III	515	622 17 1

Extras (including P.T.)

Tonneau cover and rail	£5 8 9
Hardtop	£48 6 8
Fresh-air heater	£14 10 0
Wire wheels	£30 4 2

M.G. Midget Mk. II

at the rear are shackled to a plate bolted to the floor by way of the box section members which reinforce the boot floor.

With this half-elliptic rear springing the unsprung weight of two heavy axle brackets needed for the former quarter-elliptic parallelogram layout is eliminated, plus half the weight of the radius arms and approximately one third of the weight of the thick, wide, quarter-elliptic spring. It has been possible also to eliminate much of the body stiffening required by the old layout.

Thus the total weight saving all but makes up for the extra weight of the door glasses and window lifts, and the all-up weight of the latest cars is only 6lb more than that of their predecessors.

More prospective owners will welcome the change to wind-up windows, which in no way detract from the sporty appearance of the cars and yet add greatly to their general convenience. To fit wind-up glasses into the relatively thin doors of the Sprite and Midget without a major body redesign has called for curved side glasses. The gain is all on the side of the owner, for whom adequate elbow room is retained without any increase in external body width.

Small swivelling quarter vents with non-locking catches are standard equipment and a new, more rigid windscreen frame with full height cast aluminium pillars is fitted to provide a firm sealing abutment for the doors. A thin tie rod between the top and bottom rails of the screen frame prevents it "opening up" when the hood is tensioned and also provides a mounting for the driving mirror which was previously located on the scuttle, where it created a blind spot.

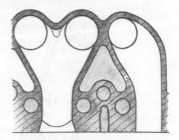

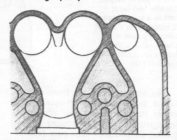

Section of the cylinder head through the ports. Above is the previous pattern, and below is the new head with better breathing capacity

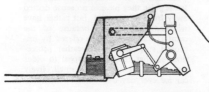

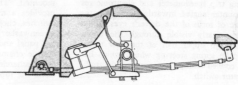

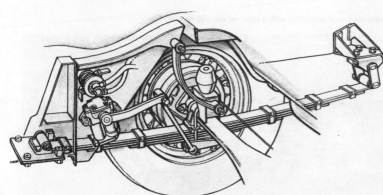

The previous type of rear suspension with quarter elliptic leaf springs and radius arms is shown in the upper left diagram. Better axle location, reduced unsprung weight and improved handling result from the new layout

Specification

ENGINE
No. of cylinders ... 4 in-line
Bore ... ... 64·6mm (2·54in.)
Stroke ... ... 83·7mm (3·30in.)
Displacement ... 1,098 c.c. (67 cu. in.)
Valve operation Overhead, pushrods
Compression
ratio ... ... 9·0 to 1 (Optional 8·3 to 1)
Max. b.h.p. (net) 59 at 5,750 r.p.m.
Max. b.m.e.p.
(net) ... ... 140 p.s.i. at 3,250 r.p.m.
Max. torque (net) 62 lb. ft. at 3,250 r.p.m.
Carburettor ... Twin S.U. HS2
Fuel pump ... S.U. Electric
Tank capacity ... 6 Imp. gallons (27 litres)
Sump capacity ... 6·5 pints (3·7 litres)
Oil filter ... ... Full-flow wich renewable element
Cooling system Pressurized system centrifugal
pump, fan and thermostat
Battery ... ... 12 volt, 43 amp. hr.

TRANSMISSION
Clutch ... ... Borg and Beck hydraulically
operated, single dry plate, 7·25in.
dia.

Gearbox ... ... Four-speed, synchromesh on 2nd,
3rd and top. Central floor change
Overall ratios ... Top 4·22; third 5·73; second
8·09; first 13·51; reverse 17·32
Final drive ... Hypoid bevel, ratio 4·22 to 1

CHASSIS
Brakes ... ... Lockheed hydraulic. Front discs,
8·25in. dia.; rear drums, 7in. dia.;
1·25in. wide shoes.
Suspension:front Independent, coil springs and
wishbones, Armstrong telescopic
dampers
rear Half-elliptic leaf springs, lever arm
dampers
Wheels ... ... Steel disc, 4 studs, 3·5in rim.
Tyre size ... ... 5·20—13 Dunlop tubeless Gold
Seal Nylon C.41
Steering... ... Rack and pinion
Steering wheel... Three-spoke, 17in. diameter

No. of turns,
(lock to lock)... 2·25

DIMENSIONS
Wheelbase ... 6ft. 8in. (203 cm)
Track: front ... 3ft. 9·75in. (116 cm)
rear ... 3ft. 8·75in. (114 cm)
Overall length ... 11ft. 4·25in. (345 cm)
Overall width ... 4ft. 5in. (135 cm)
Overall height
(unladen) ... 4ft. 1·75in. (126 cm)
Ground clearance
(laden) ... 5in. (13 cm)
Turning circle ... 31ft. 2·5in. (9·5 cm)
Kerb weight ... 14cwt (1,566lb—714kg)

PERFORMANCE DATA
Top gear m.p.h. per 1,000 r.p.m. .... 15·37
Torque lb. ft. per cu. in. engine capacity........ 0·92
Brake surface swept by linings .... 190 sq. in.
Weight distri-
bution ... F. 52·4 per cent; R. 47·6 per cent

SPRITE and MIDGET . . .

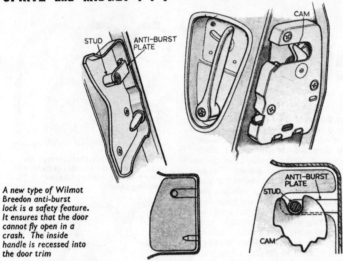

A new type of Wilmot Breedon anti-burst lock is a safety feature. It ensures that the door cannot fly open in a crash. The inside handle is recessed into the door trim

The main effect of the latest cockpit layout is to give it a designed look, rather than the appearance of having been assembled from a number of un-related components. The new facia is handsome and practical, with the matching trip speedometer and electronic rev counter angled inwards to fall on the arc of focus of the driver's eyes. Both are clearly visible through the unob-structed upper half of the new three-spoke spring steering wheel, which has a cowled column incorporating the traffi-cator switch.

The instrument panel is a steel pres-sing taking up two-thirds of the width of the facia, and on the left-hand sec-tion (right hand for left-hand-drive cars) the fuel gauge and a combined oil pres-sure gauge and coolant thermometer are mounted. This section of the panel also provides a mounting for the electrical switches, choke and heater controls and screenwasher plunger. The whole of the panel and facia is finished in black crackle enamel, surmounted by a pad-ded leathercloth roll which is extended along the tops of the doors.

On the passenger side a crushable, fibreboard parcels shelf with a padded edge provides stowage for maps and small oddments, and would collapse safely in the event of accident. The floor and transmission tunnel are covered in good quality pile carpet, and this has bound edges and rubber heel mats for both occupants.

Road Impressions

A short run in an M.G. Midget veri-fied that the ride has been very much improved, and has a great deal in com-mon with that of the larger MGB. The wider location base for the rear springs has allowed the manufacturers to put more rubber into the shackles. This makes for a quieter running as well as a better ride. Final drive vibration which was felt in older models is noticeably absent. Handling is particu-larly pleasant, light and predictable, and the necessity on certain surfaces to drive with the fingertips has gone. Particu-larly noteworthy is that there is ample elbowroom with two large people on board.

The Austin-Healey Sprite and the M.G. Midget were introduced as cheap, small sports cars suitable for young people to cut their motoring teeth on with safety and economy. In their latest guise they have in no sense drifted away from this precept, but rather have widened their' scope, because of the comfort and convenience offered by im-proved suspension and weather protec-tion, so that they now appeal to older enthusiasts looking for a small, lively car for everyday use.

Visibility is not impaired with the hood up and there is good wind protection with it removed and side windows raised

'Motor' tells you
what to look
for under the
skin of that
second-hand car

SPRITE I & II

NOT the world's most beautiful car in its Mk. I form, the Austin-Healey Sprite was introduced in May, 1958, and was quickly accepted because it represented the cheapest way of going fast and, anyhow, people soon got used to its cheeky face.

The B.M.C. A series engine, with suitable modifications, powered it in 948 c.c. form. In May, 1961 the very much prettier Mk. II appeared and, in October of the following year, the engine capacity was upped to 1,098 c.c. —these models were mechanically similar to the Mk. I.

The run continued until March, 1964, when the current Mk. III took over.

● A look around

Check the Mk. I for rust in the body welds between the wings and bonnet top and at the sides of the radiator grille. On early models, the tank/boot joint may be broken and cars used in competition can become bent under the nose. Examine proprietary plastic bonnets for accuracy of fit.

Early hoods were fixed by press-studs and the later hook-on strip arrangement is much better. A damaged rear window means a new hood: check also the stay tension. The doors are simple and give no trouble but improved catches were introduced during 1959.

Check the rubber grease retainers on the steering linkage for splits and examine the handbrake cable for stretch. It is wise to look over "extra" wiring as these cars are happy hunting grounds for the mod men.

On disc wheels, look for cracks between the studs.

● Engine running

The engine should start easily but if a Mk. I or II has been standing around for some time the mechanical petrol pump will almost certainly need priming. An electric one can be fitted if desired, as on the Mk. III.

The valve gear should be reasonably quiet but look for a blown manifold/exhaust joint. A loud rattle when starting can come from a fractured carburetter heat-shield. Over-enthusiastic tightening can break the rear lug on the manifold—check. Examine the engine-mounting rubbers for weakness.

If the timing chain rattles this can be cured by replacing the tensioner rings and/or chain and/or sprocket— it's a matter of stripping down to have a look.

Oil leaks from the rocker cover and side cover gaskets are of little account: an improved type of seal will take care of weeping at the front main bearing; but a leak from the oil filter can be serious as this may mean that the distance-piece has vibrated loose. The fixing bolts are very difficult to get at and the best scheme is to " glue " them in place with a locking cement.

● On the road

The rack-and-pinion steering is very light and the steering wheel should not be held firmly—even then it takes a while to get used to this lightness and the car should really be handled like a solo motorcycle.

If the handling seems odd, or the tyres show uneven wear, check the forward mountings of the rear springs. These locate the back axle and if they are out of line, control will suffer very badly. Also check the front upper shock-absorber mountings for tightness. There should be no steering play.

The clutch travel should be light and short—check early examples for slip. The brake pedal should have normal travel and if the brakes seem inadequate, A40 units (8 in. instead of 7 in.) can be fitted to make a considerable improvement.

Many modified cars have disc brakes with wire wheels and this increases the track with a beneficial effect on ▷47 handling.

● Brief Specification

Engine: four-cylinder o.h.v., 948 or 1,098 c.c.
Gearbox: Four-speed with synchromesh on three upper ratios.
LENGTH: 11 ft. 5 in.
WIDTH: 4 ft. 6 in.
WEIGHT: 12¾ cwt. Mk. I; 13½ cwt. Mk. II.

● New Performance

TOP SPEED: 82 m.p.h. Mk. I; 85 m.p.h. Mk. II (948 c.c.); 87 m.p.h. Mk. II (1,098 c.c.).
AVERAGE FUEL CONSUMPTION: 43 m.p.g. (948 c.c.); 37 m.p.g. (1,098 c.c.).
ACCELERATION: 0-50 through gears 14 sec. (948 c.c.); 11 sec. (1,098 c.c.). 20-40 in top 12·5 sec. (948 c.c.); 11 sec. (1,098 c.c.).
BRAKING FROM 30 M.P.H.: 30 to 31 ft.

● Identity Parade

Introduced May 1958.

Screen and hood fitting modified October 1958.

Door locks improved January 1959.

Sliding side windows standard on open models March 1960.

Mk. I discontinued May 1961 at chassis no. 50116.

Mk. II introduced at chassis no. 101.

Larger engine, disc brakes, baulk-ring synchromesh introduced October 1962.

Discontinued at chassis 38828 and Mk. III introduced.

AUTOCAR, 24 April 1964

Austin-Healey Sprite Mk III 1,098c.c.

IT doesn't take one many miles in the latest Austin-Healey Sprite to appreciate that this car's recent revisions must have been devised by designers who really drive. This is in sharp contrast to the all-too-familiar boardroom process whereby a product is made different, so that it can advance from one Mark or Series to the next, without significant improvement. The new Sprite is faster, holds the road better, rides more comfortably and is more habitable. Just the simple refinements of providing it with winding windows and door locks must surely widen its commercial scope. The Mk III Sprite was described, together with the almost identical M.G. Midget Mk II, in our 13 March issue. The M.G. costs £10 (basic) more than the Austin-Healey, £12 odd including purchase tax.

As this is essentially a sports car, many owners of earlier types of Sprites and Midgets, as well as prospective buyers who are undecided as yet between these small B.M.C. sports cars and their direct rivals from other factories, will want to know first how the latest ones go. Engine improvements described on 13 March include a modified cylinder head with larger inlet valves and re-shaped tracts to them, a higher compression ratio and new exhaust manifold. The crankshaft is considerably beefier, with 2in. dia. instead of 1·87in. main journals. Although on paper the maximum power output has risen only from 56 to 59 b.h.p. (net) at the same crankshaft speed (5,750 r.p.m.), and peak torque of 62 lb. ft. at 3,250 r.p.m. is unchanged, the Sprite under review performed considerably better than the M.G. Midget tested last November.

Mean maximum speed has risen from 89·5 to 91·8 m.p.h., which signifies that the car can reach a true 90 even in slightly adverse conditions; but the chief gain is in acceleration almost throughout the range. For example, 60 m.p.h. was reached in only 14·5sec and 80 in 31·5, whereas the

PRICES	£	s	d
Sprite Mk. III	505	0	0
Purchase Tax	105	15	5
Total (in G.B.)	**610**	**15**	**5**
Extras (inc. P.T.)			
Heater	14	10	0
Wire wheels	30	4	2
Radio	26	11	8

How the Austin-Healey Sprite Mk III compares:

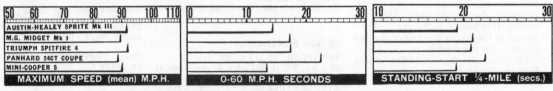

	MAXIMUM SPEED (mean) M.P.H.	0-60 M.P.H. SECONDS	STANDING-START ¼-MILE (secs.)
AUSTIN-HEALEY SPRITE Mk III			
M.G. MIDGET Mk I			
TRIUMPH SPITFIRE 4			
PANHARD 24CT COUPE			
MINI-COOPER S			

Autocar road test • No. 1971

Make • AUSTIN-HEALEY   Type • Sprite Mk III (1,098 c.c.)
(Front engine, rear-wheel drive)

Manufacturers : The Austin Motor Co. Ltd., Longbridge, Birmingham

Test Conditions
Weather......Fine and dry with 5-10 m.p.h. wind
Temperature .... 2·8 deg. C. (37 deg. F.)
Barometer .... 29·4in. Hg.
Dry concrete and asphalt surfaces.

Weight
Kerb weight (with oil, water and half-full fuel tank)
    13·94cwt (1,561lb-708kg)
Front-rear distribution, per cent F. 53·5; R. 46·5
Laden as tested............16·94cwt (1,897lb-860kg)

Turning Circles
Between kerbs .... L. 32ft 1in.; R. 30ft 10in.
Between walls .... L. 33ft 6in.; R. 32ft 3in.
Turns of steering wheel lock to lock............ 2·3

FUEL AND OIL CONSUMPTION

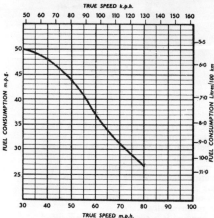

FUEL   Super Premium Grade
                (100-102 octane RM)
Test Distance........................ 1,042 miles
Overall Consumption ...... 29·7 m.p.g.
                (9·5 litres/100 km)
DIN Consumption........... 30·0 m.p.g.
                (9·4 litres/100 km)
OIL: SAE 30......... Consumption 4,000 m.p.g.

HILL CLIMBING AT STEADY SPEEDS

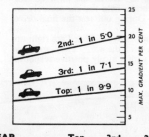

2nd: 1 in 5·0
3rd: 1 in 7·1
Top: 1 in 9·9

GEAR PULL (lb per ton)	Top	3rd	2nd
	225	310	445

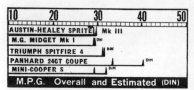

M.P.G. Overall and Estimated (DIN)				
10	20	30	40	50
AUSTIN-HEALEY SPRITE Mk III				
M.G. MIDGET Mk I	DIN			
TRIUMPH SPITFIRE 4		DIN		
PANHARD 24CT COUPE			DIN	
MINI-COOPER S		DIN		

MAXIMUM SPEEDS AND ACCELERATION TIMES

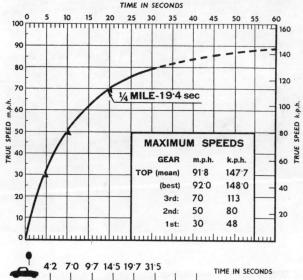

¼ MILE-19·4 sec

MAXIMUM SPEEDS		
GEAR	m.p.h.	k.p.h.
TOP (mean)	91·8	147·7
(best)	92·0	148·0
3rd:	70	113
2nd:	50	80
1st:	30	48

	4·2	7·0	9·7	14·5	19·7	31·5		TIME IN SECONDS
0	30	40	50	60	70	80	90	100	TRUE SPEED m.p.h.
	32	43	53	63	74	85	96	CAR SPEEDOMETER

Speed range, overall gear ratios and time in seconds

m.p.h.	Top (4·22)	Third (5·73)	Second (8·09)	First (13·50)
10—30	—	9·5	5·6	3·5
20—40	12·5	7·7	4·9	—
30—50	11·6	7·6	5·4	—
40—60	11·7	8·4	—	—
50—70	14·6	10·0	—	—
60—80	19·7	—	—	—

BRAKES (from 30 m.p.h. in neutral)	Pedal Load	Retardation	Equiv. Distance
	25lb	0·19g	158ft
	50lb	0·43g	69ft
	75lb	0·78g	39ft
	100lb	0·97g	31·0ft
	Handbrake	0·40g	75ft

CLUTCH   Pedal load and travel—45lb and 4in.

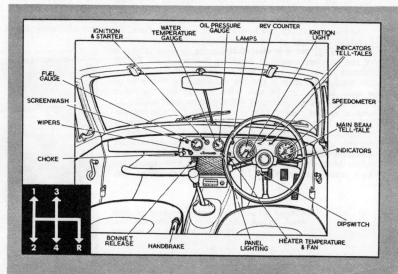

IGNITION & STARTER — WATER TEMPERATURE GAUGE — OIL PRESSURE GAUGE — REV COUNTER — IGNITION LIGHT — LAMPS — INDICATORS TELL-TALES — FUEL GAUGE — SCREENWASH — WIPERS — CHOKE — SPEEDOMETER — MAIN BEAM TELL-TALE — INDICATORS — DIPSWITCH — BONNET RELEASE — HANDBRAKE — PANEL LIGHTING — HEATER TEMPERATURE & FAN

1 3
2 4 R

AUTOCAR, 24 April 1964

Austin-Healey Sprite Mk III

While interior width has not been lost through the fitting of winding side windows, the door pockets have gone; but there is now a tray on the left under the crackle-finish facia. Speedometer and tachometer are angled slightly inwards to meet the driver's line of sight

superseded Midget took 17·2 and 36·9sec respectively. At low engine speeds, however, the carburation on our Sprite was a bit fluffy with the throttle opened wide, and it was 0·4sec slower from 20 to 40 m.p.h. in top.

Once over about 2,000 r.p.m. (30 plus in top) it cleaned up completely, and one could feel the power delivery proper coming in from about 2,500 onwards. Although the power curve peaks at 5,750 r.p.m. and we restricted ourselves to 6,000 in the indirect gears, which marks the start of the red sector on the tachometer, at this point the engine has by no means run out of breath, nor has it lost any of its customary smoothness. Indeed, one would not expect it to, since this unit is among the easiest to tune further and can be run safely up to far higher speeds. Thus one can take the red sector not as a sort of safety margin but purely as a practical limitation dictated by the standard tune.

Reverting to the acceleration figures, the measure of the Sprite III's progress is emphasized by comparing it with its larger-engined stablemates of earlier years. Although having a considerably lower maximum speed than the 1½-litre MGAs, its figures beat any of them except the twin-cam up to 80 m.p.h., and it is quicker to 60 m.p.h. than the first of the 1600s tried out in 1959. Even the twin-cam took only 2·4sec less to reach 70, and 0·8sec less to cover the standing-start quarter-mile.

Add to this agility the Sprite's compact dimensions, its lightning reactions to the controls and a new standard of road-holding, and it is clear that the car is potentially one of the quickest means of reaching B from A on British country roads. For motorway journeys 80 m.p.h. is about the comfortable limit if one has a companion to talk to or a radio to listen to, because wind roar around the cabin with the hood up increases quickly from that point. As well as making conversation difficult, this can also become fatiguing over long distances. The wind roar almost drowns mechanical noise up to and above the maximum shown—for this may creep to a true 95 m.p.h. or so with a short downhill stretch to help it there. Any inhibitions one might have about holding this engine at high r.p.m. for long periods are countered by its running refinement and,

of course, by reflecting on its competition record. A freak fault on the test car, that fortunately occurred during a very short burst of speed between two 30-limits, was that a core plug blew out of the cylinder block and let all the water out. A sudden hot smell of anti-freeze fluid and the sight of the water temperature gauge needle returning to zero provided the obvious evidence. But had this occurred during a spell of flat-out driving on a motorway it could have been disastrous mechanically.

Complementing the engine is a very splendid four-speed gearbox, its lack of synchromesh for first gear being the only grounds for criticism. This would not worry the keen driver, especially since the downward change from second is managed easily enough without a sound by double-declutching. There was no difficulty about engaging first from rest. The synchromesh is virtually unbeatable, and the lever movements are short and positive. Ratio spacings to allow maxima (at 6,000 r.p.m.) of 30 m.p.h. in first, 50 in second and 70 in third suit the car admirably. A restart was managed without taxing the clutch too hard on our 1-in-3 test hill, and the handbrake held the car securely on this slope either way round. During our test the final drive gears became rather noisy.

Front disc and rear drum brakes by Lockheed are right up to the standard set by the rest of the car. They are very powerful, smooth and stable, with a nicely positive response

Untrimmed and awkwardly shaped because of the spare wheel, the boot is for soft bags rather than suitcases. The clumsy prop is a real nuisance

AUTOCAR, 24 April 1964

Winding side windows and hinged vents of curved glass have greatly improved the Sprite's appearance, ventilation, outward visibility, weatherproofing and security against theft, with the hood raised. Wire wheels are costly extras

to a short pedal movement. A best stopping figure of 0·97g was reached repeatedly with no drama, for a pedal load of about 100lb, and there seems to be no problem with fade.

From the driver's viewpoint the most significant of all the Sprite's modifications is the substitution of conventional half-elliptic rear springs for the previous quarter-elliptics. The theoretical advantages of reduced unsprung weight (since the mounting brackets on the axle casing are much simpler and lighter) and better location of the axle are fully borne out in practice. The half-elliptics allow more travel at a softer rate, which means improved comfort and a reduction in axle hop over bad surfaces; more important, they cut out "rear-wheel steering" and the over-sensitivity of control that were criticized in previous Sprites.

Steering

Strong side winds or indifferent surfaces no longer call for concentration to keep it on course. This is a really important contribution to one's peace of mind and physical relaxation on long runs. As it is, the car now goes just where it is pointed and stays there, the rack-and-pinion steering gear providing very accurate control in return for light effort and very moderate steering-wheel movement. The mechanism requires only 2¼ turns of the wheel between extremes of lock, the turning circle being handy at about 32ft diameter between kerbs.

So easy and responsive is the steering that one can apply almost all one's concentration to the other aspects of fast driving. The Sprite is a neutral steerer in ordinary circumstances; that is to say, it neither runs wide nor swings its tail out when bustled through a corner near the limit of tyre adhesion. Occasionally a bump will push the rear axle a few inches off its natural course, and on wet roads it is this end that first loses its grip. A quick tweak on the wheel at once brings it back into line.

One could describe the ride in general terms as being a logical compromise that is firm and stable without liver-shaking harshness. The proof of the pudding is that one can motor all day without becoming too weary, and there were no complaints from our testers of backache or other discomforts. Properly shaped, unpretentious bucket seats that give support in the right places without being over-supple or bouncy suit the car's character admirably.

Over the special rippled concrete or "washboard" test

surface the Sprite behaved very well, the vibrations becoming progressively absorbed above about 25 m.p.h. and almost disappearing from 40 onwards. It coped quite well with the simulated Belgian *pavé*, too, the body remaining almost free from the scuttle shake that afflicts many open cars, but the rear springs occasionally met their rubber bump stops.

All the controls are well arranged and convenient. The pendant clutch and brake pedals have a quite short travel and their levers are long enough to ensure a very moderate change in pedal angle as they are depressed. There is plenty of space for the left foot to rest beside the clutch pedal, and the transmission housing down the middle of the car is padded in that vicinity. The relationship between accelerator and foot-brake is such that both can be operated simultaneously for downward gear changes while braking.

The 16in. steering wheel is set where it leaves plenty of space for fat thighs beneath it, yet without projecting upwards into the driver's line of sight. It is fixed at comfortable arm's reach with the driving seat right back on its slides, but drivers of above average height would have appreciated a little more fore-and-aft space. This cannot be found, since the seats already back on to a carpeted-over cross-piece of the main structure. Wire spokes are concentrated in the lower half of the steering wheel (with the road wheels running straight) to allow an unobstructed view of the two main instrument dials. The centre gear lever and pull-up handbrake to the left of the dividing tunnel are likewise conveniently placed.

An innovation is that the speedometer (which has both

Accessibility for tinkering and routine servicing is very reasonable, but the bonnet is not counterbalanced

total and trip mileage recorders) and electronic tachometer face slightly inwards to meet the driver's natural line of vision. The other dials comprise a combined instrument for oil pressure and water temperature, and a fuel gauge. So small is the fuel tank capacity that the last-named instrument's needle can almost be seen to move when the car is being hurried down a motorway. Only six gallons can be carried, which means just under 180 miles at our overall consumption figure of 29·7 m.p.g. Allowing some margin for the distance between filling-stations and any inaccuracy in the gauge, about 150 miles is the safe limit. An inconvenience during daytime, this restriction can lead to real anxiety during night runs on unfamiliar routes or where all-night stations are known to be very few. The Sprite owner who travels far from home would thus be wise to carry a suitable plastic reservoir in the boot.

Forward visibility is improved by a new screen with more curvature and by having the rear-view mirror attached to a slender strut from the scuttle to the top of the screen frame. It can be adjusted to any height to suit the driver; previously it was screwed to the top of the scuttle and obscured one's view of the left wing. Single-speed screen-wipers cover a good area and do their job properly up to the car's maximum. They are self-parking and the motor is quiet. Push-button screenwashers are standard. Protective padding runs along the top of the facia and door window sills, and the hood clips, as well as being neat, present a flat surface to a skull advancing under strong g forces. The hood is easy to operate, and stows away neatly out of sight.

Winding side windows and hinged quarter-vents of curved glass have done much for the Sprite's appearance as well as for its travelling comfort and snugness in cold weather. Now that the car also has external door handles and locks it stands a much better chance than before against thieves. Although daylight could be seen between the doors and their frames at window sill height, in fact the Sprite was found draught-free and almost completely rain-proof.

Behind the seats is some extra luggage space to supplement that in the rather Spartan boot. At extra cost one can have a seat cushion to put here for small children. A zipped tonneau cover is another extra that most owners would want, and an interior heater is not standard. That fitted to the test car was quite powerful, the proportion reaching the foot-wells or screen being regulated by trap doors at either side of the transmission tunnel. In warm weather one has to raise the bonnet and turn off the water tap to the heater before using the system for cold air. A single-speed electric booster is provided for use at low speeds when there is no ram effect through the fresh-air intake.

Powerful Lucas headlamps are right up to one's needs on dipped as well as main beams, but one has to pay extra for a headlamp flasher unit. After all, at only £611 including purchase tax for a 90 m.p.h.-plus car one cannot expect everything.

More sports cars are produced in the U.K. than in any other country in the world, and the Austin-Healey Sprite III (with its twin, the M.G. Midget) is probably unrivalled in its class for the combination of a truly sporting performance, fine road-holding with precise control and an obvious ruggedness both of the moving parts and the basic structure.

Specification: Austin-Healey Sprite Mk III

PERFORMANCE DATA

Top gear m.p.h. per 1,000 r.p.m. ....15·4
Mean piston speed at max. power.........3,160 ft/min
Engine revs. at mean max. speed.........5,970 r.p.m.
B.h.p. per ton laden.......................................69·7

▼ *Scale: 0·3in. to 1ft. Cushions uncompressed.*

ENGINE

Cylinders ...	4-in-line, water-cooled
Bore ...	64·58mm (2·54in.)
Stroke ...	83·72mm (3·30in.)
Displacement ...	1,098 c.c. (67 cu. in.)
Valve gear ...	Overhead, pushrods and rockers
Compression ratio	8·9-to-1
Carburettor ...	Two S.U. HS2 semi-down-draught
Fuel pump ...	S.U. electric
Oil filter ...	External full-flow with replaceable element
Max. power ...	59 b.h.p. (net) at 5,750 r.p.m.
Max. torque ...	62 lb. ft. at 3,250 r.p.m.

TRANSMISSION

Clutch ...	7·25in. dia Borg and Beck S.D.P.
Gearbox ...	Four-speed, synchromesh on upper three, centre remote control
Gear ratios	Top 1 : 1, Third 1·36 : 1, Second 1·92 : 1, First 3·20 : 1, Reverse 4·11 : 1
Final drive ...	Hypoid bevel, ratio 4·22 to 1

CHASSIS

Construction ...	Integral with steel body

SUSPENSION

Front ...	Independent, coil springs and wishbones, telescopic dampers
Rear ...	Live axle, half-elliptic leaf springs, lever-arm dampers
Steering ...	Rack and pinion
Wheel dia. ...	16in.

BRAKES

Type ...	Lockheed hydraulic, front discs, rear drums, no servo
Dimensions ...	F. 8·25in. dia.; R. 7·0in. dia., 1·25in. wide shoes
Swept area ...	F. 135 sq. in.; R. 55 sq. in. Total: 190 sq. in. (225 sq. in. per ton laden)

WHEELS

Type ...	Wire-spoked centre-lock (optional extra), 3·5in. wide rim
Tyres ...	Dunlop Gold Seal Nylon 5·20—13in. tubeless

EQUIPMENT

Battery ...	12-volt 43-amp. hr.
Headlamps ...	Sealed beam 40-45 watt.
Reversing lamp ...	None
Electric fuses ...	2
Screen wipers ...	Two-blade, single-speed, self-parking
Screen washer ...	Standard, manual plunger
Interior heater ...	Extra
Safety belts ...	Anchorages provided
Interior trim ...	Vinyl-treated fabric
Floor covering ...	Carpet
Starting handle ...	No provision
Jack ...	Ratchet pillar
Jacking points ...	One each side beneath door
Other bodies ...	None

MAINTENANCE

Fuel tank ...	6 Imp. gallons (no reserve)
Cooling system ...	10 pints (plus 1 for heater)
Engine sump ...	6·5 pints SAE 30 or multigrade. Change oil every 6,000 miles; change filter element every 6,000 miles
Gearbox ...	2·5 pints SAE 30. No change necessary after first 500 miles
Final drive ...	1·5 pints SAE 90. No change necessary after first 500 miles
Grease ...	12 points every 3,000 miles
Tyre pressures ...	F.18; R.20 p.s.i. (normal driving) F. 24; R. 26 p.s.i. (fast driving) F.18; R.24 p.s.i. (full load)

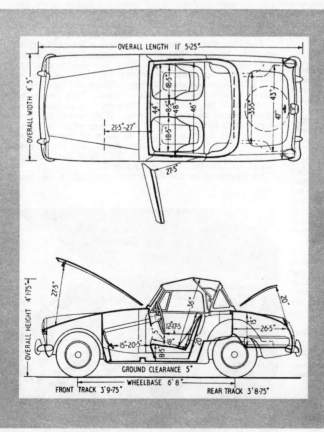

OVERALL LENGTH 11' 5·25"
OVERALL WIDTH 4' 5"
OVERALL HEIGHT 4' 1·75"
GROUND CLEARANCE 5"
WHEELBASE 6' 8"
FRONT TRACK 3' 9·75"
REAR TRACK 3' 8·75"

NEW CARS

'Spridgets' with bigger engines

65 b.h.p. for Austin-Healey Sprite and MG Midget

Austin-Healey Sprite Mk. IV

MG Midget Mk III

ALTHOUGH the changes made to the Austin-Healey Sprite and the MG Midget for the coming year are few in number, they are far-reaching in their effects on the character of these models and well merit the new mark numbers that have been given. The Sprite becomes the Mark IV and the Midget the Mark III. Not unexpectedly, there have been price increases. Both models go up by a total, when tax is included, of approximately £48, the new inclusive figures being £672 (basic £545) for the Sprite and £684 (basic £555) for the Midget.

Principal innovation is the fitting of a new engine—or more correctly, a new version of the basic BMC A-type unit. Larger in capacity by 16% compared with the present 1,098 c.c. unit, it gives a 10% step-up in power and an 11% improvement in torque. With virtually no change in weight, the new models should not only be much more potent but should perform with less effort.

The new engine has a bore and stroke of 70.63 mm. and 81.33 mm., giving a capacity of 1,275 c.c. These dimensions are, of course, identical to those of the well-known Mini-Cooper S, but although there is much in common with the S unit, the engine which is being used in the new Midget and Sprite has in fact, been redesigned in various respects, partly to make it more suitable for production in the very substantial numbers involved.

Both the cylinder block and the head have been redesigned for ease of casting without loss of efficiency. Because, however, the "Spridget" version is planned for a car designed to sell at a very popular price, the Nitralloy crankshaft of the Cooper engine is not used but a substantial "2-in." crank employed in its place. Valves, springs, conrods and so on are the same but a lower compression ratio of 8.8:1 is used and the output is 65 b.h.p. net at 6,000 r.p.m. compared with the 76 b.h.p. of the Cooper "S" version. For territories where high octane fuel is un-

obtainable, an 8.0:1 compression edition of the engine is available.

Also new is a diaphragm spring clutch designed to give lighter and smoother operation without loss of bite. As before, it is operated hydraulically but instead of the clutch and brake master cylinders being cast in a single unit, separate master cylinders are now employed. The reason for this is to enable a tandem braking system to be fitted readily if this should be required to comply with American or other overseas regulations.

The excellent close-ratio gearbox with unbeatable synchromesh in the three upper ratios and a very handy remote control is retained. So, too, is the remainder of the mechanical specification.

The big body change is to the hood which is now permanently attached instead of being arranged with detachable hood-irons and covering—all of which can be a nuisance to stow and a minor disaster in a sudden heavy shower. Furling the new hood is simply a matter of releasing it from the screen and unclipping four fasteners on the sides, when it can be folded down into a recess behind the seats. A neat cover can be buttoned in place to conceal it completely in settled weather. Erection is equally easy and weatherproofing is completed by raising the wind-up windows. An incidental added attraction of

the new hood is the fact that it has a more pleasing contour with a less abrupt angle at the rear.

With their added performance and improved weather protection, these new Sprites and Midgets should be more popular than ever in both home and overseas markets. Since the Mark I Sprite was introduced in May 1958, 160,000 Sprites and Midgets have been produced, of which 73½% (116,000) have been exported—mostly to the U.S. and Canada.

During this period, the type has steadily increased in both power and sophistication, although maintaining its basic objective of providing true sports-car motoring at minimum cost.

The original Mark I Sprite had a 948 c.c. engine and ¼-elliptic rear springs. In June 1961 the Mark II version with a much improved body was backed up by the first MG Midget version. Both types were given disc front brakes and 1,098 c.c. engines in October 1962. Then, in March 1964, a further increase in engine power (but not size) was made and winding windows were fitted, these constituting the Mark III Sprite and Mark II Midget which are now superseded and which have proved so popular as to call for the very high production rate (for sports cars) of 350 a week.

M

LEFT: *Engine has twin SU carbs, is reasonably accessible.* BELOW RIGHT: *Windows, dash are new.*

AFTER providing almost spartan motoring for soprts-car enthusiasts for something like six years, the little Austin Healey Sprite has at last had its upcomance to the ranks of the 1964 sophisticates.

It's the most comfortable, rapid and convenient Sprite so far devised— but it costs more than ever and has lost some of its character along the way.

But, of course, this is primarily a young person's car, so the number of people who are prepared to accept sidescreens and such are rapidly diminishing.

With the exception of the Lotus Super Seven—which is barely a road

SOPHISTICATED

MAIN SPECIFICATIONS

ENGINE: 4 cylinders in line o.h.v.; bore 64.6mm., stroke 83.7mm., capacity 1098c.c., compression ratio 9:1; maximum b.h.p. 59 (net) at 5750 r.p.m.; maximum torque 62ft./lb. at 3250 r.p.m.; twin S.U. carburettors, electric fuel pump, 12-volt ignition.
TRANSMISSION: Single dry-plate clutch, 4-speed gearbox with synchro on upper 3 ratios; ratios: 1st, 13.51; 2nd, 8.09; 3rd, 5.73; 4th, 4.22. Final drive, 4.22:1.
SUSPENSION: Independent front by coil springs and wishbones; live rear axle with semi-elliptic springs. Tele shockers at front, lever-arm at rear.

STEERING: Rack-and-pinion; 2¼ turns lock to lock; 31ft. 2.5in. turning circle.
BRAKES: Disc/drum, 190 sq. in. of swept area.
WHEELS: Steel disc with 5.20 by 13in. tubeless tyres.
DIMENSIONS: Wheelbase, 6ft. 8in.; track, front, 3ft. 9.75in.; rear, 3ft. 8.75in.; length, 11ft. 4.25in.; width, 4ft. 5in.; height, 4ft. 1.75in.; clearance, 5in.
FUEL CAPACITY: 6 gallons.
KERB WEIGHT: 14cwt.

PERFORMANCE ON TEST

CONDITIONS: Fine and cool, slight crosswind. Two occupants, premium fuel.
BEST SPEED: 86.7 m.p.h.
FLYING ¼-mile average: 84.2 m.p.h.
STANDING ¼-mile Average: 20.1s.
MAXIMUM in gears: 1st, 30 m.p.h.; 2nd, 50 m.p.h.; 3rd, 70 m.p.h.
ACCELERATION from rest: 0-30 m.p.h., 5.1s.; 0-40, 7.3s.; 0-50, 10.8s.; 0-60, 15.3s.; 0-70, 22.5s.

ACCELERATION in top (with third in brackets): 20-40 m.p.h., 12.1s. (6.9s.); 30-50, 11.8s. (7.1s.); 40-60, 11.6s. (7.6s.); 50-70, 14.0s. (9.9s.).
BRAKING: 31.5ft. to stop from 30 m.p.h. in neutral.
FUEL CONSUMPTION: 27.6 m.p.g over 190 miles, including all tests.
SPEEDOMETER: 2.6 m.p.h. fast at 30; 3 m.p.h. fast at 50; 5 m.p.h. fast at 70.

PRICE: £1059 including sales tax

"Best Sprite yet" is Ian Fraser's verdict after testing the more powerful Mk. III version which now has new dashboard layout and the luxury of wind-up windows

car anyway—and the Morgan, all the popular sports cars now have wind-up windows and most of the other family-car comforts.

In addition to the windows, completely revised dashboard and new rear suspension, the Mk. III also has some engine modifications which have made it stronger and more powerful by about eight percent.

There's been no significant change to the outside appearance of the car apart from the external door handles and new windscreen and quarter panels. For all intents and purposes it's the same pretty little Sprite.

As before, the car is assembled in Sydney from c.k.d. packs imported from the U.K. to which a reasonable quantity of locally-found parts and materials are added.

On the test car neither the paintwork nor the trim was particularly good inside or out, but it was no worse than previous Sprites.

The interior, nice and all as it is, comes as a bit of a shock to the eye. Everything, but everything, is black, except the seats, which are red. Somehow the seats don't seem to belong to the car; they would be much better in black, as they were in the previous models.

Cabin Comforts

Nevertheless, the seats are quite comfortably trimmed and padded, even if broadly-built people find that the bucket shape takes a pretty firm hold of them.

Both seats are fully adjustable and their squabs tilt forward to provide access to the "carry-anything-that's-not-too-big" platform in the back.

When only the driver was aboard the passenger-seat squab rattled un-

SPRITE

modern
MOTOR
ROAD
TEST

mercifully, just as it did on the Mk. II Sprite I owned a couple of years ago.

On the subject of tilting squabs, I can hardly let the opportunity pass without mentioning that when you heave the driver's-side squab forward it comes in contact with the protruding horn button and frightens the daylights out of everyone in sight.

This sort of clottish design has been put into sports cars for so long now—including the very expensive ones—that I am beginning to wonder if this is some kind of special feature about which I have a mental block.

That motor cars are a compromise could hardly be better illustrated than by the Mk. III's doors: because they have a window-winding mechanism installed in them and it takes up their full thickness, you lose the elbow room and door pockets of the old side-curtain models. Frankly, there is not much elbow room now and although there is an odds-and-ends shelf under the dash on the passenger's side, the driver has no hope of reaching it when the car is moving.

Indeed, the passenger cannot reach it either if he is wearing a safety-belt, attachment points for which are built into the Sprite.

The entire dashboard is new and a vast improvement over the old one. There is still the same number and type of instruments, but they are disposed differently and the matching speedo and tacho—one each side of the columns — are tilted in towards the column to cut out parallex error. The oil pressure and engine temperature gauges are arranged under the one dial, and the petrol gauge, which provides ample scope for parallex error, is nearer the passenger than the driver.

There's a turn-key starter on the crackle-finish dash, a manual choke, screenwasher button and a series of unlabelled toggle switches for lights, panel and wipers. The bonnet release is under the dash on the passenger's side.

There's still no ashtray in the cabin, and in view of the serious nature of tossing cigarettes and matches out of cars during the bushfire season, the omission is unfortunate.

The rear-vision mirror adjusts up and down on the central scuttle-to-screen bracing rod and gives a good rearward coverage, even when the hood is erected.

Forward visibility is somewhat

(Continued on page 39)

JAPAN v. U.K.

A contrast
between the Honda and the Sprite

IN THE white corner, ladies and gentlemen, we have the challenger from Japan. A light, lively newcomer from the Orient full of new ideas, perhaps a bit suspect on staying power over 15 rounds. In the green corner, an old stalwart friend, rugged and agricultural maybe but with proven stamina. The British defender has put on some weight recently so this is a catchweight contest. May the best car win.

The awaited introduction of the Honda S800 sports car to the British market at Earls Court last year caused speculation out of proportion to the share of the market it might achieve. Order books were filled and deliveries began shortly after, bringing a new style of motoring to our roads. Both B.M.C. and Triumph opted at the same time to increase engine size into the 1,300-c.c. class, so that the " Spridget " and Spitfire gave slightly better performance in a lazier, more effort-free manner. In contrast, the Honda engine gives 70 b.h.p. (gross) from 800 c.c., the highest power/capacity ratio of any car offered to the public in volume sale.

At a quick glance there is little difference between the Honda and Sprite, though the Japanese car is 6 in. shorter. Neither car will carry a decent-sized suitcase in the boot, though both have a fair amount of space behind the seats. The Honda's boot stays open automatically, and the 7¾-gallon fuel tank is situated forward (with the spare wheel under the floor), giving an uninterrupted space of 49 in. wide, 12 in. deep and 15 in. front-to-back, a capacity of 6.1 cu. ft. The Sprite, which we also drove for comparison, does not have an automatic stay on the boot. The luggage area is badly planned, with the spare wheel in the centre, a sloping rear wall, and a petrol filler pipe impeding the space, so that it is much more a soft-baggage compartment measuring 42 in. by 6 in. by 24 in., a capacity of 4.2 cu. ft.

The Honda's engine is the talking-point, being an all-alloy three-roller-bearing 2-o.h.c. unit fed by two twin-choke Keihin carburetters. Surprisingly it is an under-square unit with 60-mm. bore and 70-mm. stroke, giving a 4-cylinder capacity of 791 c.c. Also surprising is the fact that the compression ratio has been kept down to 9.2, so that, with the heat-dispersant qualities of the alloy head, commercial grade fuel can be used.

The seats in the Japanese car are rather firm, while providing good support, and the suspension on our test car was also firm. Various types of independent rear suspension were tried during development but the car is in production with a rigid axle, twin trailing radius arms and a transverse linkage bar, while front suspension is effected by wishbones and longitudinal torsion bars. The result is firm suspension, harsh over rough roads, and our test car at least was rather uncomfortable at low speed on average roads. There is an unwelcome amount of feed-back through the rack-and-pinion steering, noticed even at high speed.

On the credit side, the handling is very good indeed. There is practically no roll at all and the Honda is directionally stable, understeering slightly. The brakes are superb, the gearbox ratios well chosen and quick to select.

Although there is a distinct shortage of torque from the engine the ultra-low axle ratio (4.71), giving 11.8 m.p.h. per 1,000 r.p.m. in top gear, ensures clean pick-up at low speed, and the car will pull smoothly from as little as 2,000 r.p.m. in high gear. However, maximum power is developed at 8,000 r.p.m. so the driver in a hurry is well rewarded by using the gearbox freely and keeping the engine turning above 6,000 r.p.m., the peak of the rather meagre torque curve.

Though not excessively noisy, the sound of a peak-revving engine is bound to make heads turn and one cannot use full performance just anywhere. On the open road, the Honda is a joy for any sportsman, exceptionally well mannered in every department concerning safety, with the sole proviso that, needing 6,000 r.p.m. to cruise at 70 m.p.h., it is necessarily the more tiring on a long journey.

Renewed acquaintance with the Sprite was a marked contrast. The seats are much more softly padded but gave less lateral support when cornering. The steering wheel is too close to the body, although both cars had plenty of leg-room for a six-footer. Steering is a bit heavier but more direct, and in a straight line the ride is certainly more comfortable.

It was strange to return to the antique wide-ratio gearbox, still with no synchromesh on 1st, though light and quick in action. This is a much more beefy engine, however, a detuned version of the 1275S unit, delivering substantial torque at 3,000 r.p.m. and 65 b.h.p. (net) at 6,000 r.p.m. (the limit of the orange sector on the tachometer). Fed with 4-star petrol it returns about 30 m.p.g., so the running costs between the two cars are quite comparable.

While the cart-springs give a good ride, the handling of the car is unsophisticated. On good roads the Sprite settles down into an understeering state with roll-oversteer threatening but predictable, and bumps will unsettle the car more than somewhat without endangering control. The brakes are excellent, and generally the car feels rugged, reliable, and perhaps not very exciting. Other points which come to mind are the inwardly-angled dials (all the latest features from Maranello here!) and the inadequate fuel range with the 6-gallon tank. The axle ratio gives approximately 14.7 m.p.h. per 1,000 r.p.m., so that 4,800 r.p.m. are showing at 70 m.p.h. There is a fairly loud, muffled exhaust note to the Sprite, of which the driver may be blissfully unaware when the hood is raised.

Contrary to appearance, the Sprite is the lighter car (1,510 lb. " dry " compared with 1,556 lb.). The Sprite costs £672 in Britain, plus £15 for the optional heater, and surely the car deserves something better than the squeaky Dunlop Gold Seal tyres, which do nothing for the handling, even though it is the cheapest model of its type?

The Longbridge product suffers rather less from wind noise at speed when the hood is erected, and would be the car we should choose for a long journey, especially on the Continent. It takes 50 seconds to put the hood down, or about two minutes including the time taken to fix the neat cover, and one minute 20 seconds to put the hood up. The two catches on the windscreen rail did not line up properly, or this time could have been reduced.

Costing £779, the Honda is well-equipped, including a heater and Dunlop SP3 tyres. The fuel tank capacity gives it a just-adequate range. Like the Sprite, it needs servicing every 3,000 miles, but there are less greasing points. Obviously it accelerates better, reaching 60 m.p.h. in less than 14 seconds, whereas the Sprite takes about a second longer, but there is little difference in the top speeds. It takes 38 seconds to lower the hood and 45 seconds to erect it.

If the £100 price differential were spent on making the Sprite go faster and handle better, it would be a thoroughly potent machine, but still the character would be different. With its remarkable little engine the Honda is bound to appeal to sportsmen, especially those with the opportunity to drive fast without being detected, so the choice is a straight one between innovation and tradition.—M. L. C.

TRAPPER TRAPPED !

The *Rugby Advertiser* reports that a policeman set off to Overslade intent on trapping drivers by radar. The first householder whom he approached about setting up his apparatus in the drive to the house refused permission. In backing the Police Morris Traveller out onto the road to try his luck at the next house the policeman hit an on-coming Mini. The motorcycle police patrol, presumably waiting to take part in the trapping, did not help by parking opposite. The police driver was fined £10 by Rugby Court and had to pay £5 5s. towards an advocate's fee.

A letter has been received congratulating the Essex constabulary on their keen observation and efficiency. The correspondent's M.G. Midget was travelling along A127 with its bonnet insecurely fastened early one Saturday morning. He noticed this and stopped in a lay-by to fix it, before resuming a 70 m.p.h. cruising pace. At the Halfway House roundabout he was halted by one of the crew of a patrol car, who pressed down on the bonnet. Another police car had noticed it flapping and radioed back to have the driver told about it. So one sports-car driver went on his way with a good opinion of the helpfulness of the police in this area.

Bucks County Constabulary are to include advice to purchasers of cars in their county on how to prevent them from being stolen (1,272 were stolen in Bucks alone, last year). With the co-operation of dealers they will include in the car's papers a personal letter from the Acting Chief Constable and a " Bucks Constabulary " envelope containing pamphlets on Crime Prevention and on locks and alarm systems for vehicles. The County Crime Prevention Officer, Inspector L. Bishop, telephone Aylesbury 5010, ext. 113, will give additional advice. The Chief Constable of Bucks has previously taken a realistic view of motorists' problems, preferring his patrols to caution rather than convict, and so there is every chance of something useful coming out of the present campaign.

MOTOR ROAD TEST No 30/67 ● Austin Healey Sprite Mk IV

Sprightlier still

''. . . useful increase in both acceleration and tractability . . . so controllable . . . excellent gearbox . . . new folding hood not flap-free at 70 m.p.h. . . .''

PERHAPS it is because *Motor* has tested only two soft-topped cars in the past two years that we too have become a bit soft; our diet of modern, comfortable, if not always quiet, saloons and GTs has made some of us think that the better modern sports cars are those with a roof, and particularly with a sunshine roof. How nice then to be able to record that during our tenure of the Sprite, its hood was down more often than not, a tribute both to the enjoyment of open-top driving and to the British summer which is not as anti-open motoring as one might think.

Pottering round the countryside in the fresh air is just one of the delights of Sprite motoring; it gets a bit draughty over 60 m.p.h. and it helps to wear a scarf, but unless you want to do a continuous 60-plus on a motorway, say, it is not much more tiring than a hard top car. With the new folding hood erect, draughts are exchanged for noise at the same cruising speeds, as the hood is not tensioned sufficiently for a flap-free 70 m.p.h. Most people in the open car market will put up with its disadvantages quite readily as part of the appeal; less hardy passengers might well get rather bored on long journeys with the difficulties of conversation and radio listening.

The latest Sprite, the Mk. IV, has the new 1,275 c.c. engine which gives a useful increase in both acceleration and tractability without affecting fuel consumption. A maximum speed of 95 m.p.h. and a consumption better than 30 m.p.g. is more than most can

PRICE: £545 plus £126 12s. 4d. equals £671 12s. 4d. As tested, including heater, tonneau cover and flasher, total equals £694 19s. 5d.

offer particularly at that price. Its roadholding is quite good if not exceptional; it is more the way you can use all its reserves because it is so controllable that endears it to a sporting driver. The available performance is easily used and with the excellent gearbox one can maintain consistently high cross country speeds, nipping safely past any obstructions that present themselves.

For the price, one can perhaps forgive the occasional draughts and dribbles of water which come through the poorly fitting window-to-hood seals and perhaps even the continued tendency for the carpets to get wet through the floor, but not the need to open the bonnet to adjust the water valve for the heater which is an extra anyway. Although the high scuttle is beginning to feel a little dated, we all thoroughly enjoyed driving this safe little sports car—still a happy Sprite and good value too.

Performance and economy

When it was announced that the engines for the Sprite and Midget were to be increased to 1,275 c.c., a capacity used only in the Mini Cooper S at that time, we expected quite a step forward in performance from the previous 1,098 c.c. unit. However, the S engine is more specialized and expensive to produce, so it was logical to de-rate the unit and use less extravagant design and materials for the greater quantity production of Sprites and subsequently for the more expensive 1100s. In its twin carburetter form, the engine produces 65 b.h.p. at 6,000 r.p.m. against 59 at 5,750 for the 1,098 c.c. The improvement in torque is more impressive—72 lb.ft. at 3,000 r.p.m. against 62 at 3,250; this is reflec-

Austin Healey Sprite Mk IV
continued

ted in the better top gear acceleration with 40–60 m.p.h. in 10.2 sec. instead of 11.7 being the most obvious to a driver; it is surprising how quickly 60 m.p.h. comes up without any effort.

A yellow sector on the rev counter runs from 5,500 to the 6,300 r.p.m. start of the red where we changed gear during our acceleration tests. Apart from a harsh note at 4,500 r.p.m. there is little mechanical excitement to betray engine speed until it reaches peak revs—you need to watch the rev counter in first and second.

Cold starting has been instant in the recent mild weather with only half choke needed for the first half mile or so; with the usual BMC SU carburetter layout we can safely say that starting in cold weather should be just as good but with more choke. It needs nearer two miles before the temperature gauge is up to its normal reading, but there is no hesitation during this period.

We tried 4-star petrol in view of the 8.8:1 compression ratio but the engine pinked when accelerating hard from under 20 m.p.h. (possibly aggravated by the loss of the vacuum advance mechanism on this model) and occasionally ran on after town driving, so we had to use 5-star fuel. Consumption is very good for the hard driving that the Sprite inspired and 30.8 m.p.g. overall is better than the smaller unit managed. Quieter drivers may well get nearer 35 m.p.g.

Transmission

If only big brother B had the same gear ratios as those in the Sprite. It is one of the best four-speed sets in production; the ratios are well-spaced for the power, giving a useful 50 m.p.h. in second gear and seem to be well-chosen to give a really smooth change

Performance

Performance tests carried out by *Motor's* **staff at the Motor Industry Research Association proving ground, Lindley.**

Test Data: World copyright reserved; no unauthorized reproduction in whole or in part.

Conditions

Weather: Light winds up to 12 m.p.h. with occasional gusts to 20 m.p.h.
Temperature 60°-68°F. Barometer 29.42 in. Hg.
Surface: Dry concrete and tarmacadam.
Fuel: 4-star 99 octane (RM).

Maximum speeds

	m.p.h.
Mean lap banked circuit	95.1
Best one-way ¼-mile	100.0
3rd gear	68.5
2nd gear } at 6,000 r.p.m.	48.5
1st gear	29

"Maximile" speed: (Timed quarter mile after 1 mile accelerating from rest)

Mean	84.1
Best	87.4

Acceleration times

m.p.h.	sec.
0-30	4.2
0-40	6.4
0-50	9.2
0-60	13.0
0-70	19.1
0-80	27.8
Standing quarter mile	19.1

m.p.h.	Top sec.	3rd sec.
10-30	—	7.2
20-40	9.8	6.6
30-50	10.1	7.0
40-60	10.2	7.9
50-70	12.0	10.2
60-80	17.9	—

Hill climbing

At steady speed		lb./ton
Top	1 in 9.3	(Tapley 240)
3rd	1 in 6.1	(Tapley 360)
2nd	1 in 4.4	(Tapley 500)

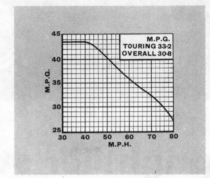

M.P.G. TOURING 33·2 OVERALL 30·8

Fuel consumption

Touring (consumption midway between 30 m.p.h. and maximum less 5% allowance for acceleration) .... 33.2 m.p.g.
Overall .... 30.8 m.p.g.
(= 9.17 litres/100 km.)
Total test figure .... 1,360 miles
Tank capacity (maker's figure) ..... 6 gal.

Brakes

Pedal pressure, deceleration and equivalent stopping distance from 30 m.p.h.

lb.	g	ft.
25	0.29	103
50	0.52	57½
75	0.77	39
100	0.96	31
Handbrake	0.41	73

Fade test

20 stops at ½g deceleration at 1 min. intervals from a speed midway between 30 m.p.h. and maximum speed (= 62.5 m.p.h.)

	lb.
Pedal force at beginning	43
Pedal force at 10th stop	45
Pedal force at 20th stop	45

Steering

Turning circle between kerbs:	ft.
Left	31½
Right	32
Turns of steering wheel from lock to lock	2¼

Steering wheel deflection for 50 ft. diameter circle .... 0.7 turns

Clutch

Free pedal movement = ¾ in.
Additional movement to disengage clutch completely = 2¼ in.
Maximum pedal load = 32 lb.

Speedometer

Indicated	10	20	30	40	50	60	70	80
True	10	19	28	37½	47	56½	66	76

Distance recorder .... accurate

Weight

Kerb weight (unladen with fuel for approximately 50 miles) .... 13.9 cwt.
Front/rear distribution 54½/45½
Weight laden as tested .... 17.7 cwt.

Parkability

Gap needed to clear a 6ft. wide obstruction parked in front:

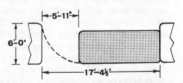

5'-11"
6'-0"
17'-4½"

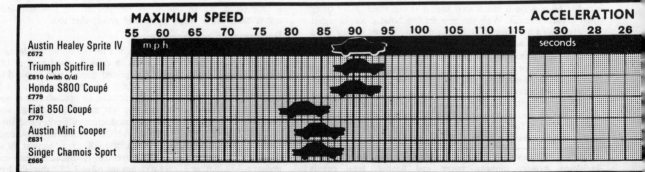

	MAXIMUM SPEED	ACCELERATION
	55 60 65 70 75 80 85 90 95 100 105 110 115	30 28 26
Austin Healey Sprite IV £672	m.p.h.	seconds
Triumph Spitfire III £810 (with O/d)		
Honda S800 Coupé £779		
Fiat 850 Coupé £770		
Austin Mini Cooper £631		
Singer Chamois Sport £665		

Neat hood bag (above) tucks the folded hood out of sight. Previous Sprites have had completely removable hoods. Lap and diagonal belt is well placed.

Tonneau cover (left) is held taut by the rail whose outline can be seen; the folded half is attached to press studs behind the seat. The seat belt emerges through the unzipped slot as shown.

Seat rake is adjusted by bolts screwed into the base of the back rest; we removed them altogether and found the angle comfortable.

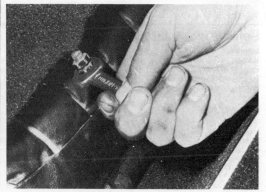

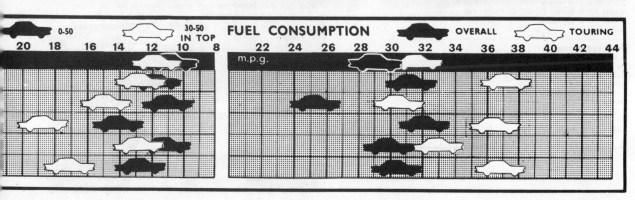

FUEL CONSUMPTION

MOTOR week ending September 9 1967

Only the chrome strip at the base of the hood identifies the 1,275 c.c. Mark IV. Good hood "glass" stays clean and uncreased if you follow folding instructions; no blind spots.

Austin Healey Sprite Mk IV
continued

however fast you move hands and feet, but the faster the better. The lever is in just the right place and the movement sufficiently short to stay well placed whatever the gear; before familiarity eases the situation, it is quite easy to nudge against first gear, particularly when moving through second to top. Despite the lack of synchromesh on first it needs only a not-too-accurate double de-clutch for noiseless engagement on the move. Good bottom end torque makes second a very adequate bottom gear unless the car is actually stationary.

At rest it pays to pull the lever back against second gear synchromesh before selecting first. Bottom gear whines a bit, but the box is quiet in the other ratios. The back axle is less so; it whines gently at low speed on light throttle openings and rumbles distantly at speeds over 80 m.p.h. The 4.22:1 ratio is retained in the 1,275s but it might have been nicer to raise it to a 3.9, say, and drop the top gear revs from the 5,200 r.p.m. at 70 m.p.h. However, this might make it impossible to start on the 1 in 3 hill which it just manages on the 4.22, so one has to accept the compromise.

Safety Check List

Steering assembly

Steering box position	Ahead of engine under radiator
Steering column collapsible	No
Steering wheel boss padded	No
Steering wheel dished	No

Instrument panel

Projecting switches	Yes
Sharp cowls	Not accessible
Effective padding	Above facia and on parcel shelf

Windscreen and visibility

Screen type	Zone toughened (laminated optional)
Pillars padded	No
Standard driving mirrors	Interior only
Interior mirror framed	Yes
Interior mirror collapsible	No
Sun visors	None

Seats and harness

Attachment to floor	Sliding runners
Do they tip forward?	Yes
Head rest attachment points	No
Safety harness	Lap and diagonal

Doors

Projecting handles	Window winder well forward
Anti-burst latches	Yes
Child-proof locks	Only two seats

Handling and brakes

Standards have changed in the nine years that the Sprite has been with us, but the design has changed too and kept up with modern handling levels even if it is not as relatively outstanding as it was in 1958. The quarter elliptic rear spring layout with no additional side location was changed to semi-elliptics in 1964 with the introduction of the Sprite III, and the entry into a corner became less of a lurch in consequence. Handling now is neutral for most of the driving that you will do on the roads; it eventually oversteers, but it can be provoked earlier either by using power at low speeds or by bumps exciting the live axle.

You can use this final oversteer to advantage if you find you are cornering too fast or if you meet an emergency in the middle. If you deliberately flick the steering wheel or put the brakes on, the tail comes gently out in a tyre-scrubbing drift which can be caught instantly on the high geared steering. If you just ease the throttle the same happens but not as drastically as on a Mini or 1100. The test car was fitted with the standard cross ply Dunlop C41s whose progressive breakaway characteristics allow this sort of indulgence; radials would improve the cornering power but might also make the oversteer situations more sudden. The C41s give good grip but squeal unnecessarily particularly on fine surfaces even with only a $\frac{1}{2}$g stop. On wet roads they still grip well although power oversteer is that much more likely. High geared steering requires little arm movement for correction and

You need a spanner if you want to change the height of the mirror, which slides on the screen bracing wire.

The left-hand pile (2.6 cu. ft.) fits into the boot and the right-hand (1.8 cu. ft) will sit behind the seats without getting in the way. Sticks on the left are for the tonneau rail.

with only 3° castor on a light motor car little effort is required; it is almost too light and a bit vague in the straight ahead position as it is difficult to sense front end breakaway in the wet, but for the majority of driving the gearing and effort is very satisfactory.

Our brake fade test produced no apparent loss of efficiency, just a smell of lining at each of the later stops. The pressures required are average and progressive with each 10 lb. producing an additional 0.1g retardation up to a maximum of 0.96g at 100 lb. In each of our two trips through the water splash, about 8 inches deep at 10–15 m.p.h., the engine died and we had to motor out on the starter, so the brakes (and the carpets) got a good soaking. However, after three ½g stops the pressures required were back to normal, having risen about 20 lb. without loss of stability.

The handbrake, placed conveniently on the left side of the transmission tunnel, is light to pull, holds the car on a 1 in 3 hill and gives a useful emergency stop at 0.41g with the rear wheels locked.

Comfort and controls

Fairly stiff and simple suspension gives a ride which is firm by modern standards but which would have been considered unusually soft in the Mk. I Sprite era. The car follows the road surface fairly faithfully without the sharper bumps being unpleasantly jerking; good seats help no doubt. On some of the worse surfaces the live axle will hop even in a straight line, but never enough to require more correction than a slight flexing of the fingers.

One of the most dated features is the driving position; for all but six-footers the steering wheel gets silhouetted against the road

Continued on the next page

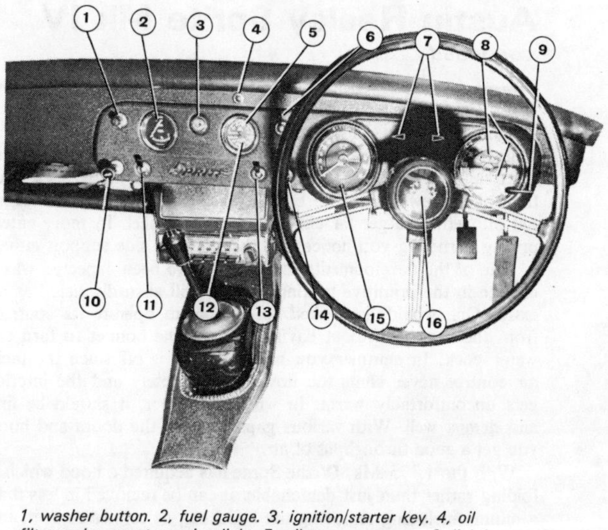

1
2
3
4
5
6
7
8
9
10
11
12
13
14
15
16

1, washer button. 2, fuel gauge. 3, ignition/starter key. 4, oil filter replacement warning light. 5, oil pressure gauge. 6, lighting switch. 7, indicator tell-tales. 8, trip and total mileage recorders. 9, direction indicator stalk with optional flasher. 10, choke. 11, wiper switch. 12, water temperature gauge. 13, panel light switch. 14, fresh air volume control. 15, dynamo warning light, 16, horn.

Specification

Engine

Cylinders	4
Bore and stroke	70.61 mm. x 81.28 mm.
Cubic capacity	1,275 c.c.
Valves	Pushrod o.h.v.
Compression ratio	8.8:1
Carburetters	Twin SU HS2
Fuel pump	SU electric
Oil filter	Purolator full flow
Max. power (net)	64 b.h.p. at 5,800 r.p.m.
Max. torque (net)	72 lb. ft. at 3,000 r.p.m.

Transmission

Clutch	Borg and Beck 6½ in. dia. s.d.p. diaphragm spring
Top gear (s/m)	1.0
3rd gear (s/m)	1.357
2nd gear (s/m)	1.916
1st gear	3.200
Reverse	4.120
Final drive	Hypoid bevel 9/38-4.22:1
M.p.h. at 1,000 r.p.m. in:—	
Top gear	15.5
3rd gear	11.4
2nd gear	8.1
1st gear	4.8

Chassis

Construction	Unitary

Brakes

Type	Lockheed hydraulic disc/drum
Dimensions	8.25 in. dia. discs, 7 in. dia. drums
Friction areas:	
Front:	18 sq. in. of lining operating on 135¼ sq. in. of disc
Rear:	33.4 sq. in. of lining operating on 55 sq. in. of drum

Suspension and steering

Front	Independent; twin transverse wishbones and coil springs
Rear	Live axle; semi elliptic leaf springs
Shock absorbers:	
Front:	Armstrong lever arm
Rear:	
Steering gear	Cam gears rack and pinion
Tyres	Dunlop C41 5.20-13 Dunlop SP41 145-13 (optional)
Rim size	3.50D-13 4J-13 (optional wire wheels)

Coachwork and equipment

Starting handle	None
Jack	Side lift type
Jacking points	One in each door sill
Battery	12 volt positive earth 43 amp hrs capacity
Number of electrical fuses	2
Indicators	Self cancelling flashers
Screen wipers	Lucas single speed electric
Screen washers	Tudor manual plunger
Sun visors	None
Locks:	
With ignition key	Both doors
With other keys	Boot
Interior heater	Optional Smiths fresh air
Extras	Hard top (£61 9s), Tonneau cover and rail (£7 7s), Heater (£14 15s), Wire wheels (£30 15s), Headlamp flasher (£1 5s), Anti-roll bar (£2 9s), Oil cooler (£8), Laminated screen (£4 18s)
Upholstery	Leathercloth
Floor covering	Carpets
Alternative body styles	None

Maintenance

Sump	6½ pints SAE 10W/30
Gearbox	2¼ pints SAE 10W/30
Rear axle	1½ pints SAE 90
Steering gear	SAE 90
Cooling system	10 pints (drain taps 2)
Chassis lubrication	Every 3,000 miles to 10 points
Minimum service interval	3,000
Ignition timing	7° b.t.d.c.
Contact breaker gap	0.015 in.
Sparking plug gap	0.025 in.
Sparking plug type	Champion UN 12 Y
Tappet clearances (cold)	Inlet 0.012 in.; Exhaust 0.012 in.
Valve timing:	
Inlet opens	5° b.t.d.c.
Inlet closes	45° a.b.d.c.
Exhaust opens	51° b.b.d.c.
Exhaust closes	21° a.t.d.c.
Front wheel toe-in	0-⅛ in.
Camber angle	¾°
Castor angle	3°
King pin inclination	6¾°

Tyre pressures:

	Standard	High speed
Front:	18 p.s.i.	22 p.s.i.
Rear:	20 p.s.i.	24 p.s.i.

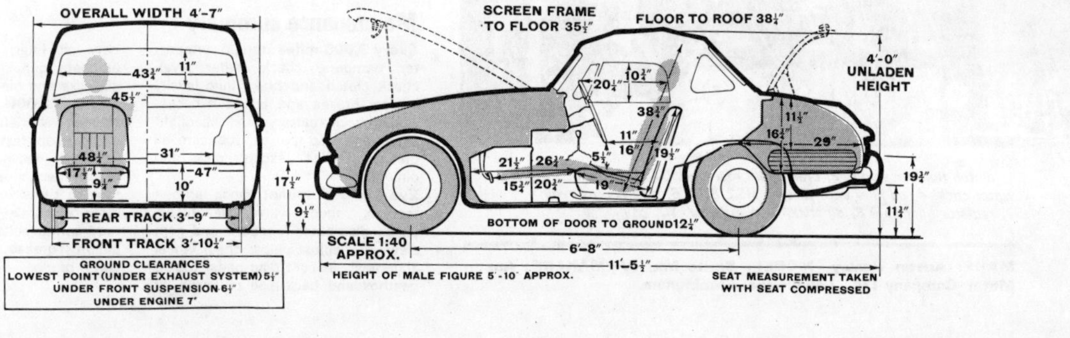

OVERALL WIDTH 4′-7″
43¾″
11″
45½″
48¼″
31″
17½″
9¼″
47″
10″
REAR TRACK 3′-9″
FRONT TRACK 3′-10¼″
GROUND CLEARANCES
LOWEST POINT (UNDER EXHAUST SYSTEM) 5½″
UNDER FRONT SUSPENSION 6½″
UNDER ENGINE 7″
SCREEN FRAME TO FLOOR 35½″
FLOOR TO ROOF 38¼″
4′-0″ UNLADEN HEIGHT
10¾″
20¼″
38¾″
11″
16″
19½″
5½″
21½″
26¼″
15¾″
20¾″
19″
11½″
16¼″
29″
17½″
9½″
19¾″
11¾″
BOTTOM OF DOOR TO GROUND 12¼″
SCALE 1:40 APPROX.
6′-8″
11′-5½″
HEIGHT OF MALE FIGURE 5′-10″ APPROX.
SEAT MEASUREMENT TAKEN WITH SEAT COMPRESSED

Austin Healey Sprite Mk IV
continued

surface and the scuttle height gives a slightly hemmed-in feeling. The seat doesn't go back very far since it comes up against the axle arch and taller drivers have to rake it right back with the bolts screwed into the base of the back rest; we took them out altogether to get far enough from the wheel. In more enterprising cornering you notice that there is little side support either.

One of the developments that might have been expected was a change in the primitive heating system, still absurdly listed as an extra. One would have liked to be able to operate its controls from the cockpit without having to open the bonnet to turn the water cock. In summer you have to leave it off since the facia air control never shuts the flow off completely and the interior gets uncomfortably warm. In winter, however, it should be fine and demist well. With various gaps between the doors and hood you get a good throughput of air.

With the 1,275 Mk. IV the Sprite has acquired a hood which is folding rather than just detachable. It can be removed in less than a minute including removing the hood bag or tonneau cover, and folding it takes only a little longer. If you follow the instructions, the plastic windows remain uncreased; these give good all-round visibility to the rear and no distortion in the mirror, which slides on the screen tensioning wire for height adjustment.

With a clean screen forward visibility is good, but the short wipers necessary for the shallow glass leave large areas dirty which is troublesome when the screen has dried. Night time visibility is well up to the car's performance and the foot operated dipswitch is well-placed. There is room for the left foot alongside the clutch and the brake and organ accelerator pedal are well spaced for heel and toeing.

One accepts that soft top sports cars are going to be noisier than closed ones, and the Sprite certainly is once you get over

More or less unchanged since the demise of the original bug-eyed headlights, it could be a Mark III from this view. MG Midgets have a central chrome strip on the bonnet top.

65 m.p.h. or so. The hood vibrates with the wind buffeting and at maximum speed it becomes almost unbearable—it is possible that our hood had less than usual tension. Radio volume needs a significant increase at around 60 m.p.h. but beyond that it can't compete without becoming a major distraction. With the hood down the noise is similar, but you get a draught round the back of the neck whether side windows are up or not—a scarf becomes normal open wear for anything but hot weather. But around town and country where high speed bursts are more short lived, the freedom of an open top is very pleasant; you can't have everything unless you pay more.

Fittings and furniture

The facia design in crackle-black finish is neat and simple with the speedometer and rev counter slanting inwards to the driver; other dials for water temperature combined with oil pressure and fuel level are easy to see. Although the three switches are unlabelled, they are easy to learn with the wiper switch under the washer button, and the light switch at top right with the separate panel light alongside the heater control, which brings on the fan when pushed right in and turned clockwise. A new warning light on the Mk. IV heralds the need for an oil filter change as on the 1100s.

The interior is liberally covered with well-fitting carpets, but they still seem to get wet after heavy rain—presumably up through the floor—and smell. Space in the boot has been a little restricted by the folding hood, but when down there are no hood sticks to put in the boot and you get more in than you used to. We managed to get 2.6 cu.ft. of our luggage in with space for oddments to spare against a 3.1 cu.ft. before with the hood up. There is more space behind the seats for a further 1.8 cu. ft., and a parcel shelf under the facia on the passenger's side.

Servicing and maintenance

A vestigial tool kit contains a pillar-type jack, wheel trim remover, and plug spanner, so you won't get very far with your own servicing. This is required every 3,000 miles and involves greasing ten nipples and an oil change if you are using a monograde oil. Other items at this service are simple checks on fluid levels, battery and tyre pressures; the 3,000 service is not beyond the scope of the home mechanic without his even getting very dirty. At 6,000 miles you have to check axle and gearbox levels plus a more comprehensive check on engine running gear.

Accessibility under the bonnet is good for the items you need to check regularly. **M**

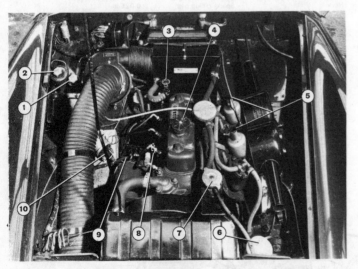

1, clutch fluid reservoir. 2, brake fluid reservoir. 3, heater temperature water cock. 4, oil filler cap. 5, twin HS2 SUs. 6, washer reservoir. 7, radiator filler cap. 8, dipstick. 9, distributor. 10, coil.

MAKE: Austin Healey. **MODEL:** Sprite Mk. IV. **MAKERS:** Austin Motor Company Ltd., Longbridge, Birmingham.

Maintenance summary

Every 3,000 miles: top up carburetter dampers, check water level, check clutch and brake fluid levels, inspect brakes and adjust if necessary, check battery and headlight alignment, top up oil, lubricate all grease nipples (except rack and pinion).

Every 6,000 miles: check fan belt tension, check valve clearances, check distributor functions and gap, clean and adjust plugs, check wheel alignment, inspect disc pads, top up gearbox and back axle oil levels, fit new oil filter, change engine oil, lubricate dynamo rear bearing and all locks and hinges.

Every 12,000 miles: fit new air cleaner elements, change engine oil filler cap, test and clean crankcase breather valve, renew sparking plugs, check steering and suspension moving parts for wear, inspect and blow-out brake drums, check rear road spring bolts, lubricate rack and pinion grease nipples, lubricate water pump.

MOTOR TESTED

Still great fun

Smooth responsive engine; flickswitch gearchange
but no synchro on first; good roadholding,
accurate light steering, predictable handling;
improved ride; poor facia layout

It's rare for *Motor's* staff to be unanimously enthusiastic about a car. But they all agreed that the latest version of the Spridget is a splendid little sports car. It is great fun to drive as well as being practical—a drawer-full of woolly vests is no longer an essential prerequisite to ownership.

The external appearance has remained substantially the same since 1961 when the squared-off lines of the Mk II replaced the oft-lamented frog-eye look of the Mk I. In 1962 the engine capacity was increased to 1098 cc, the Mk III with half, instead of quarter, elliptic rear springs was announced in 1964 and remained in production until 1966 when it was replaced by the Mk IV. This had a 1275 cc engine and a folding hood. In late 1968 BLMC slipped in a new final drive ratio without telling us; the ratio was raised from 4.22 to 3.9:1. For 1970 several detail

Price: £692 plus £213 14s. 9d. tax equals £905 14s. 9d. Extras fitted to test car: tonneau cover and rail £11 15s.; radial ply tyres £9 2s. 9d. Total as tested: £926 12s. 6d. Extras available oil cooler £13 1s. 1d.; front anti-roll bar £3 18s. 4d.; hardtop £65 5s. 7d.; wire wheels £32 12s. 9d.

improvements were made, mainly on the outside: new bumpers front and rear, a new radiator grille, black side winders, and Rostyle-type wheels. Inside reclining seats were fitted as standard. Modifications for 1971, outlined in last week's issue, include an uprated heater, cockpit improvements and stays for the bonnet and boot lids.

For its age the BLMC 1275 cc A Series engine is remarkable. With its undersquare dimensions you would expect it to pull strongly from low engine speeds—which it does, witness the 30-50 mph time in top of 9.6 sec. This compares well with the time for the last test car (with the lower final drive ratio) which took 10.1 sec. under similar test conditions. The throttle can be floored from speeds as low as 15 mph in top without the engine hesitating; it pulls so strongly that you don't need bags of revs to motor quickly. This low-speed torque is not obtained at the sacrifice of top end performance either. Our car didn't have many miles on the clock when delivered and BLMC engines tend to take a fair time to loosen up so we would expect to get slightly better times on a fully run-in example—we did 0-50 mph in 9.3 sec. whereas 9 sec. would probably be nearer par. Acceleration times are almost the same as those for the lower-ratioed sprite with the exception of that to 60 mph which is now slower (13.5 against 13.0 sec.)—with the revised final drive ratio the change from second to third now occurs between 50 and 60 mph whereas the change point used to come at just under 50 mph. Times for the standing quarter-mile are almost identical at 19.3 and 19.1 sec.

These figures put the Sprite near the top of the acceleration tables for small sports cars; only the Ginetta G15, with its Imp engine, is fractionally quicker at 8.9 sec. The Cooper S on the other hand, with its very special 1275 engine, does 0-50 mph in 7.7 sec. Round a full lap of the MIRA banked circuit the Sprite did a creditable 95 mph with the tachometer hovering in the orange sector at 5750 rpm. The engine is delightfully smooth at the top end, belying its undersquare dimensions, so you have to keep a watchful eye on the tachometer needle when really pressing on. But for most situations 5500 rpm, the start of the "orange" is sufficient.

We achieved fractionally over 30 mpg over a limited test mileage so owners who drive the car in anger should get around that figure and those who drive more gently should record nearer our

touring figure of 36.3 mpg; with a six-gallon tank this gives 210 miles. The engine is not only very smooth, but also surprisingly quiet. Some drivers thought the exhaust was too quiet, even quieter than that fitted to most saloons. The Sprite exhaust system has received some attention since our last test with a final silencer clearly visible *across* the tail of the car.

With the hood down (it's very easy to lower and erect) 70 mph is a fairly relaxed cruising speed as mechanical noises are lost to the atmosphere and there's only wind roar around the screen pillars to disturb things—with the side windows up there's not much buffeting either. Put the hood up and there is a lot of whistling noise particularly round the side windows. In some conditions the panel above the rear window flapped though on the whole the fabric is very taut. The hood itself is draught-free and waterproof. Visibility is good (though the screen is rather shallow), including the rear three-quarters view, often a problem with soft tops. The general cacophony with the hood up is further heightened by strident whines from the transmission, particularly in the indirect gears. The back axle on our car whined and groaned a bit, too, but we think this is

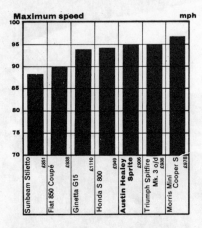

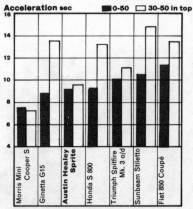

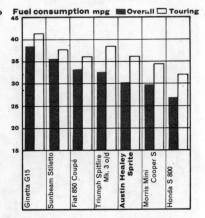

Performance tests carried out by *Motor's* staff at the Motor Industry Research Association proving ground, Lindley.

Test Data: World copyright reserved; no unauthorized reproduction in whole or in part.

Conditions

Weather: Dry and sunny; wind 4-11 mph
Temperature 58.5-62 °F.
Barometer: 29.95 in Hg.
Surface: Dry tarmacadam
Fuel: Premium 98 octane (RM) 4 Star rating

Maximum Speeds

	mph	kph
Mean lap banked circuit	95.0	153.0
Best one-way ¼-mile	96.8	156.0
3rd gear	73	118
2nd gear } at 6000 rpm	52	84
1st gear	31	50

"Maximile" speed: (Timed quarter mile after 1 mile accelerating from rest)

Mean	94.7
Best	96.8

Acceleration Times

mph	sec
0-30	4.0
0-40	6.5
0-50	9.3
0-60	13.5
0-70	19.1
0-80	28.5
0-90	45.7
Standing quarter mile	19.3
Standing Kilometer	36.2

mph	Top sec	3rd sec
10-30	—	7.1
20-40	9.9	6.8
30-50	9.6	6.8
40-60	9.8	7.4
50-70	11.7	9.4
60-80	16.0	

Fuel Consumption

Touring (consumption midway between 30 mph and maximum less 5 per cent allowance for acceleration)

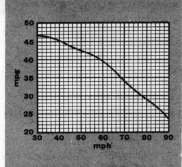

Overall	36.3 mpg
	30.2 mpg
(=9.37 litres/100km) Total test distance	673 miles
Fuel tank capacity	6 gallons

Speedometer

Indicated	10	20	30	40	50	60	70
True	9.5	19	28.5	38	47.5	57	66
			80	90			
			74.5	83.5			

Distance recorder 1.5% fast

Weight

Kerb weight (unladen with fuel for approximately 50 miles)
	13.9 cwt
Front/rear distribution	54½/45½
Weight laden as tested	17.7 cwt

Engine

Block material	Cast iron
Head material	Cast iron
Cylinders	4 in-line
Cooling system	Water; pump, fan and thermostat
Bore and stroke	70.61mm. (2.78in.) 81.28mm. (3.2in.)
Cubic capacity	1275 cc (77.8 cu. in.)

Main bearings	3
Valves	Pushrod operated ohv
Compression ratio	8.8:1
Carburetters	Twin SU HS2
Fuel pump	Electric; SU AUF206
Oil Filter	Purolator full flow
Max. power (net)	64 bhp at 5800 rpm
Max. torque (net)	72 lb.ft. at 3000 rpm

Transmission

Clutch	Borg and Beck 6½in dia sdp diaphragm sprung

Internal gearbox ratios
Top gear	1.000
3rd gear	1.357
2nd gear	1.916
1st gear	3.200
Reverse	4.140
Synchromesh	On 2, 3, 4
Final drive	Hypoid bevel 3.9:1

Mph at 1000 rpm in:
Top gear	16.5
3rd gear	12.2
2nd gear	8.62
1st gear	5.15

Chassis and body

Construction	Unitary

Brakes

Type	Lockheed hydraulic disc lining/drum
Dimensions	8.25in. dia disc, 7in. dia drum

Friction areas:
Front	18 sq. in. of disc operating on 135½ sq. in. of disc
Rear	33.4 sq. in. of lining operating on 55 sq. in. of drum

Suspension and steering

Front	Independent; twin transverse wishbones and coil springs
Rear	Live axle; half elliptic leaf springs

Shock absorbers:
Front	} Armstrong lever arm
Rear	
Steering type	Rack and pinion
Tyres	Michelin ZX 145SR13
Wheels	Pressed spoke
Rim size	4½J

untypical. We would be prepared to overlook many shortcomings in the transmission for the excellent change, possibly the quickest and most positive you can get. There's still no synchromesh on first but you don't have to be a demon double de-clutcher to get it in without a crunch; and it's not needed very often on the move anyway as the engine pulls so well from low revs in second. The ratios are well spaced with third good for 73 mph at 6000 rpm, just 250 rpm under the limit.

Although there are no changes to the suspension we thought the ride of this car much improved. Opinions on how best to label it varied from well-damped but bouncy to well-rounded but wooden. It's firm but certainly not jarring like that of early examples of the marque; over most surfaces it soaks up irregularities with ease. Round bumpy corners, though, the Sprite can be thrown off line (a penalty of stiff springs and low weight) but it catches itself very quickly. On smooth corners the cornering powers are high; our Sprite was fitted with Michelin ZX radial tyres on the new and very handsome wheels. (Why should anyone want to fit wire wheels which are heavier, weaker, and brutes to clean?) Under power the car understeers mildly, though oversteer can be induced under power; on a semi-trailing throttle gentle oversteer sets in at the limit. The optional front

anti-roll bar was not fitted to our test car; this would promote more understeer and perhaps make the car even safer in inexperienced hands. Even without it you would have to be very foolish or unlucky to get into trouble.

The steering is very light and responsive and provides good feel—the driver can sense how close to the limit are the front wheels. We would prefer a smaller steering wheel as the driver's right elbow tends to come too close to the door panel—two inches less diameter would be ideal. The leather rim is pleasant to grip, though.

With its full complement of improvements the Sprite is now comprehensively equipped. The driving position is still rather cramped but if you slide the seat forward more than you otherwise might the backrest can be reclined to get a reasonable straight arm position. The seats are very comfortable but not very strong on lateral support. All the switches, which are haphazardly strewn across the facia, are within easy reach but you still have to get under the bonnet to regulate the heater hot water valve. The output is tremendous. Other recently added amenities are an ash tray on the transmission tunnel (at last BLMC have realized that some sports car owners smoke), a courtesy light under the facia, and a further light in the boot.

The snug, simple cockpit is quite comfortable. Although the seat does not go back far, you can lean back into an extended arm position, below

The small boot is already partly filled by the spare wheel and tools. It now has an automatic light and a stay to hold the lid open

AUSTIN-HEALEY SPRITE/MG MIDGET, 1958-1970

Good handling and simplified design characterize these inexpensive sports cars

BY THOS L. BRYANT

FORMER R&T PUBLISHER John Bond once wrote, "To be successfully manufactured and sold, for minimum price, a car has to be of utmost simplicity in order to keep manufacturing costs low. Sports cars will never sell in the same quantity as family-type cars, so the argument that a sports car can sell as cheaply as a VW is not entirely valid" ("Miscellaneous Ramblings," July 1958). John was discussing the introduction of the new Austin-Healey Sprite, announced in May 1958 and destined to be as successful in its own way as the medium-size Austin-Healey 100 and 3000.

In the flush of success with the Big Healeys, Donald Healey decided to produce a smaller, more economical sporting car in the least expensive price range. As with the Big Healey, he based the Sprite on an existing sedan, the Austin A35, from which he took the 948-cc overhead valve 4-cylinder engine. This unit was slightly tuned for the Sprite with twin SU carburetors, special valve springs, improved exhaust valves and modified crankshaft bearings. This small displacement engine put out 48 bhp at 5000 rpm and 52 lb-ft of torque at 3300 rpm.

A 6-in. single dry-plate clutch connected the engine to a 4-speed manual gearbox with synchromesh on 2nd, 3rd and 4th. Ratios were 3.63 for 1st, 2.37 for 2nd, 1.41 for 3rd and 1.00:1 in 4th. The rear axle ratio was 4.22:1.

The rack-and-pinion steering system went from lock to lock in just 2.3 turns, giving the car very quick steering that took some getting used to initially. In our first road test of a Sprite (August 1958) we said, "In fact, the steering is nearly perfect for the purpose, and light and accurate besides."

The front suspension was also taken from the Austin A35 and consisted of lower A-arms and coil springs with lever-type hydraulic damper arms providing the upper suspension link. The solid rear axle was located by quarter-elliptic springs and lever-type shock absorbers. The Sprite came with 7-in. diameter drum brakes and 13 x 3½-in. steel wheels shod with 5.20-13 bias-ply tires at all four corners. This all worked quite well and cornering characteristics were close to neutral with a small amount of understeer at moderate speeds. It was very difficult to get the rear end to break loose and when it did it could be controlled quite easily.

While all of the drivetrain components and underpinnings were very conventional, the Sprite body was uniquely odd in appearance—so much so, in fact, that after awhile it began to look rather attractive! This apparent contradiction struck most of us in those early Sprite days as most of the motoring journals of the time had unkind remarks for the shape and design of the car. Soon, the bulging headlights and smiling grille were characterized as giving the Sprite a frog-like appearance and it became known as the frog-eye or Bugeye Sprite. Originally, Donald Healey's design had called for retractable headlights but when BMC actually began producing the car, this design was deemed too expensive and they were left perched in the middle of the hood.

The body of the car was a pressed steel shell and the entire

or perhaps tertiary importance.

The Sprite carved a new niche for itself in the sports car world, offering superior and economical performance for a price comparable to the least expensive sedans of the day. Almost immediately, Sprites began to appear at sports car races all over the world and soon dominated H production racing in the U.S. Who could ever forget those days of the late Fifties and early Sixties when a gaggle of the little cars would take off sounding for all the world like a horde of angry bees chasing a hive-robbing bear! Not only did club racers turn to the Sprite; such big names as Stirling Moss, Walt Hangsen, Bruce McLaren,

Austin-Healey Sebring Sprite.

Sprite dashboards weren't known for their over-instrumentation.

front end was hinged at the cowl to give easy access to the engine, steering and front suspension. The rest of the Sprite was fairly neat and clean with a simple, slightly sloping rear deck unmarred by a trunk lid. Entry to the trunk was from within the car and although the seatbacks were hinged to move forward, access to the luggage space was limited. John Bond described the appearance of the Sprite as a "hybrid of TR-3, Berkeley and Crosley Hotshot" and we are inclined to let it go at that.

The original Sprite was a classic roadster with removable soft top and side curtains. It was reasonably roomy inside with more pedal and leg room than the MGA but getting inside to make use of that room could be rather challenging, especially for a driver more than 5 ft 10 in. tall. The top came down far enough to restrict vision to the sides somewhat and rainy weather often pointed up a few places where the fit was not absolutely water tight, but then this was a sports car in the traditional sense of the word and comfort was of secondary

Briggs Cunningham and others competed in works cars or the Sebring Sprites of John Sprinzel.

Sprite Mark II

THREE YEARS after the introduction of the original Sprite and some 49,000 cars later, the Mark II version was unveiled in May 1961. Gone were the frog eyes, replaced by conven-

Austin-Healey Sprite Mark II.

tionally located headlights in fixed fenders, along with a wider grille and a hood that opened without lifting the entire front body just like most other cars. The rear was also restyled with a trunk lid that opened from outside and a 12-in. cut in the back of the cockpit for luggage or a small child.

There were also changes to the engine, including an increase in the compression ratio from 8.3 to 9.0:1, larger throats in the SU carburetors, larger intake valves and a change in the exhaust valve timing. The result was more power (50 vs 48 bhp) without loss of torque. The gearbox was also revised; the close-ratio gears used on the Sebring Sprites in competition and available as an option for a year or so were now standard in the new car.

To the avid Bugeye Sprite fanatic, the Mark II was an abomination. To the rest of the motoring enthusiast world, however, the new car was a definite improvement: "Of course, the new model may be accused of some minor loss of personality, but no one can deny that the Sprite II is better looking" (R&T, August 1961). The Mark II was also a more convenient car to live with because of its outside opening trunk and better use of space. R&T concluded that the Mark II, like the original Sprite, "offers more fun per dollar than anything we have driven for a long time."

Only a month after the announcement of the Sprite II, the same car was brought out under the MG banner as the Midget. The only differences were in the nameplates and a few minor trim details and this practice was to continue until the eventual demise of the Sprite name in 1970, when the Midget continued on by itself.

Sprite 1100

FOUR-AND-a-half years after the introduction of the Sprite, a new 1100 model was shown at the London Motor Show in October 1962. The new Sprite (and Midget) had been upgraded with an increase in engine displacement from 948 to 1098 cc, which raised the horsepower rating from 50 to 55 at 5500 rpm. The clutch diameter was increased by 1 in., front brakes were now disc rather than drum, and reshaped and more thickly padded seats plus the addition of carpeting helped to make the Sprite more comfortable.

The additional engine displacement was the result of an increase in bore (2.54 vs 2.48 in.) and a new, longer-stroke crankshaft very similar to the one used in the MG 1100 sedans. The displacement increase made the Sprite more pleasant to drive because of the extra torque available (61 lb-ft at 2500 rpm compared with 52.5 at 2750 in the Mark II).

Although the new seats were certainly more comfortable and the noise level had been reduced by the carpeting, the Sprite was still characterized by many of its original features: no wind-up windows, separate key and starter (the latter a pull cable rather than button), no door locks or outside door handles and no glovebox. The only lockable portion of the entire car was the trunk.

In terms of performance, the Sprite 1100 was a much better car. Top speed improved by only a few mph but the change in the torque characteristics offered top gear hill climbing and easier passing than in previous Sprites. This new found performance could be used with increased confidence as a result of the change to front disc brakes. The former drum brakes were marginal when the car was being driven near the limit. Handling was unaffected by any of these changes and the Sprite (and Midget) was still one of the most responsive cars on the road.

Perhaps more amazing than anything else was the fact that the new Sprite buyer was still getting all of this for less than $2000! In the period from May 1958 to October 1962, the Sprite's list price had only gone from $1795 to $1985. And *Road & Track* was still saying that this car offered more fun per dollar than any other, even after 4½ years.

Sprite Mark III

MARCH 1964 brought the introduction of the Mark III Sprite (Mark II Midget which was one number behind) and

this new model reflected the need to bring the Sprite up to date with the modern sports car. Major improvements included wind-up windows, swiveling vent wings, updated instrument panel and further improvements in interior trim.

The rear suspension came in for revision with a change from the quarter-elliptic springs to semi-elliptics to reduce the tricky roll oversteer inherent in the original design. There was also a minor improvement in engine performance (stepped up to 59 bhp) through improved manifolding and the use of the MG 1100 cylinder head.

Sprite Mark IV/Midget Mark III

ONCE AGAIN the London Motor Show was the arena for the display of the new Sprite/Midget, this time in 1966. The car now became a thoroughly modern sports car with a proper

convertible top that could be raised and lowered without dismantling. Another engine transplant had taken place and the Sprite/Midget now had a 1275-cc powerplant similar to that used in the Mini Cooper S but detuned from 75 bhp to 65. This detuning allowed lower production costs because a normal forged crankshaft could be used in place of the more expensive nitrided steel crank of the S for example, while still maintaining the Sprite's reputation for reliability and long life. The net increase of 6 bhp over the Mark III Sprite (Mark II Midget) was enough to make a surprising improvement in performance as the new Sprite/Midget would accelerate to 60 mph in 14.7 seconds versus 18.3 sec for the previous model.

The crisp handling which had always been a characteristic

of Sprites remained and there was still some roll oversteer built into the rear suspension that made the car great fun to drive sideways. The ride was still a bit jouncy over uneven surfaces but it was truly sporting in nature and aficionados of the breed didn't mind it at all and in fact felt (and still feel!) that it was necessary or you might as well have been driving a large sedan.

The Sprite/Midget cars remained little changed from this setup until 1975. Of course, the Sprite version was discontinued in 1970. The Midget continued without any drastic changes except for the addition of more and more emission controls and safety items such as the over-large bumpers of today, until the 1975 model which received the 1493-cc Triumph Spitfire engine with slightly different exhaust manifolding. Emission controls had become stringent enough that the increased displacement was capable of putting out 55.5 bhp at 5000 rpm.

For the purposes of our discussion here, we have elected to cut off our report with 1970 for two reasons: that was the last year for both the Sprite and the Midget; and the increasing emission and safety regulations have taken some of the fun out of driving the more modern Midgets. They still have reasonable handling, are relatively lightweight and thrifty of fuel, but in talking about a Used Car Classic we also have to give consideration to purchase price and post-1970 car prices are generally out of the bargain class.

Car selection tips

As with most British sports cars of the time, the early Sprite/Midget is a remarkably sturdy and simple car. The engine and transmission having come from a sedan of some years' standing, they were time-tested and of proven reliability. The twin SU carburetors have a tendency to be touchy in adjustment so many times a car that does not seem to be working properly may just need a delicate hand applied to the carburetors. Also, the linkage runs right into the carburetor throat and there have been cases where the opening becomes worn, allowing air to seep in and upset the mixture. The use of some rubber grommets

can cure this malady. One of the few weak spots in the engine is the center main bearing on the crankshaft. If it's at all suspect, replace it.

All of the Sprite/Midgets covered in our time period have a non-synchromesh 1st gear. While the gearbox is sturdy, a heavy-handed driver can wreak damage on the unit, especially 1st, and it may be necessary to consider rebuilding it. On the other hand, we have been told by Sprite owners that they have put considerably more than 100,000 miles on their cars without the gearbox showing signs of wear.

Rust is one of the most important things to look for in buying any car and it's true of the Sprite too. The potential buyer may be fortunate and find a car that has a number of holes drilled in the rocker panels and the bottom edge of the hood (Bugeye models)—these are to permit water to drain out and prevent rusting.

Prices for used models vary from area to area of the country. The Bugeye is rapidly approaching classic status and the prices are beginning to reflect this. However, a running Bugeye that needs restoration can occasionally be found in the $600–800 range in southern California, but the usual price is $200–400 more than that. The fully restored Bugeye can bring as much as $2000 and more. Prices will generally be somewhat higher

TYPICAL ASKING PRICES

Year & Type	Price Range
1958–61 Austin-Healey Sprite	$600–1200
1961–62 Austin-Healey Sprite II & MG Midget	$500–1200
1963 Austin-Healey Sprite 1100 & MG Midget 1100	$400–1200
1964–65 Austin-Healey Sprite III & MG Midget II	$500–1500
1966–70 Austin-Healey Sprite IV & MG Midget III	$800–1800

PERFORMANCE DATA
From Contemporary Tests

	1958 Austin-Healey Sprite	1961 Austin-Healey Sprite II	1963 Austin-Healey Sprite 1100	1967 MG Midget III
0–60 mph, sec	20.8	19.6	18.3	14.7
0–80 mph, sec	35.5*	49.0	42.5	31.0
Standing ¼ mi, sec	21.8	21.5	20.9	19.9
Avg fuel economy, mpg	34.0	34.0	33.0	24.0
Road test date	8-58	8-61	8-63	9-67

*0–70 mph

BRIEF SPECIFICATIONS

	1958 Austin-Healey Sprite	1961 Austin-Healey Sprite II	1963 Austin-Healey Sprite 1100	1967 MG Midget III
Curb weight, lb	1460	1540	1560	1560
Wheelbase, in.	80.0	80.0	80.0	80.0
Track, f/r	45.4	45.8	47.2	46.3
	44.8	44.8	45.0	44.8
Length	137.0	136.0	138.0	137.4
Width	54.0	54.0	54.0	56.5
Height	48.0	48.8	47.8	48.6
Fuel capacity, gal.	6.0	7.2	7.2	7.5
Engine type	ohv inline 4	ohv inline 4	ohv inline 4	ohv inline 4
Bore x stroke, mm	63.0 x 76.2	63.0 x 76.2	64.5 x 83.8	70.6 x 81.3
Displacement, cc	948	948	1098	1275
Compression ratio	8.3:1	9.0:1	8.9:1	8.8:1
Bhp @ rpm, SAE gross	48 @ 5000	50 @ 5500	55 @ 5500	65 @ 6000
Torque @ rpm	52 @ 3300	52.5 @ 2750	61 @ 2500	72 @ 3000
Gearbox	all models: 4-speed, non-synchro 1st gear			
Final drive ratio	4.22:1	4.22:1	4.22:1	4.22:1

in other parts of the country where these particular models are less readily available. Prices on newer Sprites and the MG Midgets will run anywhere from $800 on up, peaking at about $1800.

The Sprite/Midget series of cars is perhaps one of the most logical ones for inclusion in our Used Car Classic series of reports. They are simple, relatively easy to maintain, and, just as when they were new, return more driving fun per dollar than just about any sports car we can think of. If you are the proper size to fit inside one, you couldn't do much better. 🏆

DRIVING IMPRESSIONS

PHOTO BY DOROTHY CLENDENIN

Once again we find ourselves indebted to Ken Schwartz of the Long Beach (California) MG Club for leading us to a Used Car Classic owner who was willing to have us photograph and drive his car. Eddie Martinez runs a speedometer repair shop in Long Beach, owns two Bugeye Sprites and writes music and performs in musical productions. He is one of those rare persons who seems to enjoy life just a little more than the rest of us and his Sprites provide him with a lot of enjoyment—and frustration, he adds.

Eddie has been a sprite owner for 12 years and both of his Bugeyes are of 1959 vintage, both are painted bright yellow and both have received his personal attention in interior improvements. These include re-doing the dash, adding a center console and installing a vinyl-covered plywood bulkhead between the seats and the trunk. Eddie claims this last item has cut down on the noise level considerably and he is justifiably proud of his work.

To the accompanying snide comments and laughter of Eddie and R&T Managing Editor Dottie Clendenin who came along as the official photographer, I gingerly eased my portly 6 ft 2 in. bulk into Eddie's roadster. His second car had the hardtop on it and I wasn't even about to try getting into that one! Gad, but these are tiny little devils. I soon found that I was indeed in (no need for a seatbelt here as it would take more than a collision to pry me out) and that I could operate the pedals. I could not however put my left foot anyplace once I had activated the clutch and let it up, so I drove along holding it in the air just above the pedal. The controls fell readily to hand—there was no place else for them to fall—and with a turn of the key and a pull on the starter we were off.

Eddie mentioned to me as we were motoring along that I looked sort of funny in the car—I suppose he meant that I bore a strange resemblance to a trained circus bear driving a kiddy car—but I was undaunted, dividing my time between bending down to look through the windshield and craning upward to look over it. The day was one of those magnificent California days after a rainstorm, with a freshness to the air we rarely enjoy. The wind was in my face and the exhaust was singing with a healthy note. "This is what it's all about," I told myself as my left leg began to cramp up from being suspended in air for half a mile.

The ride was sheer sports car delight—jouncy and stiff, giving the driver and passenger intimate knowledge of each and every surface irregularity along the way. At the same time, however, there is a feeling of maneuverability and control so that the bumps fade away, replaced by a fiendish desire to cut and slice through and around all those behemoths blocking the way. The 948-cc in-line 4-cylinder engine revs freely up to about 4000 rpm and then begins to hint at a bit of strain. Eddie said that the crankshaft in his car was beginning to make trouble, so we didn't run the engine up to the 6000-rpm limit. The handling is close to neutral and getting the tail to hang out takes a definite effort. Once you do, it's very easily controlled—in fact, you really have to work at it to get in over your head driving a Sprite, which is why they have always been so outstanding for the young sports car enthusiast learning the ropes.

The Bugeye has generally been considered an unappealing design but I've never agreed with that—it's strange enough to have a beauty all its own. The smiling front end, which teenage girls tend to label "cute," is actually a grin with a touch of a leer in it. And that's precisely what driving the Sprite is like. It's not fast, not terribly comfortable, not very refined. So why are all those Sprite/Midget owners grinning?

—Thos L. Bryant

OWNER IMPRESSIONS

Mike Griswold was getting married so I bought the Bugeye Sprite from him for $400. Then Bill Holley and I nursed the car from the wedding in Salt Lake City back to Madison, Wisconsin, sleeping under the stars and occasionally in the rain, eating cheap greaseburgers and only making it home because buried behind a pile of recap carcasses at the Goodyear store in Cody, Wyoming was one dusty 5.20-13, which they sold to me for cost.

Privation—it was a fitting introduction to my Sprite. That car was an adventure from the first time Holley hit a pot hole in Utah and we realized the right front shock was broken. That car taught me to be a very good diagnostic mechanic.

Yet, I've never again gotten as much pure automotive joy as I did from the Blue Bugeye. It was just me, my swimming trunks and this car with the top and side curtains I could remove and stow behind the seats in under 30 sec. The early morning runs in the cool, damp Wisconsin mornings with the wind knotting my hair and fighting to get inside my nylon ski jacket are still very alive. It was a summer of cut-off Levis, cut-off sleeve sweat shirts, white tennis shoes (no socks) and driving this little British roller skate to Elkhart Lake, Meadowdale or the USAC races at Milwaukee. The little bugger even crapped out one night so I could forsake it for a blind date and meet the lady who is now my wife.

Every reaction of that roadster was crisp and immediate—a sudden sneeze could prompt a lane change. Best of all, the car was joyfully simple, which is why they ruined it when they added roll-up windows and a fold-down top. Complication was the very antithesis of the Sprite. Why must we reject simplicity and call its complicated replacement "sophisticated?" The British, of all people, should know better. I still look at Bugeyes lovingly and occasionally think of buying another, this time in British Racing Green, with wire wheels and a Nardi steering wheel. —John Lamm